THE POETRY
OF THE AMERICAN CIVIL WAR

THE POETRY OF THE AMERICAN CIVIL WAR

Edited by LEE STEINMETZ

MICHIGAN STATE UNIVERSITY PRESS

Library of Congress Catalogue Card Number: 59-15220

*
*
*
*
*

MANUFACTURED IN THE UNITED STATES OF AMERICA

This book is dedicated to Doris, Will, and Sam

PREFACE

This anthology attempts to present, for the first time, a comprehensive view of American Civil War poetry written and published in America at the time of the conflict. There is, it seems to me, a general impression current that American poets during the Eighteen-Sixties were content to let the fabricators of a few marching songs enjoy a virtual monopoly in the creation of war verse. The impression is erroneous. It would be a mistake to assume that all or even a majority of poets chose to dedicate whatever talents they possessed to the war cause. But of the nearly one thousand poets who published volumes of poetry in America during the Sixties, well over two hundred treated the war in one way or another. Some poets, in the fashion of Whitman and Melville, devoted volumes of poetry exclusively to the war. Many others tucked one or two perfunctory war lyrics away in the middle of fat volumes of sentimental verse, surrounding them with poems which celebrated such phenomena as the beauties of a May morning on earth and the greater beauties of a May morning in Heaven.

Most of this "literary" war verse is, as one might suspect, aesthetically inferior. Read as social commentary it is usually interesting, frequently amusing, occasionally hilarious. The interpretation given the war by these poets—many of whom were housewives, medical doctors, teachers, preachers, bankers, journalists, schoolboys and schoolgirls—is particularly valuable as social commentary because they considered themselves representative of society. It is certain that the interpretation these poets gave the war was precisely the interpretation they felt was shared by most Americans.

The five chapters into which I have divided the poetry are those which the nature of the poetry suggested. To have categorized the poetry by author would have been eminently unhelpful because most of these forgotten poets have little to recommend them individually. To have divided the poetry into chapters dealing with Northern verse and Southern verse would have been to indulge in distinctions without differences, since Northern and Southern war poetry—with the obvious exception of divergence over the slavery issue—is so similar. Since poets North and South, despite surface similarities in their poetry, were so violently partisan, however, I have whenever possible included within the different chapters analogous poems by Northerners and Southerners. Thus, in Chapter I, a reader may listen to the Northern poet Henry Abbey's description of the return of the fallen dead in "Returned from War," and the Southern poet Mrs. Caroline Augusta Ball's similar description of how the owner of "The Jacket of Grey" was laid to rest.

The first four chapters represent aspects of the war which greatly interested poets of the time. I have included a chapter on verse narratives both because the enormous popularity of this genre seemed to call for separate treatment, and also because I thought it would be interesting for readers to see how many war themes the writers of these long verse narratives were able to include in their stories of the war.

I have tried to make the various chapters mutually independent. Within each of the five chapters, the poems, together with my commentary, tell something of a story, and, while there is nothing to keep readers from dipping into the volume at random, they may find some interest in going through a given chapter from beginning to end.

In arranging the poems into chapters, I have made no virtue of consistency, since any attempt to categorize a body of verse such as that included in this book is admittedly arbitrary and to a degree artificial. Readers will find Dexter Smith's elegy on Lincoln included in the chapter on Slavery, even though Chapter II devotes a section to Lincoln elegies; excerpts from verse narratives in various chapters, even though an entire chapter treats these narratives; the Deity invoked in many poems other than those included in Chapter II. My only justification for this slight degree of over-lapping lies in its having allowed me to present the war poetry in a more complete light than would otherwise have been possible.

In my prefatory remarks on individual poems, I seldom have attempted anything approaching a complete analysis, but usually have confined myself to commenting on aspects of a poem which resulted in my including it in the chapter where it is found.

Readers will notice that occasionally poems whose context suggests that they were written during the war were published subsequent to the end of the war. It was a common custom during the Eighteen-Sixties, as it was before and after, for poets to gather together in a published volume poems which had previously been published in magazines and periodicals. Several poets during the decade specifically told their readers in prefaces that this was the way their volumes of verse had come into being. This fact, coupled with the inevitable time lapse between date of composition and date of publication, makes it a safe conjecture that the great majority of these poems, unless the context suggests otherwise, were written during the actual time of the conflict.

PREFACE

As I was in the process of deciding what poets to represent, the voices of well-known poets and the voices of forgotten or nearly-forgotten poets presented rival claims. With two exceptions, I listened to the forgotten voices. While poets such as Longfellow, Whittier, Lowell, and Holmes penned some war verse, their works are readily available, and hence scarcely need reiterating. Readers have only to reach for the nearest bookshelf to follow again the various fortunes of Lowell's Biglow, Sawin, Wilbur and company, or to renew acquaintance with Longfellow's beautiful youth who was "Killed at the Ford." Similarly, a poem such as Mrs. Howe's famous battle hymn, it seemed to me, stood in no need of a renewal of its perpetual lease on life. One contribution of this book, it is hoped, will be its allowing the reader to compare the representative selections it contains with war poems already familiar to him.

The two exceptions to this principle of selection are Whitman and Melville. To have represented these poets with anything like the completeness which their worth suggests would have been impracticable; while to have compiled an anthology of Civil War poetry without mentioning them would have approached, if not surpassed, literary heresy. My compromise was to include one Whitman poem and one Melville poem. While "Vigil Strange I Kept" and "Apathy and Enthusiasm" help tell the stories in Chapters I and II, I have included these readily available poems primarily by way of an excuse for the remarks I wished to make about their authors.

In editing the texts of the poems, I have largely limited myself to pointing out obvious errors in spelling. Some poets whose works appear in this book employed punctuation inconsistently; some took frequent liberties with syntax; some consciously affected archaic and poetic spelling. Repeated editorial comment concerning poetic liberties of this sort would, I felt, serve no indispensable purpose, and might stand between the reader and what the poets had to say.

In making a book, one puts himself gratefully under various obligations. It seems appropriate, in connection with a book dealing with nineteenth century America, that my indebtedness should reach back to the nineteenth century itself. Brown University's Harris Collection of American Poetry and Plays, which provided the material from which this book was made, had its beginning in the nineteenth century when Caleb Fiske Harris (1818-81), a native Rhode Islander and former student at Brown University, retired to Providence after twenty years of business in New York. Harris became a rare book collector and, in the course of time, augmented his already rich collection of American poetry and drama by purchasing the library of Judge Albert Gorton Greene of Providence. On the death of Harris his library was thrown on the market, and a cousin,

Senator Henry Bowen Anthony, purchased the American poetry collection intact. On his death in 1884, Senator Anthony, a graduate of Brown University in the Class of 1833, bequeathed the collection to Brown University, where it has grown to become unrivalled in its field. Without the Harris Collection, which sprang from an interest in their country's culture on the part of Harris, Judge Greene, and Senator Anthony, the making of this book would have been a patent impossibility.

I feel a particular indebtedness to the staff of the John Hay Library of Brown University, and to its Librarian, Professor David A. Jonah, for making the Harris Collection available to me, and for their repeated kindnesses.

My indebtedness to the more than two hundred American poets who, during the Eighteen-Sixties, wrote their poetry of the war, is incalculable. I have formed an affection for these poets which is confessedly out of all proportion to the artistic merit of most of their works. These poets, it is my belief, left us an imaginative record of our forefathers' response to the Civil War which cannot be exactly duplicated by any other accounts of the Rebellion which have come down to us. It is this imaginative record which this book attempts to recreate.

L.S.

EASTERN ILLINOIS UNIVERSITY
September, 1959

CONTENTS

Preface vii

1. THE WAR SCENE 1
   - I The Work of Death 1
   - II Sadly Silent Near the Dead 21
   - III They Had Heard the News of the Battle 24
   - IV To Think that You Died Alone 27
   - V Vigil Strange 28
   - VI They Bear Him Gently Home 32
   - VII Not E'en the House of God was Spared 34
   - VIII Home, Home Again! 41

2. THE HOLY WAR 51
   - I God of the True-Hearted 51
   - II But God He Keeps the Middle Way 54
   - III To the Plain Where the Blessed City Lies 60
   - IV In Glory Sleep! 64
   - V Lincoln Is Dead! 66
   - VI Purchased with Our Jackson's Blood 80
   - VII Thy Pale and Perished Flowers 82

3. SOCIAL COMMENTARY 85
   - I Rightful Order into Ruin Hurled 85
   - II The Glowing Wonders of Secession 99

4. SLAVERY 115
   - I Since Mercy Fell by Tyranny 115
   - II Gaunt Treason 117
   - III On None Dependent, Sovereign, Free 118
   - IV This Broad Domain that Freedom Craves 121
   - V The Thirsty Lash, with Sharp, Steel-Pointed Thong 123
   - VI The Festal March of Iron 130
   - VII Most Glorious Southern Land 142
   - VIII Magical Mesh, to Entangle a World 143
   - IX The Book of Books We Confidently Quote 146

CONTENTS

X All Scripture is Useful in its Place 161
XI Your Father, Boy, Was Eager 173

5. STORIES OF THE WAR 175
I She Gave a Shriek and Cried Aloud 175
II Their Earthly Paths No More Shall Sever 222

BIBLIOGRAPHY 257

THE POETRY

OF THE AMERICAN CIVIL WAR

Chapter One: The War Scene

I. THE WORK OF DEATH

Although Civil War poets frequently used the war as a convenient sounding-board for their ideas concerning society, religion, man's place in the universe, a considerable number strove to capture something of the immediacy of war and its impact on soldiers and their families. Very few of the poems which resulted from this effort, however, approach a vivid realism, since poets, in keeping with the sentimental and melodramatic temper of their era, characteristically employed a highly colored diction in describing the war scene.

The clash of arms provided one of the more popular subjects. Some poets poetically described specific battles which had captured their imaginations. Others, usually in amusingly sketchy fashion, recounted the military highlights of the entire war. A third group of poets treated battles in what might be termed the history-of-the-campaign approach. These poets were usually soldiers who put into verse, frequently of a humorously poor quality, the history of their regiment. The full title of George S. Rutherford's *Poetic History* (Muscatine, Iowa, 1863) typifies the aim of these soldier-poets: *The Poetic History of the Seventh Iowa Regiment, Containing All Its Principal Marches, and All the Battles They Have Been Engaged in, from the Day of Their Entering Service to the Present Time. Composed and Written by One of Their Number Who Has Passed through, or Borne His Part in, Nearly All the Scenes He Has Described.* George E. Reed's *Campaign of the Sixth Army Corps Summer of 1863* (Philadelphia, 1864) and the anonymous *A Journal of Incidents Connected with the Travels of the Twenty-second Regiment Conn. Volunteers, for Nine Months. In Verse. By an Orderly Sergeant* (Hartford, 1863) lie in the same tradition. That these poets accomplished their task in thirty-five pages or less indicates that one should not expect an over attention to detail from these veterans of the campaign.

The re-unions of regiments, which were being held before the decade closed, afforded other soldier-poets an excuse to give poetic histories of the campaigns. E. E. Ewing thus wrote *The Story of the Ninety-First. Read at a Re-union of the Ninety-First Regiment Ohio Volunteer Infantry, Held at Portsmouth, Ohio, April 8, 1868, in Response to the Toast, "Our Bond of Union."* (Portsmouth, O., 1868); and

Samuel B. Sumner read *A Poem Delivered at the Reunion of the Forty-ninth Regiment Massachusetts Volunteers, at Pittsfield, Mass., May 23, 1867* (Springfield, Mass., 1867).

Excerpts from George S. Rutherford's *Poetic History of the Seventh Iowa Regiment* represent the treatment given the war by various soldiers. Entering service July 16, 1861, the regiment, at the time Rutherford wrote his history in 1863, had seen action in the major engagements of Donelson, Shiloh, and Corinth. Although Rutherford describes these engagements, he is careful to avoid the impression—too frequently given by poets whose knowledge of army life had been garnered second-hand—that regiments did nothing except engage in one colorful, melodramatic clash of arms after another. Dividing his poetic history into twenty-four sections, Rutherford devotes ten sections to battles, five to the frequently hum-drum and inconvenient life in camp, nine to the inevitably unpleasant marches the regiment was obliged to make. Rutherford's history, then, taken as a whole, constitutes an honest if amusingly prosaic attempt to tell the folks back home what it was like to be a member of the Seventh Iowa Regiment. What prompted Rutherford to tell his story in verse can be explained partially, if at all, through a realization that during the period of the Civil War the province of poetry was considerably wider than it has since become.

Rutherford begins his history by describing various movements in and around St. Louis. Next the poet describes the trip to Fort Henry and the Battle of Donelson. Following the surrender of the fort, the Seventh Iowa make a trip up the Tennessee River, camping at Mineral Landing. Then follows the excerpt printed below, in which Rutherford pictures the regiment marching, fighting, and living the every-day life of a military camp. Following these parts of the poem, Rutherford closes by describing the march to Iuka and the Battle of Corinth, during which battle, the author informs us, he received a ball in his leg, which set him "to spinning like a top on its peg." Rutherford closes by asking rhetorically, "Who can define what the future will be," and suggesting that, whoever may be in that enviable position, " 'Tis not us poor mortals to a dead certainty."

THE WORK OF DEATH

from THE POETIC HISTORY OF THE SEVENTH IOWA REGIMENT

* * *

Trip to Pittsburg Landing

Again our good regiment got under way,
And reached this good Landing in five or six days.
Thus, having arrived there all sickly or lame
We gladly did enter the forest again.

There the Seventh recovered their vigor once more,
By roaming the forest which here lines the shore,
For their senses were greeted with floral perfume
From sweet smelling blossoms the North has in June.

Battle of Shiloh

Soon war-clouds o'ershadowed this place of delight,
Whose horrors will sicken our once peaceful sight
From this battle now pending, long talked of before,
Will display all its fury on this peaceful shore.

The 6th, like a maiden all blooming and bright,
Dawned on us in splendor and gladdened our sight;
While drawn up in order and dressed in deep blue
According to custom for Sunday's review.

Our quick ears were greeted with war's sullen roar,
With its fatal delusions and streams of red gore—
Then our Colonels got orders and we must away,
To stand by our brothers in this bloody fray.

We advanced through the forest to give them our aid,
And soon found our brethren in battle arrayed.
Assuming the place by Generals assigned
Our presence was needed to fill up the line.

It was here our poor patience was severely tried,
For many long hours by war's bitter tide
With its many lead balls and canister shot
Killed and crippled our comrades on that very spot.

The tide of this battle first vered [*sic*] to the right;
And long rolling volleys in this quarter did light.
Sending death and destruction wherever it came.
Destroying on both sides by its withering flame.

Our men could not stand such a fire, you know,
But fell from the range of this terrible blow;
Swinging round from the front to establish new lines,
Made the rebels flank movement a success at the time.

Elated at this they bore down on our left,
And here as at first they met with success;
For our army fell back as a matter of course,
As the rebels press on them with superior force.

No other alternative for us could avail,
Than to break from the center and quickly turn tail
To avoid being taken we must break to the rear
And rally again on some other point near.

A few gallant soldiers were ready at hand
When our Colonel gave orders to make a new stand;
For a hundred brave hearts were not scattered by flight,
But stood by our banners that dark Sunday night.

The lurid light flashed as their batteries play,
And the missiles tore through our encampment to-day
Till our gunboats and seige guns, with terrible roar,
Made these haughty rebels retire from this shore.

Then as evening gave way to the shadows of night
The darkness was broken by streaks of red light
From bomb shells describing their course through the air,
Making sleep for the rebels a shabby affair.

Thus "night was made hideous" to friend and to foe
By half hour discharges from the gunboats below,
Together with thunder and rain pouring fast,
And the rattle of hailstones completed the blast.

Second Day's Battle

The Army of Buell came forth with the light,
And soon put a different face on this fight,
For those who had pushed us so hard the first day,
Before these fresh veterans fled off in dismay.

From seven till three, with steady advance,
Our cannons and muskets both play on their ranks—
This field being sprinkled with hundreds of dead
General Beauregard's army ingloriously fled.

Victory perched on our banners on this bloody field,
Yet by Patriot's blood was this victory sealed;
And mothers and maidens are weeping in pain
O'er their husbands and lovers so ruthlessly slain.

The Seventh Iowa, when the battle was o'er,
Returned to their quarters sadly jaded and sore
On Tuesday evening, and quickly they found
Their tents filled with wounded from the late battle ground.

No other alternative being at hand,
Our lodging was made on this rain spattered land
For nearly a week, with no shelter at all
But the forest above us to break the rain's fall.

A week of such treatment was bitter at best;
But the boats bore the wounded to some place of rest,
And leaving our tents to the owners once more,
The lords of these quarters moved in as before.

The rains at this season set in with a rush,
Making causeways and bottoms a vortex of slush,

Keeping back for a season our engines of war,
Till the sun dried the mud and the roads were repaired.

Brave Halleck came to us in Shiloh at last,
Making noise and confusion events of the past;
While his plain, honest face with intelligence shines,
As he makes observations along our whole line.

From the dawn of the morn to the shadows of night,
All men are kept busy preparing to strike
Another good blow for our country and flag

When order attended our army once more,
All firm and majestic they marched from the shore,
Over hills and on causeways, by them lately built,
And through tangled thickets for the enemy felt.
Against the arch traitors at Corinth, with Bragg.

It was thus by building our roads as we went,
Many days on this journey by our army was spent
Before we arrived within reach of the foe,
Who, before us, fell back to Corinth below.

When the distance to Corinth was just seven miles,
We threw up entrenchments and rested awhile;
Our General displaying good caution and care
In the lunch he intended should fall to their share.

But they slowly retired from our pioneers,
Who were backed by an army of brave volunteers,
Sent there for protection from the enemy's fire,
And these molesters of labor were compelled to retire.

A few days pass by and the way is made clear,
And our mighty army through the wilderness steer;
Yet this little journey, like others, must end
Where spades and good axes are made to defend.

More roads are made passable ere we advance
To a point of attack—a good one perchance—

THE WORK OF DEATH

Building long lines of breastworks for soldier's defense,
Where blood might be spilt ere we should go hence.

Now we listen to skirmishes made on their wings,
Where musket shots rattle and grim cannons ring;
'Tis the death knell of many, who by these missiles fall,
Pure victims to Liberty's loud trumpet call.

Again preparations are made to advance
To the last line of breastworks, whose moments enhance
The hour of battle, which the rebels avoid,
While moving their baggage they had not destroyed.

The axes rang sharply along the whole line,
While Parrot guns thundered and muskets did shine;
And spades in the trenches were handled with speed,
As danger did thicken men felt their whole need.

They worked like true veterans, reeking with sweat,
First with spades, then with guns, as they never worked yet
Since the day they enlisted for country and flag—
There was no time for shirking or for any to lag.

Before we could finish this desirable job,
To strengthen the pickets our Company plods,
While the rest of the Regiment handle their steel,
And finish the pits with commendable zeal.

The night was disturbed by the scattering fire
From both lines of pickets, which was not required
To make the night pleasant to our Company's men,
Who heard the balls whistle above now and then.

But morning brought with it, as usual, relief,
With coffee and crackers to soften our grief,
And what was still better for soldiers oppressed,
By a want of their slumber, a season of rest.

Now for several nights we had frequent alarms;
When we ran to the breast works and seizing our arms

Prepared for the worst which a battle could bring
To an army at night possessing their things.

By miniature battles on the right and left wings,
With the center on picket these days were put in.
Till at last one fine morning an explosion was heard,
Whose tones plainly told of the flight of these birds.

When battle no longer could crown our just hopes,
Our brigade was transferred to the Army of Pope;
When our boys hurried off to Booneville away,
Which we used up in moving for five or six days.

This camp, like a desert, is choking with thirst,
Where creeks are dead water, and it some of the worst
Of any we tasted in our marches thus far,
Through the Land of Rebellion, now blasted with war [.]

A part of our drink was obtained from mud wells
In the beds of dry creeks in these Southern dells,
Where soldiers had dug in the hopes to obtain
A little good water while they might remain.

March to Camp Montgomery

Again we have orders, from high sources, to march,
Which we heed as before and pack up to start,
With our faces turned backward as if in retreat,
Our Division moves on through the terrible heat.

Oppressed by the heat and all covered with dust,
Through this smiting heat was our Regiment thrust
Toward our destination, from morning till eve,
Leaving some by the roadside you'd better believe.

The hour arrived when the sun ceased to burn,
When those by the wayside could safely return
To their places in camp, if they had survived
This terrible march, where some lost their lives.

We halted, at length, in a fire-scorched field,
Where poor tired Nature her sceptre did wield,
For all were soon wrapped in slumbers profound,
Rolled up in our blankets on the dew covered ground.

Refreshed we awaked at the close of the night,
Rejoiced in beholding sweet Heaven's pure light;
And as the bright sun-light peeped over the hills,
We completed this journey of four or five miles.

Arrived at Camp Montgomery—Every Day Life

Arrived in good season at our journey's end,
On a fine swell of woodland, where labor would blend
To make this place airy and embellish the scene,
Which we had selected in this forest glade green.

Our days were divided by duties, though slight,
They filled up the season from morning till night;
With police and guard duty and four hour's of drill,
It was the business the Seventh was called to fulfill.

No water being handy but what we could bring
From poor dirty creeks and bad tasting springs,
It was Company A who conceived a bold plan
To dig in the earth for this blessing to man.

By means of hard labor we soon did succeed
In obtaining the blessings which we so much need,
For in finding this treasure our bosoms did swell,
When we saw the pure water running into the well.

Our labors were crowned with such speedy success
That others, by these true facts, were impressed
To enter with spirit into this paying game,
When two wells repaid them well for the same.

Now all of the Seventh, by necessity led,
Contrived a nice plan for baking their bread;

And from hasty materials did the best that they could,
By building ovens of sticks and clay mud.

Thus the Summer, in garrison duty, was past,
For three months, at least, flew rather fast,
Bringing Autumn's cool evenings unto us, and lo,
We were ordered to Northeast Corinth, as you know.

Three Companies, now, were ordered to go
In different directions, above and below,
And in the selection there happened to be
Included the companies A, K and C.

The rest of the Seventh was now left behind,
To keep our place good from the evil inclined;
Now Company K was the first one to leave
For her destination, as you may perceive.

Their course was to march five miles to the East,
Down onto the railroad and the pickets increase,
And remain in position till ordered away
To join with their comrades for some bloody fray.

The time had now come for the others to start,
And A, with their consort, for Corinth departs,
With their arms and their baggage and utensils complete;
We pulled up at length in the principal street.

We stood on the platform while our officers go
To General Ord, his opinion to know
Concerning these companies under command,
Who patiently waited for the business in hand.

The clouds in black masses excluded the light,
While rain burst upon us with the darkness of night:
This drenched our good garments and adding its weight
To the other impediments which rain can create.

In different directions through puddles of slush
Our officers led us to the General's house, with a rush;
And he kindly pointed to an empty old house,
Where we should take shelter in the home of the mouse.

THE WORK OF DEATH

We proceeded to measure our length on the floor,
And sleep came to visit our eyelids once more.
Sending all off to Dreamland in whose regions we roam,
Forgetting our lodging till morning had come.

Now all of our comrades soon sprang to their feet,
And in washing their faces shook off their late sleep,
Making ready to travel along the highway
Leading out to our station for the rest of the day.

Captain Smith and his Company filed to the left
On the road out to Hamburg for the present to rest,
And establish his pickets on that part of the line
To watch out for stragglers on the road for some time.

The day was far spent and the sun getting low
When orders came for us to pack up and go
A little way forward to an old cotton field
To the line of our pickets with its duties revealed.

Here with double guard duty by day and by night,
We worked for the Nation, and strove for the right.
Now again we are moving, but the distance is short,
To our new position as I shall report.

Our Company hailed this position with glee
With half of its labors on Company C.
And here we all labored both morning and night,
Together in friendship defending the right.

The voice of our Colonel now bade us return
To join our old comrades, as you may learn,
For the march to Iuka to battle with Price,
Whose tribe was assembled through this rebels advice.

* * *

The land war appealed to the imaginations of poets more than the war at sea, colorful and significant as was this latter aspect of the conflict. The sea fights of the war would have gone virtually unchronicled in the poetry of the time had it not been for Henry Howard Brownell, who served under David G. Farragut on board the *Hartford* both at the taking of New Orleans, April 24, 1862, and at the capture of Mobile Bay, August 5, 1864. Among other poems concerning the war at sea, Brownell commemorated those two major naval engagements, the former in "The River Fight," the latter in "The Bay Fight." These two poems are notable, if scarcely memorable, not only because they represent an aspect of the war which other poets neglected, but also because Brownell imbued his sea poetry with an amount of realistic detail unusual for his time.

In "The River Fight," Brownell vividly describes the setting and, later, lets the reader hear the orders of the commander as he prepares for the engagement. Throughout the poem Brownell gives considerable attention to the details of the ship and to the actual course of events, his poem constituting an historically accurate account of the engagement. But Brownell's is not quite a photographic realism. The reliance on exclamation marks, the generally heightened diction, the emphasis on the melodramatic aspects of the struggle, combine to suggest that Brownell has selected those elements of the battle which will prove most colorful to the reader.

The poem is from *War Lyrics and Other Poems* (Boston, 1866).

THE RIVER FIGHT

(Mississippi River, April 24, 1862.)

Do you know of the dreary Land
  If land such region may seem,
Where 'tis neither sea nor strand,
Ocean nor good dry land,
  But the nightmare marsh of a dream—
Where the Mighty River his death-road takes,
'Mid pools, and windings that coil like snakes,
(A hundred leagues of bayous and lakes,)
  To die in the great Gulf Stream?

No coast-line clear and true,
(Granite and deep sea blue,)
  On that dismal shore you pass—
Surf-worn boulder nor sandy beach,

But ooze-flats far as the eye can reach,
With shallows of water-grass—
Reedy savannas, vast and dun,
Lying dead in the dim March sun—
Huge rotting trunks and roots that lie
Like blackened bones of the Shapes gone by,
And miles of sunken morass.
No lovely, delicate thing
Of life o'er the waste is seen—
But the cayman couched by his weedy spring,
And the pelican, bird unclean—
Or the buzzard, flapping on heavy wing
Like an evil ghost, o'er the desolate scene.

Ah, many a weary day
With our Leader there we lay,
In the sultry haze and smoke,
Tugging our ships o'er the bar—
Till the Spring was wasted far,
Till his brave heart almost broke—
For the sullen River seemed
As if our intent he dreamed—
All his shallow mouths did spew and choke.

But, ere April fully past,
All ground over at last,
And we knew the die was cast—
Knew the day drew nigh
To dare to the end one stormy deed,
Might save the Land at her sorest need,
Or on the old deck to die!

Anchored we lay—and, a morn the more,
To his captains and all his men
Thus wrote our stout old Commodore—
(He wasn't Admiral then:)

GENERAL ORDERS

"Send your to' gallant masts down,
Rig in each flying jib-boom!
Clear all ahead for the loom

Of traitor fortress and town,
Or traitor fleet bearing down.

In with your canvas high—
We shall want no sail to fly!
Topsail and foresail, spanker and jib,
(With the heart of oak in the oaken rib,)
Shall serve us to win or die!

Trim every hull by the head,
(So shall you spare the lead,)
Lest, if she ground, your ship swing round,
Bows in-shore, for a wreck—
See your grapnels all clear, with pains,
And a solid kedge in your port main-chains,
With a whip to the main-yard—
Drop it, heavy and hard,
When you grapple a traitor deck!

On forecastle and on poop
Mount guns, as best you may deem—
If possible, rouse them up,
(For still you must bow the stream)—
Also hoist and secure with stops
Howitzers firmly in your tops,
To fire on the foe abeam.

Look well to your pumps and hose—
Have water-tubs, fore and aft,
For quenching flame in your craft,
And the gun-crews' fiery thirst—
See planks with felt fitted close,
To plug every shot-hole tight—
Stand ready to meet the worst!
For, if I have reckoned aright,
They will serve us shot, both cold and hot,
Freely enough, to-night.

Mark well each signal I make—
(Our life-long service at stake,
And honor that must not lag!)
Whate'er the peril and awe,

In the battle's fieriest flaw,
Let never one ship withdraw
  Till orders come from the Flag!"

Would you hear of the River-Fight?
It was two, of a soft spring night—
  God's stars looked down on all,
And all was clear and bright
But the low fog's chilling breath—
Up the River of Death
  Sailed the Great Admiral.

On our high poop-deck he stood,
  And round him ranged the men
Who have made their birthright good
  Of manhood, once and agen—
Lords of helm and of sail,
Tried in tempest and gale,
  Bronzed in battle and wreck—
Bell and Bailey grandly led
Each his Line of the Blue and Red—
Wainwright stood by our starboard rail,
  Thornton fought the deck.

And I mind me of more than they,
  Of the youthful, steadfast ones,
  That have shown them worthy sons
Of the Seamen passed away—
(Tyson conned our helm, that day,
  Watson stood by his guns.)

What thought our Admiral, then,
Looking down on his men?
  Since the terrible day,
    (Day of renown and tears!)
  When at anchor the Essex lay,
  Holding her foes at bay,
When, a boy, by Porter's side he stood

Till deck and plank-shear were dyed with blood,
'Tis half a hundred years—
Half a hundred years, to-day!

Who could fail, with him?
Who reckon of life or limb?
Not a pulse but beat the higher!
There had you seen, by the star-light dim,
Five hundred faces strong and grim—
The Flag is going under fire!
Right up by the fort, with her helm hard-a-port,
The Hartford is going under fire!

The way to our work was plain,
Caldwell had broken the chain,
(Two hulks swung down amain,
Soon as 'twas sundered)—
Under the night's dark blue,
Steering steady and true,
Ship after ship went through—
Till, as we hove in view,
Jackson out-thundered.

Back echoed Philip!—ah, then,
Could you have seen our men,
How they sprung, in the dim night haze,
To their work of toil and of clamor!
How the loaders, with sponge and rammer,
And their captains, with cord and hammer,
Kept every muzzle ablaze!
How the guns, as with cheer and shout
Our tackle-men hurled them out,
Brought up on the water-ways!

First, as we fired at their flash,
'Twas lightning and black eclipse,
With a bellowing roll and crash—
But soon, upon either bow,
What with forts, and fire-rafts, and ships—
(The whole fleet was hard at it, now,
All pounding away!)—and Porter

Still thundering with shell and mortar—
'Twas the mighty sound and form
Of an Equatorial storm!

(Such you see in the Far South,
After long heat and drouth,
As day draws nigh to even—
Arching from North to South,
Blinding the tropic sun,
The great black bow comes on—
Till the thunder-veil is riven,
When all is crash and levin,
And the cannonade of heaven
Rolls down the Amazon!)

But, as we worked along higher,
Just where the river enlarges,
Down came a pyramid of fire—
It was one of your long coal barges.
(We had often had the like before)—
'Twas coming down on us to larboard,
Well in with the eastern shore—
And our pilot, to let it pass round,
(You may guess we never stopped to sound,)
Giving us a rank sheer to starboard,
Ran the Flag hard and fast aground!
'Twas nigh abreast of the Upper Fort,
And straightway a rascal Ram
(She was shaped like the devil's dam)
Puffed away for us, with a snort,
And shoved it, with spiteful strength,
Right alongside of us, to port—
It was all of our ship's length,
A huge crackling Cradle of the Pit,
Pitch-pine knots to the brim,
Belching flame red and grim—
What a roar came up from it!

Well, for a little it looked bad—
But these things are, somehow, shorter
In the acting than the telling—

There was no singing-out nor yelling,
Nor any fussing and fretting,
No stampede, in short—
But there we were, my lad,
All a-fire on our port quarter!
Hammocks a-blaze in the netting,
Flame spouting in at every port—
Our Fourth Cutter burning at the davit,
(No chance to lower away and save it.)

In a twinkling, the flames had risen
Half way to main top and mizzen,
Darting up the shrouds like snakes!
Ah, how we clanked at the brakes,
And the deep steam-pumps throbbed under,
Sending a ceaseless flow—
Our top-men, a dauntless crowd,
Swarmed in rigging and shroud—
There, ('twas a wonder!)
The burning ratlins and strands
They quenched with their bare hard hands—
But the great guns below
Never silenced their thunder!

At last, by backing and sounding,
When we were clear of grounding,
And under head-way once more,
The whole rebel fleet came rounding
The point—if we had it hot before,
'Twas now, from shore to shore,
One long, loud thundering roar—
Such crashing, splintering, and pounding,
And smashing as you never heard before!

But that we fought foul wrong to wreck,
And to save the Land we loved so well,
You might have deemed our long gun deck
Two hundred feet of hell!

For all above was battle,
Broadside, and blaze, and rattle,

THE WORK OF DEATH

Smoke and thunder alone—
(But, down in the sick-bay,
Where our wounded and dying lay,
There was scarce a sob or a moan.)
And at last, when the dim day broke,
And the sullen sun awoke,
Drearily blinking
O'er the haze and the cannon-smoke,
That ever such morning dulls—
There were thirteen traitor hulls
On fire and sinking!

How, up the river!—though mad Chalmette
Sputters a vain resistance yet.
Small helm we gave her, our course to steer—
'Twas nicer work than you well would dream,
With cant and sheer to keep her clear
Of the burning wrecks that cumbered the stream.

The Louisiana, hurled on high,
Mounts in thunder to meet the sky!
Then down to the depth of the turbid flood,
Fifty fathom of rebel mud!
The Mississippi comes floating down,
A mighty bonfire, from off the town—
And along the river, on stocks and ways,
A half-hatched devil's brood is a-blaze—
The great Anglo-Norman is all in flames,
(Hark to the roar of her tumbling frames!)
And the smaller fry that Treason would spawn,
Are lighting Algiers like an angry dawn!

From stem to stern, how the pirates burn,
Fired by the furious hands that built!
So to ashes forever turn
The suicide wrecks of wrong and guilt!
But, as we neared the city,
By field and vast plantation,
(Ah, mill-stone of our Nation!)
With wonder and with pity
What crowds we there espied

Of dark and wistful faces,
Mute in their toiling-places,
Strangely and sadly eyed—
Haply, 'mid doubt and fear,
Deeming deliverance near—
(One gave the ghost of a cheer!)

And on that dolorous strand,
To greet the victor-brave
One flag did welcome wave—
Raised, ah me! by a wretched hand,
All outworn on our cruel Land—
The withered hand of a slave!

But all along the Levee,
In a dark and drenching rain,
(By this, 'twas pouring heavy,)
Stood a fierce and sullen train—
A strange and a frenzied time!
There were scowling rage and pain,
Curses, howls, and hisses,
Out of hate's black abysses—
Their courage and their crime
All in vain—all in vain!
For from the hour that the Rebel Stream,
With the Crescent City lying abeam,
Shuddered under our keel,
Smit to the heart with self-struck sting,
Slavery died in her scorpion-ring,
And Murder fell on his steel.

'Tis well to do and dare—
But ever may grateful prayer
Follow, as aye it ought,
When the good fight is fought,
When the true deed is done—
Aloft in heaven's pure light,
(Deep azure crossed on white)
Our fair Church-Pennant waves
O'er a thousand thankful braves,
Bareheaded in God's bright sun.

Lord of mercy and frown,
Ruling o'er sea and shore,
Send us such scene once more!
All in Line of Battle
When the black ships bear down
On tyrant fort and town,
Mid cannon cloud and rattle—
And the great guns once more
Thunder back the roar
Of the traitor walls ashore,
And the traitor flags come down!

Flag Ship *Hartford,* March, 1864.

II. SADLY SILENT NEAR THE DEAD

Most poets dramatized the reactions and fate of the individual in battle rather than the mass movements of armies and navies. The fate of the individual most frequently was death. Actual historical events and poetic tradition combined to produce this emphasis. The War of the Rebellion was, in terms of men killed, quite literally a costly war. Added to this is the fact that mid-nineteenth century poets conceived death as the most poetic of subjects, whether they were writing about war between Northerners and Southerners, war between the Flesh and the Spirit, or war between God and Satan for the souls of men. In Amherst, at the very time of the conflict, Emily Dickinson was penning her enigmatic messages from beyond the poetic grave. Whitman, in a footnote to his 1876 preface, was shortly to state: "I am not sure but the last inclosing sublimation of Race or Poem is, what it thinks of Death . . . ." Throughout the Eighteen-Sixties, appreciably more poems treated death than any other subject. Add to these factors the honor which, since the time of Homer, has attached itself to death in battle, and it becomes more than understandable why the poets' warrior-heroes seldom lived to tell of their exploits.

Mrs. Mary Evelyn David, writing under the pen name of Mollie E. Moore, gives a typical treatment of death in battle in "Chickamauga." This Southern poet obviously is less interested in describing factually the course of a bloody encounter which took thirty thousand casualties in dead and wounded than in focusing attention on battle as a prelude to death.

The poem is from *Minding The Gap and Other Poems* (Houston, 1867).

CHICKAMAUGA

The sharp, clear crack of rifles, and the deep
  Loud thunder of artillery; the flash
Of bayonets, and the arrowy sweep
  Of keen-edged sabres; the most fearful clash
Of meeting squadrons, and the pride
Of hostile banners! How they fought who died
          By the River of Death!

Morn dawned upon the field, the bugle's blast
  Wound out its shrilly summons, and the word
Leaped down the lines, and fiery hearts beat fast:
  Two gallant armies bared the murderous sword,
And fearless breasted battle's bitter waves,
And eager thousands sought their nameless graves
          By the River of Death!

And many eyes grew dim; the labored breath
  Fled many a young and gallant breast;
And many an arm grew rigid there: but Death
  Urged on the carnage, and they knew no rest,
Those panting hosts. Our banner kept its pride,
But its blood-stained stars tell how they fought, who died
          By the River of Death!

And Texas' fearless sons were there: they bared
  Their bosoms to the shock and met the tide,
As their own forests meet the storm; they dared
  Their splendid foe with all his bannered pride:
Their hearts were in the struggle, for they thought
On their free fair homes in Texas, as they fought
          By the River of Death!

His heart beat high amid the deepening strife,
  That stalwart Texan's heart! His manly breast

Caught in its veins a new, a holy light,
   As on that reeking plain, where crest met crest,
A thought of Texas, with her lovely plains,
Came o'er his heart like music's soothing strains,
            By the River of Death!

The free fair plains of Texas, and her hills
   With rich dark valleys sleeping soft between;
Her moss-hung forests and her willowy rills,
   Her streams like silver in the noonday sheen;—
The free, fair plains of Texas! how the thought
Of all their beauty nerved him as he fought
            By the River of Death!

His boyhood's home amid the shadows lying,
   Beneath his own, his sunny western skies!
His mother and his sisters! 'Mid the dying
   How is it that a new fire lights his eyes,
As these thoughts sweep like lightning through his breast?
. . . . The day drags on: the strong arms know no rest
            By the River of Death!

By the River of Death! 'Twas there he fell
   As only Freedom's own can fall! his eye
Still lit with triumph, and his heart, as slow
   It ceased its own faint earth-born melody,
To battle's raging chorus keeping time—
The "infinite, fierce chorus"—that mad chime
            By the River of Death!

A single thought o'ershadowed him, his eye
   Grew troubled for one moment, then 'twas o'er—
"His fair young wife, his dark-eyed boy, to die
   Far from them!" The cannon's lordly roar
Broke on his ear, his eye caught back its pride,
His lax hand grasped his falling gun: he died
            By the River of Death!

He died, and night with clouded skies looked down
   Upon his burial. The torch-light red
Glared fitfully about; they gathered 'round,

His comrades, sadly silent near the dead.
They wrapped him in his blanket,—song nor prayer
Awoke the stillness, as they laid him there
By the River of Death!

Buried upon the field! 'Tis meet, for why
Should warriors rest where peaceful churchyards are?
Why should they sleep where battle's trumpet-cry
Was never heard, nor breath of glorious war?
Upon their field of glory, on the plain
Where Death's strange voice hath hushed the noble slain,
There let them lie.

At home, the sweet young wife droops like a flower,
His prattling babe hushed sadly by her knee—
His boy, his laughing boy, whose earthly dower
Is fatherless childhood! Ah, sunbeams flee
That darkened hearth, and free the shadows stray,
Shadows born there since that fatal day
By the River of Death!

The camp-fire in the distant wood gleams red,
The soldiers group about the ruddy light,
And count in softened tones the noble dead—
The dead! "It thinned our ranks so, that last fight!
The brave who fell like brothers, side by side!"
And then his comrades tell how well he fought, who died
By the River of Death!

III. THEY HAD HEARD THE NEWS OF THE BATTLE

A contingent of poets portrayed the experience of battle; a complementary contingent depicted the impact of the war on those left at home. Many books of war poetry contained a poetic portrait of the soldier's family waiting for news from the battle field. Just as a combination of forces caused death to become a popular subject among war poets, so various forces impelled poets to turn toward the fireside. A strong domestic current flowed throughout the literature and thinking of mid-nineteenth century America. Culture centered pre-eminently in the home. The plots of the extremely popular sentimental novels of the era usually revolved around domestic situations. The word "household," itself, enjoyed a wider currency then than now. Poets who pictured domestic affections spoke of themselves as "household poets." Houghton-Mifflin's extremely popular Household Edition of nineteenth century poets carries suggestion in its title.

As a part of their emphasis on domestic scenes, poets defined separation as an inevitable concomitant of domesticity. In the popular long verse narratives, for example, separation of the hero and heroine constituted a *sine qua non.* In large part poets employed the subject of separation as a convenient means of focusing attention on man's sensibilities. It is not surprising, then, that poets should make poetic capital of the inevitable separation brought on by the war.

In "The Soldier's Fireside, after a Battle," an anonymous poet who signed his work M. T. C. draws a typical picture of the kind of anxiety experienced by the families of those who are fighting.

The poem is from *Flowers from the Battle-Field, and Other Poems* (Philadelphia, 1864).

THE SOLDIER'S FIRESIDE, AFTER A BATTLE

Suggested by a scene in a soldier's family, after the battle of Chancellorsville

They sat by the dying embers,
As the daylight fled away,
A sister, a wife, and a mother,
With hearts too heavy to pray.

Around the walls and the ceiling
The shadows clustered and clung,
Till the room seemed a chamber of mourning
With funeral drap'ry hung.

They had heard the news of the battle,
But not the names of the dead,
And in thought they were seeking their loved one
On a battle-field trampled and red.

The mother, in widow'd garments,
Sat upright with face of stone,

Striving bravely to bear both sorrows,
  Her country's grief and her own.

Bent low was the wife's slight figure,
  And her face, by her falling hair
And her clasped hands, was hidden,
  In the depth of her despair.

Between these two, on the carpet,
  The sister had knelt down,
With the large tears slowly stealing
  From beneath the lashes brown.

But the baby of the household,
  Who had missed her evening game,
Was fast asleep on the hearth-rug,
  Unconscious of grief or shame;

The rosy lips were parted,
  As the breath came softly through,
And the golden curls fell backward,
  From the temples veined with blue;

And she seemed a holy vision,
  An angel with Hope's pure light,
Sent down to dispel the terror
  That clouded their souls that night.

The very fire in the chimney
  Seemed trying to cheer their gloom,
For a sudden blaze set dancing
  All the shadows in the room.

The mother's brow grew softer,
  The sister faintly smiled,
And the wife lost half her anguish,
  As she gazed upon the child.

Each thought of the loving Father
  Who makes the brave soldier His care,
And their doubt and despair were routed
  By the holy power of prayer;

And the morning proved that the baby
  Had brought them a vision true,
For they had good news from their loved one,
  And hope for their country too.

IV. TO THINK THAT YOU DIED ALONE

The soldier's family pictured in "The Soldier's Fireside, after a Battle" (see page 25), in receiving "good news from their loved one," found itself in an extraordinary position. In keeping with their penchant for death, poets customarily pictured those at home receiving news that was anything but good. Laura C. Redden's "Left on the Battle Field" parallels many poems in which women grieve over the deaths of loved ones in battle.

The poem is from *Idyls of Battle and Poems of the Rebellion* (New York, 1864).

LEFT ON THE BATTLE-FIELD

Oh, my darling! my darling! never to feel
  Your hand going over my hair!
Never to lie in your arms again,—
  Never to know where you are!
Oh, the weary miles that stretch between
  My feet and the battle-ground,
Where all that is left of my dearest hope
  Lies under some yellow mound!

It is but little I might have done
  To lighten your parting pain;
But 't is bitter to think that you died alone
  Out in the dark and the rain!
Oh, my hero love!—to have kissed the pain
  And the mist from your fading eyes!
To have saved one only passionate look
  To sweeten these memories!

And thinking of all, I am strangely stunned,
  And cannot believe you dead.

You loved me, dear! And I loved you, dear!
  And your letter lies there, unread!
You are not dead! You are not dead!
  God never could will it so—
To craze my brain and break my heart
  And shatter my life—I know!

Dead! dead! and never a word,
  Never a look for me!
Dead! dead! and our marriage-day
  Never on earth to be!
I am left alone, and the world is changed,
  So dress me in bridal white,
And lay me away in some quiet place
  Out of the hateful light.

V. VIGIL STRANGE

Out of the mass of war poetry produced during the Eighteen-Sixties, two books stand pre-eminent. One is Herman Melville's *Battle-Pieces and Aspects of the War* (New York, 1866); the other is Walt Whitman's *Drum-Taps* (New York, 1865).

Whitman's book, for one thing, is unusual in that its central philosophy gives the poems a cumulative effect. Whitman's recurring note—the unity and greatness of America to come from the struggle—echoes from poem to poem. In "From Paumanok Starting I Fly like a Bird" Whitman declares that his purpose is

> To sing first, (to the tap of the war-drum if need be,)
> The idea of all, of the Western world one and inseparable,

In "Song of the Banner at Daybreak," the banner and pennant, symbolic of the entire country, declare,

> We may be terror and carnage, and are so now,
> Not now are we any one of these spacious and haughty
>   States, (nor any five, nor ten,)

In "Rise O Days from your Fathomless Deeps" Whitman exhorts,

Thunder on! stride on, Democracy! strike with vengeful stroke!
And do you rise higher than ever yet O days, O cities!

Whitman's short poem, "Long, Too Long America" states the theme throughout.

Long, too long America,
Traveling roads all even and peaceful you learn'd from joys and prosperity only,
But now, ah now, to learn from crises of anguish, advancing, grappling with direst fate and recoiling not,
And now to conceive and show to the world what your children en-masse really are,
(For who except myself has yet conceiv'd what your children en-masse really are?)

The well-known "Over the Carnage Rose Prophetic a Voice" opens with the optimistic lines,

Over the carnage rose prophetic a voice,
Be not dishearten'd, affection shall solve the problems of freedom yet,
Those who love each other shall become invincible,
They shall yet make Columbia victorious.

Whitman closes this poem by declaring that no living thing will so cohere as the country following the conflict.

This theme, central in a number of poems, is implied in the tone of others. The jubilant manner with which Whitman greets the war in "Eighteen Sixty One," "First O Songs for a Prelude," and "City of Ships" implies that good, rather than ill, is to come from the war. Whitman's awareness—an awareness far greater than that of his sentimental peers—of the suffering caused by the war gives his positive assertion a conviction it would otherwise lack. When a poet can describe the agony of the wounded as Whitman does in "The Wound-Dresser," a reader is not inclined to accuse him of indulging in unthinking sentimentality in asserting that good, not ill, will result from the conflict.

Interestingly, Whitman's *Drum-Taps*, coming though it does from a poet who has contributed some of the most moving symbolic poems in the language, is refreshing because of its frequent realism. Whitman employs his well-known cataloguing technique effectively in several war poems. His "First O Songs for a Prelude," for example, depicts the country's response to war in part as follows:

To the drum-taps prompt,
The young men falling in and arming,
The mechanics arming, (the trowel, the jack-plane, the blacksmith's hammer, tost aside with precipitation,)
The lawyer leaving his office and arming, the judge leaving the court,
The driver deserting his wagon in the street, jumping down, throwing the reins abruptly down on the horses' backs,
The salesman leaving the store, the boss, book-keeper, porter, all leaving;

Whitman here dramatizes the action vividly and, although the expression contains ordinary phraseology and an uncomplex attitude, Whitman avoids the stereotyped phrases utilized by most poets. "The Wound-Dresser" is another poem whose minute realism gives penetrating insight into the actual conduct of the war.

But Whitman had maintained in his 1855 preface that "folks expect of the poet to indicate more than the beauty and dignity which always attach to dumb real objects . . . they expect him to indicate the path between reality and their souls." Consequently, he was not always content with a mere surface realism, however minute and graphic. In *Drum-Taps,* Whitman occasionally experiments with language, using the unusual combinations of words which is an earmark of his style. That *Drum-Taps* contains less experimentation than some of Whitman's other poetry suggests that the poet allowed his emotional involvement in the war to lessen the aesthetic distance between himself and his work. Nevertheless, Whitman is able, in "First O Songs for a Prelude," to characterize war as "the red business." Whitman's use of homely phrases such as this in poems possessing the sonorous rhythms of the Old Testament gives such poems an unusual emotional range.

Whitman's artistry with language is particularly evident in his "Vigil Strange I Kept." In using the subject of the soldier slain in battle, Whitman placed himself in a popular tradition. The superiority of Whitman's poem over all other poems on this subject lies in his definition of the phrase "vigil strange." Whitman consciously builds up an ambiguity in the word "vigil," a word having both military and religious connotations. Since the narrator is keeping watch over a soldier slain in battle, he feels that his vigil should be of a military nature: a guarding of the corpse from harm. Yet the vigil, from the first verse, seems "strange." Although this strangeness never leaves (the fifth verse from the end speaks of "Ending my vigil strange"), the word assumes religious connotations as the poem progresses, so that midway through the poem Whitman can speak of "Vigil wondrous and vigil sweet," and later of "Vigil of silence, love and death." Thus the "Vigil strange" near the close of the poem has acquired definition, possessing a richer meaning than the "Vigil strange" of the opening verse. Few of the slain who were strewn throughout the war verse of the Sixties have been quite so honored as Whitman's "dear comrade."

VIGIL STRANGE I KEPT ON THE FIELD ONE NIGHT

Vigil strange I kept on the field one night;
When you my son and my comrade dropt at my side that day,
One look I but gave which your dear eyes return'd with a look I shall never forget,
One touch of your hand to mine O boy, reach'd up as you lay on the ground,
Then onward I sped in the battle, the even-contested battle,
Till late in the night reliev'd to the place at last again I made my way,
Found you in death so cold dear comrade, found your body son of responding kisses, (never again on earth responding,)
Bared your face in the starlight, curious the scene, cool blew the moderate night-wind,
Long there and then in vigil I stood, dimly around me the battlefield spreading,
Vigil wondrous and vigil sweet there in the fragrant silent night,
But not a tear fell, not even a long-drawn sigh, long, long I gazed,
Then on the earth partially reclining sat by your side leaning my chin in my hands,
Passing sweet hours, immortal and mystic hours with you dearest comrade —not a tear, not a word,
Vigil of silence, love and death, vigil for you my son and my soldier,
As onward silently stars aloft, eastward new ones upward stole,
Vigil final for you brave boy, (I could not save you, swift was your death,
I faithfully loved you and cared for you living, I think we shall surely meet again,)
Till at latest lingering of the night, indeed just as the dawn appear'd,
My comrade I wrapt in his blanket, envelop'd well his form,
Folded the blanket well, tucking it carefully over head and carefully under feet,
And there and then and bathed by the rising sun, my son in his grave, in his rude-dug grave I deposited,
Ending my vigil strange with that, vigil of night and battle-field dim,

Vigil for boy of responding kisses, (never again on earth responding,)
Vigil for comrade swiftly slain, vigil I never forget, how as day brighten'd,
I rose from the chill ground and folded my soldier well in his blanket,
And buried him where he fell.

VI. THEY BEAR HIM GENTLY HOME

Poets frequently brought the battle-field and the home together by depicting the dead soldier brought home from war. A comparison of the tone possessed by the two following poems affords insight into how similarly North and South reacted to the Great Leveller. "Returned from War," by the Northern poet Henry L. Abbey, is from *May Dreams* (New York, 1862); "The Jacket of Grey," by the Southern poet Mrs. Caroline Augusta Ball, is from *The Jacket of Grey, and Other Fugitive Poems* (Charleston, 1866).

RETURNED FROM WAR

Shrouded by his country's flag,
  And in martial garments dressed,
Came the soldier to his home,
  With his sword upon his breast.

Stepping to the muffled drum,
  Pass the guard on either side:
All the people as they come,
  Whisper how the warrior died.

Of his deeds, what words can tell?
  But in battle, 'mid the van,
Cheering on the fight, he fell
  For the common cause of man.

He shall lead the charge no more—
  Scale the rampart to the gun;
For they bear him gently home,
  To his wife and little one.

THEY BEAR HIM GENTLY HOME

She, who through her bridal vail [*sic*],
  Looked and called him dearest, best!
Bends above him in her tears,
  With her head upon his breast.

She has sorrow for her part:
  Grief alone to her is sent,
Blighting all her summer heart,
  And the roses of content.

What if victory crowned the day?
  She will heed you not nor stir:
He has fallen in the fray:
  He was all the world to her.

THE JACKET OF GREY

Fold it up carefully, lay it aside;
Tenderly touch it, look on it with pride;
For dear must it be to our hearts evermore,
The jacket of grey our loved soldier boy wore.

Can we ever forget when he joined the brave band,
Who rose in defence of our dear Southern land,
And in his bright youth hurried on to the fray,
How proudly he donned it? the jacket of grey.

His fond mother blessed him and looked up above,
Commending to Heaven the child of her love;
What anguish was her's, mortal tongue cannot say,
When he passed from her sight in the jacket of grey.

But her country had called, and she would not repine,
Though costly the sacrifice placed on its shrine;
Her heart's dearest hopes on its altar she lay,
When she sent out her boy in the jacket of grey.

Months passed, and war's thunders rolled over the land,
Unsheathed was the sword, and lighted the brand;
We heard in the distance the sounds of the fray,
And prayed for our boy in the jacket of grey.

Ah! vain, all, all vain were our prayers and our tears,
The glad shout of victory rang in our ears;
But our treasured one on the red battle field lay,
While the life-blood oozed out on the jacket of grey.

His young comrades found him, and tenderly bore
The cold lifeless form to his home by the shore;
Oh, dark were our hearts on that terrible day,
When we saw our dead boy in the jacket of grey.

Ah! spotted and tattered, and stained now with gore,
Was the garment which once he so proudly wore;
We bitterly wept as we took it away,
And replaced with death's white robes the jacket of grey.

We laid him to rest in his cold narrow bed,
And graved on the marble we placed o'er his head,
As the proudest tribute our sad hearts could pay,
He never disgraced the jacket of grey.

Then fold it up carefully, lay it aside,
Tenderly touch it, look on it with pride;
For dear must it be to our hearts evermore,
The jacket of grey our loved soldier boy wore!

VII. NOT E'EN THE HOUSE OF GOD WAS SPARED

Sherman's army, in its march to the sea, briefly occupied Columbia, South Carolina. On the night of February 17, 1865, fire swept a large part of the city. Controversy still smoulders concerning the origin of the fire, which Southerners universally attributed to Sherman and his men. By the time Sherman's march had become history, the devastation wrought by his army had caused his name to become a byword in the South.

NOT E'EN THE HOUSE OF GOD WAS SPARED

The fact that most of the military action of the Civil War took place in the South gave Southern poets a subject not open to their Northern counterparts. The fearful destruction in the South had ravaged a land looked upon by its people as little short of Paradise. It is small wonder, then, that Southern poets found a place in their war verse for an expression of grief over the desolation visited upon their land by the Northmen; or that Mrs. Elizabeth Otis Marshall Dannelly, in taking up her pen to sing of the Lost Cause, should have selected the dramatic burning of Columbia to epitomize Northern depravity.

Of equal interest with the poet's strictures against the rapacious invaders is her picture of the tone of Columbia society and the nature of its people. Here Mrs. Dannelly reflects accurately the way Southerners regarded their ante-bellum civilization.

Destruction of the City of Columbia, South Carolina. A Poem by a Lady of Georgia was published in Charleston during 1866.

DESTRUCTION OF COLUMBIA

Methinks there'll be emblazoned on the dismal walls of Hell,
A record base, whose fiery words of fiendish deeds will tell,
Through ages of eternal woe, to demons black with crime,
How once on earth degraded men o'erleaped the bounds of time,
And though they dwelt in human flesh, incarnate devils turned,
When maddened by infernal hate, they plundered, killed and burned,
Methinks the "Prince of Darkness" with a wild sardonic grin,
Will point exultant to a crime that won the prize from sin,
And glory in a monument that tells his direful sway,
O'er Northmen, who with burning torch swept happy homes away.
They came a motley multitude, a God forsaken band,
With vengeance rankling in each heart, and blood upon each hand,
And as they stood with glittering steel on Carolina's banks,
"Vae victis!" was the fiendish shout that sounded through their ranks.
They looked across Savannah's stream with fury glaring eyes,
And trembled in their eagerness to pounce upon their prize.
In muttered curses mingled with *"the howlings of delight,"*
They longed to strike with bloody hand the stunning blow of might,
And as they neared with dashing speed Columbia so fair,
The heavy tramp, and cannon's roar that thundered on the air,

Gave warning to her people that a conflict had begun,
Whose deadly stroke would do its work before another sun.
A carriage then was seen to leave which bore a flag of white,
And men, within whose bosoms burned the consciousness of right;
The Army reached, in proper form, a noble hearted Mayor
Surrendered all, and begged the foe their lovely city spare.
The sacred promise sought was given, but soon a shout arose,
Which told, alas! of pledges broke, and treachery of foes.
Behind them desolation told the fury of their wrath;
The light of burning homesteads threw a glimmer o'er their path;
The smiling fields all trampled lay beneath the horseman's tread;
And cattle o'er a thousand hills lay mangled, bleeding, dead.
Half naked people cowered under bushes from the blast,
And shivered as the midnight wind with icy breathings past;
Fair maidens whose luxurious lives had known before no blight,
With faces pale as marble stood, beneath the pall of night;
While "crimson horrors" lighted up the wintry midnight sky,
As on the ebon wings of smoke their burning homesteads fly;
Till village after village, by ascending flames were traced,
And rising on the mourning clouds, with fiery arms embraced.
The treasured stores of art, and taste, defiled and ruined lay,
Rare paintings which had long withstood the touch of Time's decay,
Rich tapestry of velvet soft, besmeared with ink and oil,
Where dainty feet once lightly tread, is now among the spoil;
Rare furniture, superbly carved, pianos grand in tone,
Beneath the ruffian's crushing stroke, sent up an echoing moan;
The gardens, types of Paradise, in tropic verdure dressed,
All trampled by the vandal's steed, lay ruined with the rest;
The cries of starving children rose upon the smoky air,
And wild ascended piteous screams of women in despair;
As far as human eye could reach a blackened desert lay,
And o'er a stricken people hung the shadows of dismay.
On, on, they dashed, with mad'ning speed, *"woe to the conquered"* cried,
"We'll crush rebellion's spirit now and Carolina's pride;
We'll burn her cherished capital; we'll rob her of her gain,
And woman's prayers, or piteous cries shall reach our ears in vain."
No summons for surrender came, but thick and rapid fell,
Into Columbia's very heart the treacherous bursting shell;
The flying fragments bearing death to innocence and mirth;
To children sporting, free from care, around the social hearth;
To helpless women, feeble age, and victims of disease,

Who fell with terror, stricken down upon their bended knees.
An aged sire, with wrinkled brow, and silken locks of white,
Was wounded by a missile sent which took away his sight.

The wild excitement on the street, the universal haste,
The people flying to and fro, the rush, the wreck, the waste,
The "wilderness of baggage" sent on wagons to the train;
The hundreds striving to get off, but striving all in vain;
The children, and the helpless babes, of every age and size,
Who added terror to the scene with sharp and fearful cries;
The women trembling pale with fright, who knew, alas! too well,
The weaker sex no mercy claimed from men in league with hell,
Will be a sight remembered long, and long on history's page,
The record will be handed down to tell of Yankee rage.

A loud explosion ushered in that long remembered day,
The Depot at the dawn of light in smouldering ruins lay,
A prelude to the tragic act, the dark infernal plot,
Which left upon the Northern name a black, eternal blot.
The clock upon the Market-hall had struck the hour of ten
On Friday, that eventful morn, when entered Sherman's men.
High o'er a captured city now, the "stars and stripes" they place,
To witness scenes of violence, of burning, and disgrace;
A banner that once proudly waved, the standard of the free,
Now floats above the tyrant's ranks, the type of infamy,
To take upon its sullied folds a deeper, darker, stain,
Than blood of brothers in the cause of holy freedom slain;
To wave above infernal scenes, fit prototypes of Hell,
And with its colors dyed in crime, a mute approval tell;
A flag that once o'er Washington a hallowed shadow threw,
When in the cause of liberty his gleaming sword he drew;
A flag upon whose azure blue the brightest stars that gleamed,
Arose from where the Southern blood in crimson rivers streamed;
Whose glory fled, when 'neath its fold no longer could we stand;
When first it ceased to wave above a free, and happy land.

The thieving wretches, one and all, their pillage now began,
Assisted by the officers exalted in command.
Woe to the honest passer-by, who carried watch and chain,
His arguments of prior right were uttered all in vain,
For Yankees ignore all but gold, and no compunctions feel,

'Tis but the "nature of the beast" to *swindle, lie,* and *steal.*
New boots, and shoes, or coats and hats, the same abstraction shared,
And all alike, the white and *black,* with gross injustice fared.
The jeweled hands of maidens fair were sought a brilliant prize,
And sparkling gems were taken off in spite of tearful eyes;
Engagement rings of massive gold, their diamonds, and their pearls,
Now glitter on the brawny hands of saucy Yankee girls,
And Yankee boards are shining now arrayed in silver plate,
Engraven with the honored names of South Carolina's great;
The relics of ancestral pride, by noble sires left,
Are lost, polluted, sacrificed, to groveling Yankee theft,
And Yankee cooks, and chambermaids, now since the hellish raid,
Flaunt out in Southern women's lace, and elegant brocade;
Disgracing lovely womanhood, ignoring moral law,
They wear without a blush of shame, their "trophies of the war."
But 'twere a task impossible to write the endless list,
The articles of precious goods that Southerners have missed.
We "fell among" inhuman "thieves," suffice it then to say,
That scarce a vestige of our wealth remains with us to-day.

Not e'en the house of God was spared; the sacramental cup
Was filled with liquor's burning draught for cursed lips to sup.
The sacred vessels of the Church were wrested from his hand,
As homeward-bound his steps were turned, the venerable SHAND.
They plundered on, insatiate fiends, till near the setting sun,
While Sherman looked serenely on, and whispered "boys well done."
With vengeance written on his brow, and falsehood on his breast,
He bade our noble, trusting Mayor, retire to his rest,
Assured him that a "finger's breadth" his men should never harm,
And told him how unwise his fears, how needless his alarm.
As well might one, with childish faith, believe the "Prince of lies,"
For scarce upon the tainted air his vile assertion dies,
When, lo! the rockets darting high illume the brow of night,
The signal bids the restless foe his blazing torches light;
The barbarous sign at length is given, and bursting to the skies,
The crimson flames of burning homes, in rolling volumes rise.
The doom, the awful, awful, doom, we heard the soldiers tell,
With savage chuckle through their ranks, "to-night we'll give you Hell."
With soaking balls of turpentine, and brands of flick'ring light,
They ushered in, with eager hand, the horrors of that night.
A range of burning mountains "raised their flame-capped heads on high,"

And spouts of melted lava sent their torrents to the sky;
The crumbling walls upon the air with thundering crashes broke,
As o'er them rose successive clouds of black terrific smoke;
The embers floated on the breeze like stars of glowing light,
And glittered high above the flames upon the vault of night;
The elements of Nature seemed at war with air and sky,
And in convulsive fury swept like avalanches by.
The grandeur of that awful scene no painter can portray,
But graven on the frenzied mind, forever will it stay.

Now rocking with a death-like shock, the ancient State House falls,
And buries deep the lore of time beneath her crumbling walls.
How many reminiscences of other days arise:
Here once assembled beauty, wealth, the honored, and the wise;
'Twas here the voice of Preston rang with eloquent appeals,
And battled for that principle, that never, never, yields;
The mighty Haynes here nobly plead in freedom's holy cause,
And labored for his country's fame, its happiness and laws;
McDuffie stirred the people with his blistering words of fire,
They quailed beneath his strong appeals, the maiden and the sire;
And here spoke Carolina's son, her noblest, proudest boon,
Who rocked the Western hemisphere, the eloquent Calhoun.
Long is the bright, untarnished list of Carolina's great,
But ruined lies her Capitol, the glory of the State.

In deep despair the women rush with madness to and fro,
Receiving naught but taunting words, and insult from the foe;
They strive to rescue from the flames a relic, but in vain,
A demon grasps the captured prize and hurls it back again.

Within a silent chamber now, where burns the lamplight pale,
And prayers from anxious watchers rise upon the midnight gale,
There rests upon a downy couch a fragile form so white,
And lying closely by her side, just opening to the light,
Peeps out a tender little bud, a tiny infant face,
And love, in silence, reigns supreme within that hallowed place.
The demons rush with curses wild into the darkened room,
And carry to the being there a sad and fearful doom.
They grasp her thin and trembling hand to seize the shining rings,
And terror o'er her livid face its ghastly palor [*sic*] flings;
They seize the watch beneath her head; they steal her fleeting breath,

For lo! her eyelids gently close; she sleeps the sleep of death.
Another suf'rer pale, and wan, is writhing in her pain,
She craves the mercy of the fiends, but pleads, alas! in vain,
With cries of murder on their lips, and glaring torch they came,
And wrapt the drapery of her room in sheets of crimson flame.
Upon a matrass [*sic*], rudely borne into the chilling air,
While icy winds are sweeping by, she meekly suffers there,
And bears in patient agony, while cursing lips condemn,
What woman by the stern decree had suffered once for them.

A widow with her "little all," a bag of meal and flour,
Had sadly watched her earthly store through many a weary hour,
When with a brow unknown to shame, a rascal bore away
The earnings scant and pitiful, of many a toilsome day.
He brandished in her mournful face a shining Bowie knife,
And threatened, as she plead and prayed, to take away her life.

Nor did the hardened wretches spare the children in their play,
When closed the night, and dawned in gloom, another mournful day,
A group of merry little ones caressed a sprightly pet,
A greyhound with its glossy hair, and sparkling eyes of jet,
When passing by, a bandit threw a missile at its head,
And howling, bleeding, at their feet the little dog fell dead.

A slow procession on that night with faces deadly pale,
Around whose fragile figures hung the long, black, sweeping veil,
The nuns in silent sorrow left the holy shrine of prayer,
While o'er their faces pale as death was spread a lurid glare;
With trembling steps they sadly sought the "city of the dead,"
As from the hot and crumbling walls they terror-stricken fled,
And there mid hallowed, sacred, dust, mid tombstones cold and white,
They passed, in bitterness of heart, that long remembered night.

In Sidney Park, where once the gay and happy city thronged,
There huddled, in promiscuous crowds, the old, the young, the wronged;
The sick lay fainting on the ground, and to the mothers clung,
In almost idiotic fright, their babes and helpless young.
They fancied here a safe retreat from crumbling walls to find,
But, lo! redoubled horrors break upon the frenzied mind,
When hot, into their ghastly midst, with darting speed there falls,
Hurled wildly from the heights around the flashing fiery balls.

But there are crimes far blacker still, too base, alas! to tell,
Too vile to e'en escape the lips, too near allied to Hell.
To contemplate would cause a blush on woman's cheek to burn,
The thoughts of such infernal deeds her purity would spurn.

But night removed her sombre veil, and morning came at last,
Like maniacs the people stood and thought upon the past;
It seemed a wild excited dream, a vapor of the brain,
Too awful for reality, too fraught with mad'ning pain.
But weary limbs and aching feet, as shelterless they roam,
Remind the wanderers, pale and faint, they have, alas! no home.
Ah! who can paint the shocking scene, the desolation wild,
The black despair that reigned supreme where happiness once smiled.
The sun revealed a languid ray of sympathetic light,
As though his soul had sickened o'er the horrors of the night;
He would not cast a radiant smile into the face of gloom,
Or mock the dismal soul that mourned its sudden awful doom.
His brightest smiles were far too bright in silvery light to fall,
Upon the frowning ruins there, the black and tottering wall.

But o'er such scenes of blood and wreck my weary Muse grows faint,
No longer would she human crimes and human sorrows paint,
Nor would she peer beyond the stage o'er which the curtain falls,
The act behind congeals the blood, the tragedy appalls.
A glance upon the outer screen is all she dare bestow,
Where only types of monstrous crimes in fainter outlines glow.
So sad and awful are the scenes, whose traces cannot die,
The ruling spirit of the wreck would fain his work deny.
When devils that possessed his soul upon that awful night,
By softer feelings of the heart are put again to flight,
With human eye he views the deed, in terror stands aghast,
And on the name of Hampton brave the fearful blame would cast.
Thorns fester in the Southern heart, and do you ask me why?
"Time cannot teach forgetfulness," the *past* can *never* die.

VIII. HOME, HOME AGAIN!

A regularly scheduled meeting a century ago, such as that of a library or alumni association, as well as a special occasion to commemorate the founding of a town, to lay a monument, to graduate college seniors, to dedicate a public building or cemetery, included the reading of a poem. In every instance this poem, written by a member of the group, addressed the assembly and commented on the occasion, frequently mentioning by name various dignitaries who were present. Many such poems were subsequently printed, either by themselves or in pamphlets as part of the proceedings of the meetings. Oliver Wendell Holmes' occasional poems are survivors of this genre. These poems of address, intended to appeal to listeners in a given situation, ordinarily lose their immediacy when removed from the occasion. Holmes himself realized their ephemeral nature, writing in the 1849 edition of his poems that "many of the lesser poems were written for meetings more or less convivial, and must of course show something like the fire-work frames on the morning of July 5th."

Since poets laboring in this vineyard traditionally commented on the happenings of the moment, it is not surprising that many poems of address written during the Eighteen-Sixties make some mention of the war, and that a good number devote themselves exclusively to comment on the struggle. In the early days of war undergraduate after undergraduate informed commencement gatherings that the present called for action, not for learning alone. As the war progressed such occasional poems became somewhat less exuberant, but after Appomattox the exuberance returned in the form of rejoicing over war's end. Typical is B. H. Barnes' *Poem, Read at the Soldiers' Welcome, Franklin, Delaware Co., N.Y., August 5th, 1865* (Binghamton, N.Y., [1865]). Barnes carefully praises the returning heroes for their contribution to victory, but throughout his address the poet's relief—undoubtedly shared by the returning patriots—at the end of bloodshed is evident. Testimony to the effects of four years of war is afforded by comparing the melodramatic call-to-arms poems of 1861 with poems, such as Barnes', which rejoice that soldiers may now come home.

POEM, READ AT THE SOLDIERS' WELCOME, FRANKLIN, DELAWARE CO., N.Y., AUGUST 5TH, 1865

The heroes of a hundred fields
  Are gathered here to-day;
And banners wave, and cheers applaud
  The patriot array.

HOME, HOME AGAIN!

Proud parents boast their noble sons;
  Fond wives their husbands, dear;
And loyal maidens smile sweet praise
  On every volunteer.

Loud cornet-blare and throbbing drums—
  Soft Zephyr's bland caress—
Bright eyes, swift pulses, pealing songs,
  Bespeak our happiness.

The birds are gayer—brighter flow
  The brooklet's wave and foam—
And th' way-side cattle *seem* to low
  The Soldiers' "welcome home!"

O, cheerfully, the patriot leaves
  Home, comfort, *all,* to share
The toils and dangers of the field,
  If duty calls him there.

And well he bears War's stern fatigues—
  Counting privations light—
May he but gain his Country's thanks,
  Through triumph for the right.

But when the tidings of release
  From faithful service come,
The warrior *wings* his eager feet
  To taste the joys of home.

With sparkling eye he hails each hill
  And well-remember'd peak—
How cool the Northern breezes fall
  Upon his bronzed cheek!

Forgotten, are his years of toil—
  Wounds, prison, hunger, pain—
No room in Joy's full harmony
  For Sorrow's sad refrain.

Home, home again! the sweet tho't wakes
  Glad music in his soul—
And consciousness of *duty done*
  Pours wine in Pleasure's bowl.

Surrounded by the loving ones
  That come at Friendship's call,
The soldier sings his wild war-songs,
  While evening shadows fall.

Young children, nestled on his knee—
  Fair maiden at his side—
Or wife, or mother, sire or friend,
  With patriotic pride

List to the warrior's thrilling tales
  Of camp, and march, and fight;
Until the young hours of the morn
  Are nearer than the night.

Welcome, brave hearts! we gladly press
  The victor's glowing palm!
Come, brothers, crowned with honor, peace,
  And Freedom's blessed calm!

* * *

Three years ago the trumpet-call
  Of Liberty out-rang!
And from the hills of Delaware,
  A thousand patriots sprang

To check the tide of Treason's flood,
  That rolled its angry waves,
Cap'd with Rebellion's bloody foam,
  Up, from the land of slaves!

Our peaceful skies were dark'ning fast—
  Home trembled with alarms!
And freemen felt the hour must have
  The strength of their strong arms.

HOME, HOME AGAIN!

The loyal farmer left his fields,
  Just shorn of golden grain—
The blacksmith flung aside his sledge—
  The carpenter, his plane:

The merchant closed the ledger's lids,
  With clenched and nervous hands—
And clerk, and squire, step'd proudly forth
  In Uncle Sam's brogans.

The pale-eyed student doff'd his gown,
  And don'd the blouse of blue;
Eager to grapple with the wrong
  And prove his courage true!

And th' preacher, from his wonted place,
  Pray'd God protect his flock;
And clasp them tenderly the while
  He clasp'd the musket-stock!

Stout, brawny limbs and thick-set beards;
  Betok'ning manhood's prime—
The slender, stripling forms of youth;
  That show'd no touch of time—

Came pouring down, thro' gorge and glen—
  From vale and rock-bar'd steep—
And from the deep, green hemlock woods,
  Where frighten'd cascades leap.

All, with one mission—grandly high!
  One purpose to perform;
As pure as ever prompted prayer;
  Or nerved a patriot's arm—

All rallied 'round the dear old flag,
  For which their fathers bled!
And vow'd to follow and defend
  Tho' marching to the dead!

We trusted you—you'd faith in us—
  As one, our fates were sealed—

O, how we watched your steady tramp,
Forth to the battle-field!

What time war's wild tornado howl'd
Its fury through the years,
We asked, "God shield from every harm
Our noble volunteers."

"But should the cruel battle-blast
E'er lay our darlings low,
Aye let them fall, as they have lived—
Their faces to the foe!"

And when, anon, the lightning flash'd
Glad tidings for the free,
We made these rugged hill-sides ring
With cheers for victory!

The hopes and fears of those wild years
Are not forgotten yet—
Still, with their ling'ring memories,
Our eyes are sometimes wet.

And, Soldiers, when your letters told
(No word of murm'ring meant)
Of all your suff'rings for the cause,
In hospital and tent;

How trill'd the chords of woman's heart!
How fast her needles flew!
What sweet remittances of love,
And faith, and *courage,* too!

I need not tell—the warrior's breast,
Like a rich treasure-store,
Is full of fond remembrances;
Worth more than golden ore.

Yes, woman's countless, kindly deeds,
Borne to our braves, afar—
Have cancel'd half the wrong and woe
And misery of war.

HOME, HOME AGAIN!

Ay, in the granaries of God,
  Is garner'd Virtue's grain,
That ne'er had grown on Freedom's soil
  Without her battle-rain!

And when, alas! some fallen lad—
  To roll of muffled drum,
Timed to the pattering dirge of tears—
  Came to his Northern home;

Wrap'd in the banner he had borne
  Against the cannon's breath—
Came, from his comrades far a-field,
  On the long parole of death;

We laid him where his fathers sleep;
  'Neath Freedom's spreading trees—
And left him with the birds, and flowers,
  And grateful memories.

* * *

Still boom'd the guns! and louder rang
  Bold Freedom's trumpet calls!
And other thousands swept along
  To man her breaching walls.

Still play'd the shifting game of war:
  And, driv'n from cliff to crag,
The 'wilder'd eagles dared not fold
  Their wings on either flag;

Until God taught the Nation this;
  Through strife, defeats and pains—
"Your day of triumph ne'er shall dawn
  On th' slave's unbroken chains!"

O then that firm, but generous hand—
  True, honest, sure, though slow—
Gain'd Heaven's smile; and dealt the wrong
  Its heaviest, deadliest, blow.

And they that wore the galling yoke,
  In this and other lands,
Beheld the morning star of Hope;
  And stretched their joyful hands!

And from the dust, the toil-bow'd slave,
  His eye on Freedom's form—
Stood up! and bared his ebon breast
  To treason's fiercest storm.

Thus side by side—On! marching on—
  The Union patriots trod:
Down-bearing every hand that fought
  Humanity and God!

Then arch'd the bow, with promise bright!
  Our eagles, from the sun,
Perch'd proudly on the starry flag;
  And victory was won!

O, if the mighty dead are given
  Their angel-brows to grace
With glorious actions here perform'd,
  To free and bless the race;

Then does the crown of Lincoln shine
  Resplendent as the sun!
And heaven is songful for the deed
  Our martyr'd Chief has done!

Soldiers, no higher honors crave—
  None nobler wait for ye,—
Than wreath your names with his who wro't
  This work of Liberty.

Soldiers, your work is done! and well;
  It bears the seal "Complete!"
For they who trampled on the flag
  Are pleading at your feet.

But, should the clouds of war again
  O'ercast our land with gloom,

HOME, HOME AGAIN!

Go, consecrate your swords anew
  At Abra'am Lincoln's tomb!

*   *   *

Nor history's page, nor poet's pen
  Can e'er recount the deeds
Wrought by the gallant Union host
  To serve their Country's needs.

But every brave of every race,
  Or color, clime or name;
Has earn'd the royal right to hold
  His title-deed of fame.

Whether before the cannon's mouth—
  By bayonet or shell—
Or, by the stealthy picket's fire,
  The faithful soldier fell:

Or, on the dusty, weary march—
  By Southern prison-damps—
Amidst the fever-breeding chills
  Of cheerless winter camps:

Or, whether, down th' Atlantic main,
  Where blist'ring sunbeams dart
Fierce, poison'd arrows of disease,
  That fasten in the heart—

The noisome, pestilential plague
  Out-stretch'd his yellow hand;
And grasp'd a patriot's life, and hid
  A soldier in the sand:

It matters not: no tithe of worth
  Shall ever fade or fall—
A People's heart-felt gratitude
  O'erflows with thanks to all.

Soldiers, your battle-work is done!
  The strife is over now—

From plowing red Rebellion's ranks,
  Come, follow Freedom's plow!

As you have nail'd the old flag fast,
  Redeeming thus your pledge—
Come kindle up the smould'ring forge;
  And swing the rusty sledge!

As you have smooth'd the track for Truth,
  Now shove the smoothing plane!
And, student, from the scroll of blood,
  Turn to your books again.

Thus, we will plow, and hew, and forge;
  As in the days gone by:—
Free, happy, joyous, thanking God
  For Peace and Liberty!

Chapter Two: The Holy War

I. GOD OF THE TRUE-HEARTED

Some poets, at least in a portion of their war verse, portrayed the war in natural rather than in supernatural terms. But nineteenth century American society was not pre-eminently humanistic; it was pre-eminently Christian. And since religion loomed large in the life of society, poets, adapting the war to the attitudes of the time, more often than not gave the war a religious reading. In conceiving their war as a Holy War poets and society were following a pattern familiar throughout the course of Western civilization. Homer and the ancient Hebrews alike had dramatized the advisability of Divine aid in battle. The biblical concept that the hand of God might be seen in every human activity made it traditionally necessary for Christians to consider Him a partner in warfare. Christians of the Eighteen-Sixties thus cherished a tradition of cosmic warfare reaching back to the beginnings of their religion. John, in his apocalyptic vision, had seen war as God's ultimate instrument in judgment. The Puritans had conquered a wilderness and subjugated the Indians in the name of God. Nineteenth century Americans, in keeping with their forefathers, saw no contradiction in worshipping the Prince of Peace and a God of War.

Poets interpreted the religious aspects of the conflict optimistically, although the inevitable minority voice made itself heard. G. W. Nichols, a Wisconsin dentist, suggested in *Reconstruction: A Poem* (Beloit, 1868), that the war had been brought on to purge America of its ills; and in the title poem of *The Branch: A Sacred Poem, and Other Poems* (Philadelphia, 1862), William George Caldcleugh interpreted the book of Revelation as a prophecy of the War of the Rebellion, and confidently predicted the approach of the Scriptural millenium. But Nichols and Caldcleugh were, if one may use a metaphor which would have pleased both, voices crying in the wilderness. Their poetic contemporaries shouted—or rhymed—them down, vehemently asserting that God favored the North, or the South, as the case might be, and that if any millenium were to result from the conflict, it would appear in the form of an improved, more progressive society which would emerge when Thirsters after Righteousness had crushed the Serpent.

So imbued were poets with a sense of God's concern in the conflict that references to the Deity turn up everywhere in the war poetry of the decade. Among the call-to-arms poems which the North manufactured in such prolific quantity, the poem which appealed to the young men of the country solely in secular terms was exceptional. Clara H. von Moschzisker, in an untitled poem, has no intention of sending "husbands, brothers and sons" forth to battle, armed only with their own strength.

The poem is from *Poems* (Philadelphia, 1868).

March, march down to the battle field,
Husbands, brothers and sons, marching forward in order.
March, march, to perish, but ne'er to yield,
All the Blue Jackets are over the Border.
O'er them the Stars never dimmed in their keeping,
Save when the blood of their bearers gushed forth,
Bear them still proudly on o'er hill and dale and glen,
Fight for them, die for them, men of the North!

Darkened the bright hearths in city and hamlet,
Whitened the cheeks and lips quivering there,
In agonized fear of the doom that each morrow
May bring to the noble, the loved and the fair.
Gone from the mountains whose free air inspired them,
Gone from the vales where in childhood they played,
God of the true-hearted, guard them, o'er shadow them.
Strike through each arm, make victorious each blade!

March, march down to the battle field,
Husbands, brothers and sons, marching forward in order.
March, march to perish, but ne'er to yield,
All the Blue Jackets are over the Border.

A Rhode Island regiment enlisted God on its side in an official manner. Their chaplain, the Reverend Frederic Denison, in a series of war hymns, *Army Hymns; Written for the Third Regiment R. I.*

Heavy Artillery, by Their Chaplain (Providence, 1863), repeatedly asserted that God favored the North. His "Army Hymn" is typical.

ARMY HYMN

O thou enthroned above the skies,
  To whom all rule belongs;
To thee shall suited worship rise
  From trusting mortal tongues.

When desolating wars assail,
  When wrong defies the right,
We raise to thee our just appeal
  And ask for conquering might.

The bow and spear were powerless
  Against thy hosts of old;
To-day our loyal armies bless
  And make thy servants bold.

Ordain success to crown our arms
  And hasten righteous peace:
Preserve our land from future harms
  And spread abroad thy grace.

The policy of sending soldiers off to battle under the guardianship of God was by no means the exclusive province of chaplains such as the Reverend Denison (see above). John Savage indicated in "The Patriot Mother" that belief in divine intervention in military affairs had permeated the households of the era.

The poem is from *Faith and Fancy* (New York, 1864).

THE PATRIOT MOTHER

I.

When o'er the land the battle brand
  In freedom's cause was gleaming,
And everywhere upon the air
  The starry flag was streaming,
The widow cried unto her pride,
  "Go forth and join the muster;
Thank God, my son can bear a gun
  To crown his race with lustre!
Go forth! and come again not home,
  If by disgrace o'erpowered;
My heart can pray o'er hero's clay,
  But never clasp a coward!"

II.

"God bless thee, boy, my pride, my joy,
  My old eyes' light and treasure—
Thy father stood 'mid flame and blood
  To fill the freeman's measure.
His name thy name—the cause the same,
  Go join thy soldier brothers!
Thy blow, alone, protects not one,
  But thousands, wives and mothers.
May every blessing Heaven can yield
  Upon thy arms be showered!
Come back a hero from the field,
  But never come a coward."

II. BUT GOD HE KEEPS THE MIDDLE WAY

Apart from Whitman's *Drum-Taps,* only one book of war poetry produced by the Eighteen-Sixties rises above its fellows. This book is Herman Melville's *Battle-Pieces and Aspects of the War* (New

York, 1866). One reason for the superiority of some of Melville's war poems over those of most of his contemporaries lies in Melville's habit of juxtaposing passages varying greatly in tone, a technique which gives these poems a richer texture than was usual at the time. The setting for "Donelson" is an area around a bulletin board in an unspecified Northern city. Townspeople gather here to learn of Grant's progress in taking Fort Donelson. By alternately reporting the terse announcements posted on the board, and then himself commenting on the crowd's reactions, Melville effects an imaginative tension between the battlefield and the home.

Great suffering through the night—
A stinging one. Our heedless boys
Were nipped like blossoms. Some dozen
Hapless wounded men were frozen.
During day being struck down out of sight,
And help-cries drowned in roaring noise,
They were left just where the skirmish shifted—
Left in dense underbrush snow-drifted.
Some, seeking to crawl in crippled plight,
So stiffened—perished.

* * *

The stillness stealing through the throng
The silent thought and dismal fear revealed;
They turned and went,
Musing on right and wrong
And mysteries dimly sealed—
Breasting the storm in daring discontent;
The storm, whose black flag showed in heaven,
As if to say no quarter there was given
To wounded men in wood,
Or true hearts yearning for the good—
All fatherless seemed the human soul.

The consciously conventional poetic quality of the second stanza, conveyed by such phrases as "mysteries dimly sealed," by the alternating length of line, and by the much greater regularity of rhythm, contrasts markedly with the prosaic diction, the cold, reportorial style, and rough, uneven rhythm, approximating free verse, of stanza one. This juxtaposition of stanzas containing contrasting moods modifies the effect of such a phrase as "true hearts yearning for the good" in the second stanza. This phrase would have a sentimental effect were it surrounded by nothing but similar phrases. Here the emotion it suggests contrasts startlingly with the unlovely images of the first stanza. An artistic tension, rather than sentimentalism, results. In "The Armies of the Wilderness," Melville employs the same technique, alternating detailed scenes of fighting and camp life with short, lyric, philosophical passages commenting on the action. These lyric passages function similarly to the chorus in Greek tragedy. The lyric quality of these choruses throws into relief the prosaic quality of the descriptive passages and the somber events they chronicle.

A path down the mountain winds to the glade
  Where the dead of the Moonlight Fight lie low:
A hand reaches out of the thin-laid mould
  As begging help which none can bestow.
But the field-mouse small and busy ant
  Heap their hillocks, to hide if they may the woe:
By the bubbling spring lies the rusted canteen,
  And the drum which the drummer-boy dying let go.

Dust to dust, and blood for blood—
  Passion and pangs! Has Time
Gone back? or is this the Age
  Of the world's great Prime?

Melville's book of war poetry, like Whitman's, achieves a total cumulative effect through having an underlying theme. In emphasizing America's future greatness Whitman was much nearer his contemporaries than was Melville. The somber view of human destiny implicit in Melville's novels echoes throughout *Battle-Pieces*. Melville consistently decries the unthinking emotional hysteria engendered by the war. The note Melville sounds most frequently is the lack of discernment on the part of youth who, having never known war, regard it as a colorful, medieval pageant. Melville, in poem after poem, stands opposed to the prevailing temper of his time, which held that the war was a Holy War. To Melville, the war was decidedly Unholy, or, at best, mundane. Melville's comment, in "The March into Virginia," that "All wars are boyish, and are fought by boys," runs counter to the general insistence that all wars were god-like and were made by God. In "Shiloh," writing of the battle and of the slain, Melville states:

Skimming lightly, wheeling still,
  The swallows fly low
Over the field in clouded days,
  The forest-field of Shiloh—
Over the field where April rain
Solaced the parched ones stretched in pain
Through the pause of night
That followed the Sunday fight
  Around the church of Shiloh—
The church so lone, the log-built one,
That echoed to many a parting groan
    And natural prayer
  Of dying foemen mingled there—
Foemen at morn, but friends at eve—
  Fame or country least their care:
(What like a bullet can undeceive!)
  But now they lie low,
While over them the swallows skim,
  And all is hushed at Shiloh.

Readers, we may be certain, did not appreciate the point of view in the verse, "What like a bullet can undeceive!" To most, a bullet was not an undeceiver but God's call to a glorious martyrdom.

One of Melville's most artistic statements of the theme which underlies much of *Battle-Pieces* is "The Conflict of Convictions."

THE CONFLICT OF CONVICTIONS
(1860-1)

On starry heights
  A bugle wails the long recall;
Derision stirs the deep abyss,
  Heaven's ominous silence over all.
Return, return, O eager Hope,
  And face man's latter fall.

Events, they make the dreamers quail;
Satan's old age is strong and hale,
A disciplined captain, gray in skill,
And Raphael a white enthusiast still;
Dashed aims, whereat Christ's martyrs pale,
Shall Mammon's slaves fulfill?

(Dismantle the fort,
Cut down the fleet—
Battle no more shall be!
While the fields for fight in aeons to come
Congeal beneath the sea.)

The terrors of truth and dart of death
  To faith alike are vain;
Though comets, gone a thousand years,
  Return again,
Patient she stands—she can no more—
And waits, nor heeds she waxes hoar.

(At a stony gate,
A statue of stone,
Weed overgrown—
Long 'twill wait!)

But God His former mind retains,
  Confirms his old decree;
The generations are inured to pains,
  And strong Necessity
Surges, and heaps Time's strand with wrecks.
  The People spread like a weedy grass,
  The thing they will they bring to pass,
And prosper to the apoplex.
The rout it herds around the heart,
  The ghost is yielded in the gloom;
Kings wag their heads—Now save thyself
  Who wouldst rebuild the world in bloom.

(Tide-mark
And top of the ages' strife,
Verge where they called the world to come,

The last advance of life—
Ha ha, the rust on the Iron Dome!)

Nay, but revere the hid event;
  In the cloud a sword is girded on,
I mark a twinkling in the tent
  Of Michael the warrior one.
Senior wisdom suits not now,
The light is on the youthful brow.

(Ay, in caves the miner see:
His forehead bears, a taper dim;
Darkness so he feebly braves
Which foldeth him!)

But He who rules is old—is old;
Ah! faith is warm, but heaven with age is cold.

(Ho ho, ho ho,
The cloistered doubt
Of olden times
Is blurted out!)

The Ancient of Days forever is young,
  Forever the scheme of Nature thrives;
I know a wind in purpose strong—
  It spins *against* the way it drives.
What if the gulfs their slimed foundations bare?
So deep must the stones be hurled
Whereon the throes of ages rear
The final empire and the happier world.

(The poor old Past,
The Future's slave,
She dredged through pain and crime
To bring about the blissful Prime,
Then—perished. There's *a grave!)*

  Power unanointed may come—
Dominion (unsought by the free)
  And the Iron Dome,

Stronger for stress and strain,
Fling her huge shadow athwart the main;
But the Founders' dream shall flee.
Age after age shall be
As age after age has been,
(From man's changeless heart their way they win);
And death be busy with all who strive—
Death with silent negative.

Yea and nay—
Each hath his say;
But God He keeps the middle way.
None was by
When He spread the sky;
Wisdom is vain, and prophesy.

III. TO THE PLAIN WHERE THE BLESSED CITY LIES

Having sent their sons to battle with the assurance of God's partiality, poets were faced with the task of the disposition of the souls of those who died in battle. They accepted the task willingly. The poetry of the war era is strewn with the corpses of those who had laid their lives on Lincoln's—or Davis'—altar of freedom. These "martyred ones in freedom's war," as one poet called them, inevitably earned a heavenly reward. In part the inescapable salvation attained by the martyred soldier represents nothing more than the inescapable salvation which poets asserted to be the birthright of every mid-nineteenth century American. Many poetic pictures of Heaven implied that all Americans would "rather effortlessly" gather there. Mid-nineteenth century Americans believed in the existence of a Hell, since the Bible mentioned the place, but they believed that man, readily perfectible, could scarcely escape salvation, and that an omnipotent but kindly God would not choose to damn his children. Any contradiction inherent in the concept of a tenantless Hell did not worry Americans at a time during which church leaders themselves approached religion untheologically. Although the innate goodness of man and the beneficence of God ruled out the possibility of damnation, Americans were unwilling to forego the satisfaction derived from a contemplation of the traditional spectacle of redemption and salvation. That salvation was inescapable made it no less attractive. One needs to remember that this was a time when the camp meeting was popular.

These revivals themselves reflected the era's attitude toward salvation. It was necessary to be saved, but salvation was instantaneous and highly emotional, and it is a question whether the saved took more satisfaction in their salvation or in their ability to demonstrate their intensely emotional and highly sensitive natures.

For the soldier, salvation came simply by virtue of his martyrdom. That salvation would have come anyway did not hinder poets from taking delight in the concept of a heavenly reward for service in a Holy War. Even if poets of the period had not pictured an easy salvation for all, it is difficult to see how they could have escaped granting a berth in Heaven to soldiers who had labored in the Army of the Lord.

Thus, in a considerable body of poetry, poets fused the subjects of war and religion. A. I. Ambler, in "To a Mother," might have been addressing such a mother as that described by John Savage (see page 54).

The poem is from *Jessie Reed, and Other Poems* (Philadelphia, 1867).

TO A MOTHER

Oh mother, when with thy sorrow alone,
Thy heart goes forth with a wailing moan,
To thy darling who sleeps in a soldier's tomb.
Forever safe from the battle-gloom.
When thy voice cries out in anguish wild,
For thy pride and joy, thy first-born child;
When presses upon thee that weight of woe,
That only a mother-heart can know;
When o'er thy grief sets the summer sun,
And thy soul still yearns for the absent one:
Go forth in the night, and upward raise
To the glowing heavens thy aching gaze,
Thou wilt see a new star shining on high,
Gleaming and sparkling in the sky:
'T is the light of his glory that flames so bright,
Falling upon thy soul's dark night;
The anthems of God his spirit now sings,
And in Paradise flutter his angel-wings,
And oh! when such joy and bliss divine
Rest on the boy, canst thou repine?

Yet if still thy heart will no solace receive,
And if still thy grief finds no reprieve,
Lay thy head on thy pillow and dream,
And let the present the future seem;
Then will the glory of Jesus' love,
Guide thee up to his Kingdom above,
And in dreams amid the seraph band,
Thou shalt clasp thy loved one's holy hand.
When free from the earth and its fierce turmoils,
Thou wilt rest from its grief and rest from its toils;
When over thy son and over thee
Shall murmur the leaves of the blessed tree,
And with him in joy thou shalt dwell forever
In that Land where no death your souls can dissever;
Thus let all else be to thee as a dream,
To-night let the present the future seem,
Then will thy heart in the dawn of the morrow,
Be free from its burden of woe and sorrow,
And gladly thou'lt list to the happy mirth
Of the children who still smile around thy hearth,
And peaceful thy life thou wilt journey o'er,
Till thou bidst farewell to the earthly shore,
And on pinions from Heaven upward rise,
To the plain where the Blessed City lies,
Knocking in fear at the pearly gate,
Trembling and hoping for thy fate;
Leaving behind thee thine earthly sin,
As the angels bid thee to enter in,
And pressing near to Jehovah's throne,
Thou wilt call the lost once more thine own.

The youth who fought the war gave their experience a religious reading just as did the mothers who sent them forth to battle. The soldier in Mary H. C. Booth's "I'm Dying, Comrade" expresses attitudes which appear to have been typical in actual life as well as in poetry. Some insight into the reasons for the fury with which Americans fought the Civil War may be gained from the vision this soldier attains of the rewards of martyrdom. For not only are God and Christ going to welcome the soul, but "a hundred thousand soldiers." John Brown has replaced St. Peter at the Golden Gate, and inside wave the Stars and Stripes.

The poem is from *Wayside Blossoms* (Philadelphia, 1865).

I'M DYING, COMRADE

I think I'm dying, comrade,
  The day is growing dark;
And that is not the bob-o-link,
  Nor yet the meadow-lark:
It cannot be the distant drum;
  It cannot be the fife,
For why should drum, or bob-o-link,
  Be calling me from life?

I do not think I'm wounded;
  I cannot feel a pain;
And yet I've fallen, comrade,
  Never to rise again.
The last that I remember,
  We charged upon the foe;
I heard a sound of victory,
  And that is all I know.

I think we must have conquered,
  For all last night it seemed
That I was up in Paradise—
  Among the blest, it seemed.
And there, beside the Throne of God,
  I saw a banner wave,
The good old Stars and Stripes, my boy,
  O'er victory and the grave.

A hundred thousand soldiers
  Stood at the right of God;
And old John Brown, he stood before,
  Like Aaron with his rod:

A slave was there beside him,
  And Jesus Christ was there;
And over God, and Christ, and all,
  The banner waved in air.

And now I'm dying, comrade,
  And there is old John Brown
A standing at the Golden Gate,
  And holding me a crown.
I do not hear the bob-o-link,
  Nor yet the drum and fife;
I only know the voice of God
  Is calling me from life.

IV. IN GLORY SLEEP!

The prevalence of death and the religious reading which poets gave the war combined to make the elegy a popular genre. Many poems commemorating the dead can only loosely be called elegies, since they do not contain the sustained somber tone, the philosophical speculation, the universalizing of the experience of death, and the movement from grief to reconciliation traditionally associated with the classical elegy. Most are simply short poems lamenting the fact of death.

The Sixties, along with other eras, cherished the concept of the unknown soldier, and frequent short, lyric expressions of grief were addressed to nameless martyrs. Not infrequently, as in the case of W. T. Adams' "Ode," these poems were written to be sung as part of the dedication ceremonies connected with the raising of monuments honoring the war dead of a certain village, town, or city. As a Northerner, Adams cannot resist pointing out that the Dorchester dead "fought in freedom's fight," alluding to the cause of Emancipation; but in his closing stanza, wherein he informs God that the monument is being reared "In thy grave name," and, further, that those who have died are being given into God's keeping, Adams expresses concepts which knew no geographical boundaries.

The poem is from *Dedication of the Soldiers' Monument at Dorchester, September 17, 1867* (Boston, 1868).

ODE

by W. T. Adams, Esq.

Sung by the Children of the Public Schools.

No more the cannon peal
And clash of ringing steel
Our land o'ersweep;
But, in the soldier's grave,
The bravest of the brave,
Who died our cause to save,
In glory sleep!

On many a battle plain,
Green with their life-blood stain,
Our heroes rest.
In holy calm they sleep,
While mourning thousands weep,
And in their hearts still keep
Their memory blest.

Immortal bays we bring
Upon their graves to fling,
Heroic dead!
They fought in freedom's fight,
Dispelling treason's night,
And in their manhood's might
Their life-blood shed.

All honor to our braves,
Who sleep in hallowed graves
In southern clime,
Or at their kindred's side;
Alike they bled and died
To stay oppression's tide—
A death sublime.

Lord God of nations, here
This monument we rear,
In thy grave name.

As Thou hast blessed our land,
To Thee we give the band
Who fell by treason's hand—
And deathless fame.

V. LINCOLN IS DEAD!

In many ways the Civil War, in contrast to the gigantic and impersonal wars of the twentieth century, constituted a personalized conflict. A concept of the soldier as a cog in a vast military machine, as a cipher of little account, appears nowhere in the poetry of the Sixties. Hence, actual historical martyrs formed attractive subjects for eulogies and elegies. In the North, the martyr who enjoyed a virtual monopoly as the subject of elegies had fought with words and policies rather than with sword and musket. He was also, as the Gettysburg Address attests, himself something of a poet. Abraham Lincoln, prior to his death, had gone virtually unnoticed in the poetry of the decade, aside from a few oblique references to him in some ephemeral political satires. His death, however, captured the imaginations of Northern poets with such force that few cared to spend their talents eulogizing any of the men who, on the field of battle, had put Lincoln's war policies into execution. Some attention, to be sure, was afforded heroes other than Lincoln. Some of these expressions reflect parental love, it being not uncommon for parents of a soldier who had lost his life in battle to publish a memorial in his honor, usually containing the soldier's picture, a biography, an account of his military career and death, and a poem in his honor, obviously written to be included in the memorial, presumably at the request of the parents. Alfred B. Street thus wrote a two-page poem entitled "Lines on the Death of Lieut.-Colonel Frederick L. Tremain," which concluded an eighty-six page memorial book with the explanatory title of *Memorial of Frederick Lyman Tremain, Late Lieut. Col. of the 10th N.Y. Cavalry. Who Was Mortally Wounded at the Battle of Hatcher's Run, Va., February 6th, and Died at City Point Hospital, February 8th, 1865. By His Father* (Albany, 1865). A few other poems eulogizing specific martyrs appeared in the North. But elegies on Lincoln outnumbered elegies written for all other historical figures combined.

Only one elegy on the death of Lincoln deserves to be remembered for its high poetic quality: Whitman's magnificent "When Lilacs Last in the Dooryard Bloom'd." The superiority of Whitman's poem lies in the poet's artistry in successfully juxtaposing and reconciling contrasting moods. The mood of despair in stanza two is the reverse of the mood of calm, joyous, religious acceptance contained in the eloquent closing hymn to death. Whitman takes his reader from one mood to the other by the carefully developed evolution in thought as the poem progresses. As the funeral procession moves across the land Whitman, engrossed in grief over the personal loss of one individual, slowly sees that death, common to all, unifies rather than isolates. Whitman arrives at this conviction only after an intense struggle, symbolized by the conflicting attraction of the star and the thrush. This struggle renders more convincing his final acceptance of death.

With the exception of Whitman's elegy, poems about Lincoln made no effort to universalize the experience of Death. Rather, each poet tended to isolate some aspect of Lincoln's personality or public career. Three attitudes were dominant. Some elegists chose to emphasize various benignant aspects of Lincoln's personality. In these poems, written immediately after Lincoln's death, reside the beginnings of what skeptics have later denominated the Lincoln myth. Other poets, more metaphysical in attitude, stressed Lincoln's martyrdom. Still others, carrying the concept of martyrdom even farther, delighted in the idea that Lincoln's work was done, writing poems whose tone is reminiscent of Christ's "It is finished!" No Northern poet dared to suggest—indeed, undoubtedly never thought of suggesting—that Reconstruction formed any part of Lincoln's earthly task. To Northern poets, Reconstruction must have seemed a mundane task when contrasted with the Heaven-sent obligation of freeing the slaves.

R. H. Stoddard, in *Abraham Lincoln: an Horatian Ode* (New York, 1865), gave the fullest treatment to aspects of Lincoln's personality, although he also implied that Lincoln was a martyr, and that his earthly mission had been accomplished. Many of Lincoln's attributes as Stoddard defines them—his mildness, his homespun rustic genius, his love for the common people, his tenderness, his honesty—have formed the nucleus of most Americans' concept of Lincoln for nearly a century. If Stoddard's contemporaries had any fault to find with his portrait of Lincoln, it undoubtedly lay in the poet's attempt to draw a balanced portrait, to suggest that Lincoln, great though he was, possessed faults. Stoddard obviously includes this dimension in his portrait of Lincoln to make all the more impressive the fact that Lincoln preserved the state, the implication being that this feat infinitely more than compensated for any and all shortcomings which the man might have. Most elegists insisted that Lincoln was nothing less than Christlike in virtue and in wisdom.

ABRAHAM LINCOLN: AN HORATIAN ODE

Not as when some great Captain falls
In battle, where his Country calls,
    Beyond the struggling lines
    That push his dread designs

To doom, by some stray ball struck dead:
Or, in the last charge, at the head
    Of his determined men,
    Who *must* be victors then!

Nor as when sink the civic Great,
The safer pillars of the State,
    Whose calm, mature, wise words
    Suppress the need of swords!—

With no such tears as e'er were shed
Above the noblest of our Dead
    Do we to-day deplore
    The Man that is no more!

Our sorrow hath a wider scope,
Too strange for fear, too vast for hope,—
    A Wonder, blind and dumb,
    That waits—what is to come!

Not more astounded had we been
If Madness, that dark night, unseen,
    Had in our chambers crept,
    And murdered while we slept!

We woke to find a mourning Earth—
Our Lares shivered on the hearth,—
    The roof-tree fallen,—all
    That could affright, appall!

Such thunderbolts, in other lands,
Have smitten the rod from royal hands,
    But spared, with us, till now,
    Each laurelled Cesar's [*sic*] brow!

LINCOLN IS DEAD!

No Cesar [*sic*] he, whom we lament,
A Man without a precedent,
Sent, it would seem, to do
His work—and perish too!

Not by the weary cares of State,
The endless tasks, which will not wait,
Which, often done in vain,
Must yet be done again:

Not in the dark, wild tide of War,
Which rose so high, and rolled so far,
Sweeping from sea to sea
In awful anarchy:—

Four fateful years of mortal strife,
Which slowly drained the Nation's life,
(Yet, for each drop that ran
There sprang an armed man!)

Not then;—but when by measures meet,—
By victory, and by defeat,—
By courage, patience, skill,
The People's fixed *"We will!"*

Had pierced, had crushed Rebellion dead,—
Without a Hand, without a Head:—
At last, when all was well,
He fell—O, *how* he fell!

The time,—the place,—the stealing Shape,—
The coward shot,—the swift escape,—
The wife—the widow's scream,—
It is a hideous Dream!

A Dream?—what means this pageant, then?
These multitudes of solemn men,
Who speak not when they meet,
But throng the silent street?

The flags half-mast, that late so high
Flaunted at each new victory?
(The stars no brightness shed,
But bloody looks the red!)

The black festoons that stretch for miles,
And turn the streets to funeral aisles?
(No house too poor to show
The Nation's badge of woe!)

The cannon's sudden, sullen boom,—
The bells that toll of death and doom,—
The rolling of the drums,—
The dreadful Car that comes?

Cursed be the hand that fired the shot!
The frenzied brain that hatched the plot!
Thy Country's Father slain
By thee, thou worse than Cain!

Tyrants have fallen by such as thou,
And Good hath followed—May it now!
(God lets bad instruments
Produce the best events.)

But he, the Man we mourn to-day,
No tyrant was: so mild a sway
In one such weight who bore
Was never known before!

Cool should he be, of balanced powers,
The Ruler of a Race like ours,
Impatient, headstrong, wild,—
The Man to guide the Child!

And this *he* was, who most unfit
(So hard the sense of God to hit!)
Did seem to fill his Place.
With such a homely face,—

Such rustic manners,—speech uncouth,—
(That somehow blundered out the Truth!)
Untried, untrained to bear
The more than kingly Care?

LINCOLN IS DEAD!

Ay! And his genius put to scorn
The proudest in the purple born,
    Whose wisdom never grew
    To what, untaught, he knew—

The People, of whom he was one.
No gentleman like Washington,—
    (Whose bones, methinks, make room,
    To have him in their tomb!)

A laboring man, with horny hands,
Who swung the axe, who tilled his lands,
    Who shrank from nothing new,
    But did as poor men do!

One of the People! Born to be
Their curious Epitome;
    To share, yet rise above
    Their shifting hate and love.

Common his mind (it seemed so then),
His thoughts the thoughts of other men:
    Plain were his words, and poor—
    But now they will endure!

No hasty fool, of stubborn will,
But prudent, cautious, pliant, still;
    Who, since his work was good,
    Would do it, as he could.

Doubting, was not ashamed to doubt,
And, lacking prescience, went without:
    Often appeared to halt,
    And was, of course, at fault:

Heard all opinions, nothing loth,
And loving both sides, angered both:
    Was—*not* like Justice, blind,
    But watchful, clement, kind.

No hero, this, of Roman mould;
Nor like our Stately sires of old:
    Perhaps he was not Great—
    But he preserved the State!

O honest face, which all men knew!
O tender heart, but known to few!
    O Wonder of the Age,
    Cut off by tragic Rage!

Peace! Let the long procession come,
For hark!—the mournful, muffled drum—
    The trumpet's wail afar,—
    And see! the awful Car!

Peace! Let the sad procession go,
While cannon boom, and bells toll slow:
    And go, thou sacred Car,
    Bearing our Woe afar!

Go, darkly borne, from State to State,
Whose loyal, sorrowing Cities wait
    To honor all they can
    The dust of that Good Man!

Go, grandly borne, with such a train
As greatest kings might die to gain:
    The Just, the Wise, the Brave
    Attend thee to the grave!

And you, the soldiers of our wards,
Bronzed veterans, grim with noble scars,
    Salute him once again,
    Your late Commander—slain!

Yes, let your tears, indignant, fall,
But leave your muskets on the wall:
    Your Country needs you now
    Beside the forge, the plough!

LINCOLN IS DEAD!

(When Justice shall unsheathe her brand,—
If Mercy may not stay her hand,
    Nor would we have it so—
    She must direct the blow!)

And you, amid the Master-Race,
Who seem so strangely out of place,
    Know ye who cometh? He
    Who hath declared ye Free!

Bow while the Body passes—Nay,
Fall on your knees, and weep, and pray!
    Weep, weep—I would ye might—
    Your poor, black faces white!

And, Children, you must come in bands,
With garlands in your little hands,
    Of blue, and white, and red,
    To strew before the Dead!

So, sweetly, sadly, sternly goes
The Fallen to his last repose:
    Beneath no mighty dome,
    But in his modest Home;

The churchyard where his children rest,
The quiet spot that suits him best;
    There shall his grave be made,
    And there his bones be laid!

And there his countrymen shall come,
With memory proud, with pity dumb,
    And strangers far and near,
    For many and many a year!

For many a year, and many an Age,
While History on her ample page
    The virtues shall enroll
    Of that Paternal Soul!

Few Lincoln elegists cared to praise Lincoln in such humanistic terms as had Stoddard (see page 68), high as that praise had been. Most Lincoln elegies interpreted the President's death not simply as a martyrdom, but as a Christ-like martyrdom. Typical is "The Death of President Lincoln" by an anonymous poet who wrote under the pen-name of Neal Neff. The poet, taking positive delight in the obvious fact that Lincoln's death occurred on Good Friday, confidently proclaims that "Since the days of the Saviour, no greater than he/Graced the great halls of State, so noble and free." The poet's attitude must have gone unchallenged in the North during the Sixties.

The poem is from *Neal Neff's New National Poems, Composed by a Captain of the Line, Belonging to the 54th O.V.V.I., of the 2d Division, 15th Army Corps, of Gen. Sherman's Army, Who, While at the Front, in Moments of Idleness, Wrote for His Own Amusement.* (Cincinnati, 1866).

THE DEATH OF PRESIDENT LINCOLN

Written at Goldsboro', North Carolina, on receipt of the news of this tragic event. What a strange coincidence of Time! It will be remembered that it was on Good Friday, and on the 14th of April.

Of him who stood foremost in this mighty age,
Whose goodness is praised by the saint and the sage,
While his great-hearted kindness the poet doth sing,
Like the widow's two mites, our tribute we bring.

A long night of darkness is passing away,
Athwart the broad land comes the glorious day
Of peace and of joy and of glory and gladness,
But the brightness of morning is turned into sadness.

Yes, the joy of the nation is turned into gloom,
As true freedom's flowers just burst into bloom;
But his virtues, like flowers, doth cast their perfume,
And like a halo of glory they light up his tomb.

LINCOLN IS DEAD!

Mysterious Providence, inscrutable ways,
The victim selected, on the altar he lays,
The altar of sacrifice, freedom's oblation,
Whose blood thus atones for the sins of the nation.

On the same day the Saviour of mankind was slain
For doom'd fallen man, his pardon to obtain;
The ball of the assassin enters his brain,
A martyr he falls in the morning of fame.

How strange the coincidence, the time when he falls,
On the day over Sumpter's [*sic*] battle-scarred walls
Was both lowered and raised the flag of the free,
Laid low in the morning of his glory should be.

That citadel home of magnanimous thought,
With a nation's best interest of humanity fraught,
By a murderous missile which crashes his brain,
With his heroes of freedom, he lies with the slain.

Yes, he falls with his heroes, our chief magistrate,
Whose giant mind piloted the great ship of state
Through the battle and storm of the long dark night,
To the glorious morning, so peaceful and bright.

Says the soldier and patriot, whose bosom doth swell,
Is there not some "chosen curse" which justice can tell,
To punish the murderer whose garments doth smell
Like the fumes of the pit, so red hot from hell.

Yes, his name shall be curs'd in all future ages,
Through the tablets of time, on history's pages,
When gone to his place, the black soul of this Booth,
When millions unborn shall read the sad truth.

Since the days of the Saviour, no greater than he
Graced the great halls of State, so noble and free,
So kind yet so firm, and such powers of soul,
To seek for the nation the good of the whole.

His mantle of charity, like a halo which glows,
Melting the prejudice in the hearts of his foes,
And when vengeance is his, this mantle he throws
O'er the land of the South, to heal their sad woes.

How strange and how sad—Oh! it seems like a dream,
That his blood should thus swell the deep crimson stream
Which flow'd like a river, through the land to the sea,
Through the land of the brave, now the home of the free.

Yes, he died with his heroes, his country to save,
And the high hopes of mankind from liberty's grave,
That the soil be not curs'd by the blood of the slave,
Now the land of the free and the home of the brave.

It is understandable that poets, as a part of their picture of Lincoln's Christ-like martyrdom, should have emphasized the fitness of Lincoln's waiting to gain his martyrdom until the slaves had been liberated. Just as Christ had come to earth to free the souls of men, so Northern poets felt that Lincoln had been sent to earth to free the bodies, if not the spirits, of the Blacks. Eleazar Parmly's "Death of Abraham Lincoln" implies this parallel. Lincoln is "God's chosen one—and in his care." And although Lincoln "Lies cold and silent in the earth," he does so "Just at the time the world would raise / Its songs of triumph to his worth."

Parmly's allusion to George Washington in the last two stanzas of the elegy warrants mention. Washington, interestingly enough, appeared in the verse of the Sixties nearly as frequently as did Lincoln. In large part Washington's popularity sprang from the analogy Northern poets drew between the colonies' efforts, under Washington's leadership, to free themselves from the yoke of Britain, and the nation's efforts, under Lincoln, to free the slaves. Parmly obviously feels that the analogy between Washington and Lincoln is complimentary to the latter, an attitude which the poet shared with several contemporaries.

The poem is from *Thoughts in Rhyme* (New York, 1867).

DEATH OF ABRAHAM LINCOLN

Lincoln is dead! and all the land
  In mourning symbols is attired;
Struck by the vile assassin's hand,
  Our noble President expired.

April fourteenth—'twas near eleven,
  When through his brain the ball had passed,
And minutes twenty-two past seven,
  Next morn our chieftain breathed his last.

The people's hope, the wide world's praise,
  Lies cold and silent in the earth,
Just at the time the world would raise
  Its songs of triumph to his worth.

For nations now beyond the tide,
  Own and revere his matchless fame,
And waft o'er seas and oceans wide,
  Distinguished honors to his name.

God's chosen one—and in his care.
  Truth, love, and mercy were combined,
"For malice unto none we bear,
  But charity to all mankind."

Among the great and mighty deeds
  That cluster round his scroll of fame,
The one that others all exceeds,
  And will through time exalt his name,

Is that which swept away the stain
  Of Slavery from our land, and broke
Its bonds and fetters, stocks and chain,
  And crushed for aye its iron yoke.

When asked descendants of the slave,
  One only answer there will be,
Who to your people freedom gave?
  " 'Twas Abraham Lincoln made us free."

And that loved name will ever live,
  In all the glories it has won;
Honors to him the world will give,
  The same as to our Washington.

And even more than Washington's
  Have been our noble Lincoln's gains,
One crushed the pride of Britain's sons,
  The other, Slavery's cursed chains.

Although poets frequently stressed exclusively Lincoln's personality, or his martyrdom, or the completion of his work, a few elegists fused all of these aspects of Lincoln into a single poem as did Martha A. Parks in "A Welcome to Lincoln's Remains." Lincoln, we learn from the poem, is a "lover of righteousness," a "friend of the poor op-press'd." He is free of "malice and envy," but has "charity for every one." The poet, throughout, alludes to Lincoln as a martyr, and, near the close of the poem, advises Lincoln to rest "from thy finished labors." It is little wonder that the poet is able to go from this picture of Lincoln to the place where she can invoke him as a "Representative for God and man." If no poet went so far as to liken Lincoln to the Trinity, many Northern poets did go so far as to suggest that Lincoln had been both human and divine.

The poem is from *Echoes* (1865). Although no place of publication is given, the book is copyrighted in the state of Illinois.

A WELCOME TO LINCOLN'S REMAINS

Illinois' immortal son—
The tribute so justly won,
    Columbia has given—
In her dark hour she called thee forth,
Beloved champion of the North;
And her deep anguish proves thy worth,
        Mighty conqueror!

LINCOLN IS DEAD!

Illinois welcomes thee,
Beloved father of the "Free,"
    Thy ashes pure.
Mournfully, tenderly,
Martyr for Liberty;
With heart bruised she weeps for thee,
            Mighty President!

Spotless thy patriot fame;
No weakness mars thy name—
    Martyr sublime.
Malice and envy thou hadst none,
But charity for every one,
And tears for each suffering son,
            In thy field of Mars.

Then welcome home to rest,
Father beloved and blest,
    In thy chosen State.
Illinois you have honored long;
And your mighty deed in song,
Will gloriously pass along,
            With ages yet to come.

Yes, Illinois welcomes thee;
And with deep sympathy
    And gratitude,
She receives her honored dead—
The martyr whose blood was shed,
While he for the traitors plead,
            With lofty zeal.

Tried, scarred, bleeding country,
Ye sons of the martyred free,
    Behold the tomb,
Where Lincoln in honor rests—
The lover of righteousness,
And friend of the poor oppress'd—
            It breathes to you.

It bids you nobly on,
Until the last victory is won,
    "In life's short day."
His glorious way-marks view,
Onward, onward pursue,
The way he marked out for you—
                Columbia's patriot.

Rest, then beloved father rest;
From thy finished labors rest,
    Martyr benign.
Rest here, in honor rest;
And oh! may thy mantle chaste,
Rest on him who in anguish pass'd
                To thy illustrious place.

Representative for God and man,
Rest beloved "Father Abraham,"
    While we guard thy shrine.
While with reverence our bruised hearts glow;
While our tears still profusely flow;
While our cheeks tinge with shame to know,
                How the mighty fell.

With fidelity we'll guard the shrine,
Where reposed thy dust sublime—
    Martyr for the free.
Illinois winds will mournfully
Chant ever tenderly,
A requiem for the martyr'd free,
                Resting on her breast.

VI. PURCHASED WITH OUR JACKSON'S BLOOD

The South did not take to its poetic bosom a single hero with such ardor as the North took Lincoln. Nevertheless, isolated poems honoring various Southern military leaders appeared. Typical is Mrs. Caroline Augusta Ball's poem on the death of General "Stonewall" Jackson, who was accidentally shot by one of his own men on May 2,

1863, at the battle of Chancellorsville, and died of pneumonia a week later. In the South as in the North, death greatly enhanced one's chances of being immortalized in verse. It is typical that the poet should ignore the equally illustrious Lee in favor of the departed Jackson. General Lee, after all, had survived the conflict, and was, presumably, still able to speak for himself.

The poem is from *The Jacket of Grey, and Other Fugitive Poems* (Charleston, 1866).

WRITTEN ON THE DEATH OF OUR BELOVED GENERAL STONEWALL JACKSON

There's a wail of woe on the summer breeze,
A cry resounding o'er land and o'er seas,
A lament for the noble, the true, the brave,
Now borne to his rest in a martyr's grave.

There is mourning on Rappahannock's shore,
Where his battle cry will be heard no more;
There is mourning in camp, and cot, and hall,
For the Christian hero, beloved of all.

Ay, death has stricken a ruthless dart,
It is quivering in a nation's heart.
And our country lies bleeding 'neath the blow,
Which has laid our honored chieftain low.

The shout of victory rent the air,
We knew not that it had cost so dear;
The shout of victory is subdued,
For 'twas purchased with our Jackson's blood.

Ah, many fell on that well fought field,
To whom all honor and praises we yield;
But the sun which set on that bloody plain
When Jackson fell, will never rise again.

He won for himself a crown of fame,
He has left behind him a deathless name,
And our children's children will rise and bless
The hero who fell in the wilderness.

But what to him is the voice of fame;
And what to him is the deathless name;
And what are glory and earth's renown,
To him who has won an immortal crown?

We thought the laurel's green wreath to weave,
For him o'er whose death cold form we grieve;
But the gathered laurels must droop and fade,
For on the bier their bright leaves are laid.

Our sunny land is deep veiled in gloom,
Her fair daughters weep o'er our chieftain's doom;
E'en our gallant braves drop the tears of woe,
O'er that well loved form in the dust laid low.

Weep on, but raise the tearful eyes,
To the glorious mansions above the skies,
Where the deeply mourned his warfare done,
His last victory gained, his rest has won.

VII. THY PALE AND PERISHED FLOWERS

If the South did not deify a single individual as the North did Lincoln, it had enormous respect for the men who fought its battles. Southern poets frequently wrote elegaic poems mentioning numerous individuals who had given their lives in the Holy cause of Secession. The Viriginia poet Mrs. Cornelia J. M. Jordan, for example, in an ambitious eighty-six stanza poem entitled "Richmond: Her Glory and Her Graves," enshrined in verse no fewer than thirty-six soldiers apparently especially dear to the memory of Virginians. In "Virginia's Dead," Mrs. Jordan extends her angle of sympathy to include all fallen heroes of the Old Dominion. Mrs. Jordan conforms to a popular Southern literary tradition in praising the fallen dead while at the same time reflecting a somewhat nostalgic but nonetheless intense love for Southern cities and Southern soil. Apparently Southern poets, very shortly following the war, understood that the War of the Rebellion was to mark the close of a distinct way of life. "Virginia's Dead" thus becomes at once an elegy for the soldiers of the Confederacy and, by implication, for the South itself.

The poem is from *Richmond: Her Glory and Her Graves* (Richmond, 1866).

VIRGINIA'S DEAD

Proud mother of a race that reared
The brave and good of ours,
Lo! on thy bleeding bosom lie
Thy pale and perished flowers.
Where'er upon her own bright soil
Hosts meet their blood to shed—
Where brightly gleams the victor's sword,
There sleep Virginia's dead.

And when upon the crimsoned field
The cannon loudest roars,
And hero-blood for liberty
A streaming torrent pours;
Where fiercest grows the battle's rage
And Southern banners spread;
Where minions crouch and vassals kneel,
There sleep Virginia's dead.

Where bright Potomac's classic wave
Rolls softly to the sea,
And Shenandoah's sweet valley smiles
In her captivity;
Where Mississippi sullen rolls
His foaming torrent bed,
And Tennessee's smooth ripples break,
There sleep Virginia's dead.

And where mid dreary mountain heights
The Frost-king sternly sate,
As GARNETT cheered his legion on
And nobly met his fate;
Where JOHNSTON, LEE and BEAUREGARD,
Their gallant armies led,
Through winter snows and tropic suns,
There sleep Virginia's dead.

And where through Georgia's flowery meads
  The proud Savannah flows,
As soft o'er Carolina's brow
  Atlantic's pure breeze blows;
Where Florida's sweet tropic flowers
  Their dewy fragrance shed,
And night-winds sigh through orange groves,
  There sleep Virginia's dead.

Where Louisiana's eagle eye
  Frown's [*sic*] darkly on her chains,
And proud New Orleans' noble streets
  The Despot's heel profanes—
Where Virtue shrinks in dread dismay
  And Beauty bows her head,
While Valor spurns th' oppressor's yoke,
  There sleep Virginia's dead.

'Neath Alabama's sunny skies,
  On Texas' burning shore,
Where blooming prairies brightly sweep
  Missouri's bosom o'er,
Where bold Kentucky's lion heart
  Leaps to her MORGAN's tread,
And tyrants quail at Freedom's cry,
  There sleep Virginia's dead.

And where the Ocean's trackless waves
  O'er pallid corpses sweep,
As mid the cannon's deafening peal,
  Deep calleth unto deep;
Where ever Honor's sword is drawn
  And Justice rears her head—
Where heroes fall and martyrs bleed,
  There sleep Virginia's dead.

AUGUST 13th, 1862

Chapter Three: Social Commentary

I. RIGHTFUL ORDER INTO RUIN HURLED

Most Civil War poetry inclined toward the sentimental or melodramatic. Poets, regardless of their subject, ordinarily interpreted the war as a colorful, dramatic, emotional spectacle, as a pageant designed to bring to the surface hitherto submerged heroics. But a minority voice insisted on a hearing. A handful of poets, North and South, adopting a more hard-headed attitude toward the war than their peers, had the audacity to suggest that war, far from bringing out the divine and heroic in man, brought to light what the seventeenth century poet, Anne Bradstreet, had called man's "unregenerate part." This minority group excoriated their society variously, commenting on men and events in a manner reserved today for the syndicated columnist.

A few poets—all Northerners, interestingly enough—insisted on examining the effects of the war on the mores of their society. Most Northern poets, when moved to social commentary, became too occupied blaming the South for slavery to think about possible deleterious effects of war on the North itself. Ruth N. Cromwell, however, in a negligible poem entitled *Nancy Blake Letters to a Western Cousin* (New York, 1864), denounced war profiteering, drawing a sharp contrast between the brave men fighting in the war and self-alleged "patriots" who, by staying at home, were becoming wealthy. Ruth N. Cromwell's poem is itself a cousin to several Northern poems denouncing Northerners whose lukewarm attitude toward the war, coupled with their criticism of the Lincoln administration, caused them to be looked on as Southern sympathizers, and earned them the opprobrious title of "Copperheads." George M. Baker either felt that war and rum had entered into a conspiracy against Man, or that the war, uppermost in the thinking of the decade, would provide an impressive backdrop for a temperance lesson. Whatever his motive, Baker, in a narrative poem entitled *An Old Man's Prayer* (Boston, 1868), depicted a group of volunteers who, about to leave for war, imbibe heavily until convinced of their folly by an old man who tells them how drink has shattered his life and the lives of two of his sons, a third son having been saved from an identical fate by becoming a preacher. Baker's poem constitutes one of the very few temperance poems produced by the Sixties.

One of the most interesting Northern poems of social criticism is F. O. Sayles' *Follies of the Day, a Satire* (Springfield, Mass., 1867). By denominating himself a satirist, as did many poets who wrote social and political criticism, Sayles put himself in the company of a long line of temperamentally conservative writers who have urged reform by way of retreat to earlier modes of conduct. The nineteenth century espoused reform vigorously, but not the reactionary type urged by satirists. Crackpot after crackpot, inspired genius after inspired genius—they have been called both—insisted that the most expeditious way to usher in the millenium was not to retreat to the blundering way things used to be done, but to throw off the shackles of convention and live in a way which Western man, at any rate, had never tried. Reformers, confusingly enough, remained far apart on the question of exactly what reform was best designed to produce Heaven on earth. Where one reformer advocated free love (or perfectionism, as it was happily called), another endorsed woman's rights, a third temperance, yet others prison reform, the improved care of the insane, living from the produce of one's own labors, vegetarianism, redistribution of land. The intense abolition sentiment in the North prior to and during the Civil War constituted but one of these radical reforms.

Defined historically, very few "pure" satirists were afoot in America during the Eighteen-Sixties. Even if a poet had reservations about man's ability to bring Heaven to earth through innovation, it was difficult to remain entirely aloof from the enthusiasm of the time. Sayles' poem itself constitutes a curious blend of liberal and reactionary tendencies. In commenting on the war as only one of a number of social phenomena which needed examination, Sayles certainly took a more balanced view of the society of his time than did the majority. In his diatribes against the evils of wealth, the deleterious influence of new fashions in dress, and the corrupting power of false literature (by which Sayles means the sentimental novels so popular during his time), the poet is obviously suggesting that society retreat to an earlier time, that the changes characteristic of his era constitute a retrogression. On the other hand, his treatment of the problem of drink would have been endorsed by the most rabid of temperance advocates. Sayles' treatment of the Civil War constitutes a curious amalgamation of radical and conservative attitudes. Sayles begins by invoking the awful spectacle of "rightful order into ruin hurled," a sight which "has shocked the very world!" Such phrases intimate that the war is a mistake. But further reading discovers that the poet is, after all, somewhat a child of his time. As a Northerner, he finds it impossible to forget that the South has been guilty of the twin crimes of Slavery and Rebellion. The South with its "hellish enginery" is responsible for the war, while the North is personified as Justice. Twenty-two heroic couplets after the head-shaking at "rightful order into ruin hurled" Sayles is able confidently to rejoice over "THE DUSKY MILLIONS' ENTREE INTO LIBERTY!"

Reprinted below are Sayles' introduction and conclusion, along with the sections of the poem treating Wealth, Temperance, and the War.

from FOLLIES OF THE DAY, A SATIRE

ARGUMENT

The subjects embraced in this metrical Essay are, the inordinate desire to acquire Wealth as the true source of happiness in this life, the mistaken consequences of its acquisition, and often ruinous effects—the evil influences of Fashion—the foolishness of excessive Pride—the Drunkard—the Dram-Shop—the Temperate Drinker, and the injurious example and practices thereof—False Literature—False Critics—Impatience of Delay—the brutality of Horse-Racing—the wickedness of the Rebellion—the apparent Folly of the Mexican Emperor.

These subjects are treated briefly, as some of the prominent vices or follies of our time.

The definitions of "Folly," given by Dr. Worcester, are here adopted, and are as follows: 1. Want of understanding; weakness of intellect; foolishness; fatuity; imbecility. 2. Foolish conduct; an unwise act; indiscretion. 3. A shameful act; wicked conduct; sin. 4. Criminal wickedness; depravity.

Satire differs essentially in its character, from other metrical compositions. It is "a species of poetry peculiar to the Romans, in which the poets attacked the follies and vices of mankind in general."

Satire is "a composition, commonly in poetry, in which vice or folly is censured or exposed to hatred or contempt; an invective poem. It is applied both to persons and things, and the purpose of it is, or should be, not to vex, but to reform."

This Poem was not designed to be a work of fancy—it was intended to be made of "sterner stuff."

Whoe'er surveys the conduct of mankind,
With purpose just, and independent mind,

Sees motives that inspired and wrought the plan
Of deeds to bless the countless race of man,
And oft, the annals in the book of Fame,
Tinged deep with folly, wickedness or shame.

To praise, or flatter, is an easy task,
And welcome often,—but to strip the mask
From crime, depravity, blind selfishness,
And in true colors, paint them with success—
To face the guilty and to make them feel
Remorse, or shame, requires the nerve of steel
And censure strong, sustained by sense and skill,
To reach the object, and its aim fulfill.
  The pen of fiction wins insensate youth—
  Manhood can prize the golden pen of Truth.

Now to my task.—What conscience shall indite,
Satiric Muse, I ask thy aid to write.
From flowery landscape and the starry skies,
From mossy cascade, shut my longing eyes,—
From the soft flutter of the Zephyr's wing
That fans to sleep the infant of the king—
From realms of fancy, where the willing sense
Revels, till judgment loses competence,
Or Beauty sits enthroned in matchless might,
To woo and fasten the admirer's sight,
Keep me; but show me follies of the day,
To lash or ridicule, as best I may.

With men, a common object of pursuit
That yields a *precious* or a *poisoned* fruit,
Ripe throughout Christendom, and made to be
The bond of modern Aristocracy,
Is wealth; a blessing, were it rightly used,
A curse most damning, when it is abused.

Exact economy and constant care,
Virtues commendable, as well as rare,
With industry produce possessions vast,
That make men heirs to fortune—while they last!
Though all acquired by truly honest gain,

Amassed, are suffered briefly to remain;
For, a wise Providence whose eye surveys
Man in his thoughts, intents, and all his ways
Will break the IDOL,—a mysterious fate
All titles change, or sever his estate—
The vault where hoarded treasure lay untold,
Will yield to other hands, the heaps of gold!
These are not riches, ever to endure—
Not incorruptible, abiding, pure.

To prove that wealth affords no happiness,
Or, that it always makes enjoyment less,
Is not a problem for solution here;—
What truth sustains, is ALL that shall appear.
It needs no labored argument to show
What all intelligent observers know,
That wealth and wisdom go not hand in hand,
But may exist apart, in every land.
If Solomon of old the two possessed,
Few, since his time, have equally been blessed;
Many will seek and gain the large estate,
And claim a rank among the *truly* great;
Look now for WISDOM with unceasing care,
And found, give credit for it, any-where.

Wealth is the fruitful mother of pretence—
Excessive vanity and insolence,
And pride that swells into dimensions vast,
Forgetful of the present and the past!
It is a cloak to cover many sins—
Its glitter many a weak admirer wins,—
Its power to bribe—to awe the faint, conceals
What poverty to public view reveals,—
It is a tyrant to oppress the slave,
The just to punish, and the guilty save;
And shameful follies swell the lengthy train,
That cause HUMANITY to writhe in pain.
Dear modern CROESUS, labor still to gain
What yet can make your progeny more vain,
And nurture habits, *you* and all despise,
To be a PANORAMA for your eyes;

Yes, squander industry and gather pelf,
To make a son, more wretched than yourself,—
An idler, spendthrift, drunkard, Folly's fool,
Or leading scholar in her crowded school!

Why tempt a daughter, beautiful and young,
Whose promise moves to praise, each worthy tongue,
Her mind, unsullied, plastic, ardent, free,
A fair abode for ANGEL purity,
To be seduced by vanity's display,
And ruined by the vices of the day?
Or, won by show, to smother sober sense—
Try modes of life where luxuries commence,
And in their course a destiny fulfill,
Whose end is fated to torment, or kill,
Enfeeble, or distort proportions fair,
Which nature had designed and formed with care.
What dangers lurk around the home of wealth!
What trouble enters on the steps of stealth!

Ye who have millions, soberly reflect,
That cause will have legitimate effect,
And then believe the evidence of truth,
That riches will corrupt both age and youth;
That from this source, can spring no lasting joy,
The wise, for good, will better means employ;
They shun temptation when the way is plain,
Nor let resistance meet the foe in vain.
The *pious* Rich a modest hint deserve,
Who, *tempted,* from the path of duty swerve,
Moved by desire for earthly goods, will make
Digressions *slight,* for "filthy lucre's sake."
Transparent is their effort to deceive
Those who have sight and reason to believe.
"Vile self creeps in" behind profession's veil,
And clothes the inner man with worldly mail,
Which will not shield the soul from avarice,
Nor blind the mortal eye by artifice.

Why try to crowd your burdened coffers still?
Why seek your sated treasury to fill?

Why covet more than will your wants supply,
To ruin half your heirs before you die?
If it be true, that two and two make four,
The more you get, increases want for more.
You thirst, yet have a fountain for supply,
And, drink the ocean, you will still be dry;
In bondage—likely never to be free,
For MAMMON holds your moral destiny!
The fear of poverty and love of gain,
Compose the links in his satanic chain.

To-day, in this "Sweet Land of Liberty,"
Where all may worship God with conscience free—
Where Gospel light illumes the wide extent,
And calls mankind to sorrow, and repent—
Their sins forsake, and in salvation joy—
To hope for peace unmingled with alloy;—
Where congregations to the Temples flock,
To build their faith on the Eternal Rock,
Pride shows her power, e'en in that sacred place,
Amid the *humble suppliants* for Grace;
And, at the Master's table fills a seat,
Where meek, devout, adopted Christians meet!

There is an Eye whose universal ken
Beholds the dark hypocrisy of men!
The grosser forms, unscreened by shades of night,
Are seen with human eyes in solar light.
That stolen garb of SANCTITY ill fits
The shriveled, hideous form of hypocrites.
What deep excitement marks the fleeting hour,
And stirs the Empire city by its power;
Frauds, perjuries, and forgeries are rife,
Reported of the ranks in upper life!
The swollen, shining bubble now has burst!
The public sees iniquity accursed.
The golden speculations of our time,
Unveil their hidden elements of crime;
Still, in that trade the speculator shares,
A combat fierce engages "Bulls and Bears."

The morals, peeping from behind the screen,
Show BUSINESS ladies, acting in the scene,
Who keep important secrets dark as night,
Till time and truth expose them to the light.
So goes the world,—some art to trick the just,—
To circumvent them, and obtain their trust!
The Saviour had not where to lay his head;
And yet, of poverty He had no dread!
And wise, old Agur, whose unbiassed sense
Taught him right views of man and Providence,
Devoid of selfishness and pride, could see
That riches fostered wicked vanity,
And held dominion o'er the mental whole,
To shut the humane fountains of the soul.

Thank God, he made his blessings to depend
On laws man cannot alter or amend.
Both mind and body gain what will suffice
For health and strength, from food and exercise,—
From heat and cold, from sunshine, rain and air,—
From clothing, shelter, sleep, and prudent care,—
From proper use of all the aids of life,—
From shunning evil and excessive strife,—
From knowledge, whence the mind true wisdom draws,—
From Revelation, and from Nature's laws.
The plainest logic prove [*sic*] to common sense,
That PLENTY is a needful competence.

* * *

The drunkard, what a wreck for man to see!
What profanation of the Deity!—
He once had appetites controlled by sense,
(He may have been a man of eminence!)
His youth gave hopeful promise, while he trod
The path of soberness, ordained of God,
Till wrong indulgence overcame, at last,
His judgment, and the evil held him fast.
Then Ruin sternly stared him in the face,
And wrote upon his countenance, DISGRACE.

The dram-shop, and the brothel claimed him soon
As patron, and his sun went down at noon.

Now drunkards meet the eye, on either hand,
In every town and city in the land.
The deadly poison fires the victims' blood,
And sweeps them to destruction like a flood;
While in their mad career with conscience blind,
Brain seethed, and passion wholly unconfined,
Reason dethroned, or wandering in doubt,
The image of their God, all blotted out!
Infernal in appearance, and disgust,
Objects of terror, pity, or distrust,
With alcoholic eloquence they rail
At all who would their liberty assail;
When drunk, to break the peace at any time;
To mangle, murder, perpetrate all crime,—
The right to use the pistol, bowie-knife,
As lawful weapons in the creed of life,
And ply the lighted torch at midnight hour,
As a convenient and effectual power
To give redress, for some imagined wrong,
And prove that *honor* feels resentment strong!—
When drunkards in philosophy excel,
Mind will be tenant of the oyster-shell!

There is a sight, no pen can well portray,
No artist give it form, nor speech convey
A just conception, but a semblance slight,—
The view alone, discovers it aright—
The female tippler, who defames the name
Of woman, and becomes a loathsome shame.
From her exalted sphere of usefulness,
Assigned by gracious Heaven her race to bless,
She is transformed to fiend! Another worse
Ne'er left the lowest hell, a world to curse.

In every place where appetites abound,
Dens for infernal commerce may be found;
There, daily, nightly, sots will congregate
To settle questions that concern the State!

To purchase wretchedness, and put in use
The latest modes of personal abuse,—
To give the countenance a lovely air,
By using a cosmetic that will wear!—
To get the marks of valor in a fight
For mastery, as well as *private* right,—
To prove, as clearly as example can,
THAT ELEGANCE OF DRESS NE'ER MADE A MAN,—
To demonstrate how tender he must be,
Who treats his household with barbarity!—
To furnish paupers for the Town or State,
And for the prisons, subjects fit create,—
To show, this pleasant world is not a cheat,
But makes the *destiny of man* complete.

Shall crime increase and folly mark the age,
The laws be passive when disorders rage?
Will RULERS of the State and men in power,
Submit to bear the evils of the hour,
And wink at morals, growing in our time,
Which lead directly to acknowledged crime?

Where are the men of character and might,
Who value order and the *public* right?—
A few reformers, eloquent and brave,
Still labor with a zeal and will to save
The youth from drunkenness, and stay the tide
Of misery, now rolling far and wide.
Where is that army, once so valiant, strong,
That battled with success the mighty wrong,
And held in check its progress in that day?
Demoralized, retired, o'ercome by false dismay!

They who are cowards in a moral cause,
And fear to execute remedial laws,
From righteous censure cannot be exempt;
The guilty, even, hold *them* in contempt.
They are accountable before that bar,
Where conscience reigns and tells them, *what they are.*

You, who eschew intoxicating drink,
Have eyes to see, and brains enough to think;

Who make professions with a heart sincere,
And sign a creed to which you will adhere,
For human welfare earnestly contend,
To save a neighbor, family, or friend;
Go forth to duty,—let your motto be,
'War on the curse to all humanity.'

Can men, who once have loathed the very sight
Of the foul demon, stalking day and night,
Through all their borders, dealing woe or death,
To hopeless victims, breathe his fetid breath,
Mixed with the sweet, and wholesome, vital air,
And not detect his presence *any-where?*

Physicians hold, that they who would be cured,
To faith in remedies must be allured.
Faith works by love, the SACRED truth declares,
Why may it not, in temporal affairs?
Love changes taste, as every-body knows—
Why should it not make friends of former foes?
And is it not, at least, a prudent thought,
(Since the true Panacea may be bought,)
To keep at hand, a curative of pain,
Prepared for use, delectable and plain?
One, which will make us young when we are old;
When cold, will warm us, and *will make us cold?*
This is fair logic,—*cultured* minds can see
What is embraced in Physiology!
The crafty fiend has a peculiar charm,
Whereby he can his enemy disarm,
And make him liege, if he be weak, by art
Which bribes the stomach, spoils the brain and heart,
Subdues the minor organs, more remote,
Unseats the reason, sets the man afloat.
In his strange bark upon the seething tide,
From a due course, he often wanders wide;
Near shore, the ground-swells to his vision rise;
Then, in the vessel on "beam-ends," he lies.
In life's short voyage, wherever he may float,
For pains, *he* takes the *spirit-antidote.*

You who profess the virtue, abstinence,
Who drink the secret cup with false pretence
Of some dire ailment, or expectant ill,
A cough, a swoon, a fever, or a chill!
When under pledge, may pass awhile, as true,
But honest men will soon discover you;
When all exposed, you find no one deceived,—
What you professed, the world had disbelieved.
Then comes the sentence to remain through time,
Due perpetrators of fool-hardy crime:
That such impostors take cognomen fit,
Which is *no synonyme* of hypocrite.
Let drunkards blush to feel the deep disgrace
Of such deception in the human race!

Of all the beings living on the earth,
Since Eve was formed, and man had proper birth,
The arch dissembler with his double face,
Is qualified to fill an *honored* place,
Where shame, deceit, contempt and folly dwell,
In that dark region, proximate to hell.

* * *

That bloody field, spread out in great extent,
Embracing half of one vast Continent,
Affords a theme for the pathetic muse,
And matter which the Satirist may use.

See! rightful order into ruin hurled,—
The sight—the thought has shocked the very world!
A nation drenched in blood by civil war;
Not by a foreign power, but angry jar,
Dividing subjects into factions strong,—
One, branding human bondage as a wrong,—
One, claiming human flesh!—At length, the strife
Warmed into treason and conspired the life
Of that Republic, destined at its birth,
To be the model government of earth.

The union of the States, which blood had bought,
To sunder, made Rebellion vainly sought.—

Its hellish enginery caused blood to flow,
And fill the land with mourning and with woe;—
It wasted treasure, and it slew the brave!
Yet, loyal patriots had power to save
The sacred bond, the adamantine chain,
Unbroken,—and the triumph will remain,
The proudest monument of ages past,
And, to the end of time, shall all its glory last.
Graved on this monument by Time's own hand,
In characters that all may understand,
Is this important lesson for mankind
To read, believe, and treasure in the mind:
That Government its end will best fulfill,
Whose basis is the free and sovereign will
Of loyal subjects; and their power alone,
Makes a Republic stronger than a throne.

Here, Justice, bodied from a true design,
Is plainly wrought, and perfect in its line—
The figure of a man, whose countenance
Betrays the sculptor's purpose at a glance.
The right hand holds a dark and lengthy scroll,
Entitled, "Treason's Famous Muster-Roll;"—
The left displays a Record, brief and plain,
Which shows a Nation's loss and Freedom's gain!
In all the past, no parallel appears;
It may lie hidden in the coming years.
Now they who thither turn their eyes, may see
Rebellion's rise, and fall, and infamy!
That martyred Chief,—the climax of its crime,—
A sin and folly that will live through time!—
THE FATE OF REBELS! once successful, free,—
THE DUSKY MILLIONS' ENTREE INTO LIBERTY!

*   *   *

Extravagance in modes of life and dress—
Pursuit of wealth to gain true happiness—
False taste in literature and love of show—
A style of morals, ranging far too low!—

Intemperance, hypocrisy, and fraud
Astounding in its nature, deep and broad—
The people, careless of the public weal,
To private interest, alive with zeal,
The dupes of demagogues who thrive by tricks,
Concealed with skill in party politics—
A vanity, imposing its displays
Of silly weakness in unnumbered ways,—
These glaring follies bear important sway,
And stain the public character to-day.

Why censure Folly, now as old as Time,
And lash her wickedness in sounding rhyme?
Her progeny is countless as the face
Of man, and quite as difficult to trace.
Since Adam's sin, the broods of lighter stain
Have multiplied—increasing, they remain.
The grade of each is only known to fate—
Man separates the little and the great;
So subtle the gradations run between,
By mortal ken they cannot all be seen:
Would that the greater might be growing less,
The less, decreasing into nothingness.
All crimes are follies, not all follies crimes,
Else, how could Heaven's dread vengeance spare our times?

The Artist sets the picture in a light,
Where its position will afford a sight
Of all the beauties which his art has made,
And leave defects concealed beneath the shade.
The honest satirist will use his skill,
To reach the fountains of the heart and will,—
To place the human conduct in the light
Of Truth's pure sunshine, and in colors bright,
That when unmantled, every eye may see
In crime or folly, bare deformity;—
How evil passion urges on to sin,
Grows strong, and claims the mastery within,—
How Folly flutters in the public gaze,
And shows her weakness in a thousand ways,
That drowsy conscience, stirred to life by pain,
May choke these ills and reign supreme again.

It has not dawned, that day of sacred feast,
When crimes or follies of mankind have ceased;
Till then, so long as moral ills are born,
Let Satire paint them for the public scorn.

APRIL 8, 1867.

II. THE GLOWING WONDERS OF SECESSION

Even with his dissatisfaction concerning the manners and mores of his time, F. O. Sayles (see page 87) was unwilling to suggest that the war should not have been waged. But in *Secession or Prose in Rhyme* (Philadelphia, 1864), published anonymously as "by an East Tennessean," the Hon. T. A. R. Nelson sarcastically informed the South that secession had not created a new Southern Heaven and a new Southern earth, as its advocators had prophesied. This point of view places Nelson in the rather strong pro-Union camp which prevailed in Tennessee throughout the war, even though the state formally went with the Confederacy. It should also be noted that the poem was written as the war entered its final stages, and consequently at a time when more than one Southerner was undoubtedly trying to decide whether secession constituted at best a mixed blessing or, as Nelson avers, an unmixed curse.

Throughout his poem, Nelson portrays typical Southern attitudes prior to and during the conflict, in a manner which shows him to have been an acute observer. His poem, as is typical of the poetry of political criticism, abounds with references to specific persons and events. The extensive footnotes which Nelson appends to his topical allusions, as though fearful that these references might escape some readers unless documented, suggest something of the utilitarian nature of the poem. But even though the poem is propagandistic, the poet in Nelson chose not to overlook the aid of so useful a tool as irony, a technique employed at the beginning of the poem by the query, "What pen can trace, with just impression, / The glowing wonders of Secession,—" and continued throughout the poem. The "rights" which, according to Nelson, the South has won by seceding (the right "to have our ports blockaded," the right to have our preachers "prophesy that we, in battle, / Should slay our brethren just like cattle," the right "to let rude soldiers seize / Your milk and poultry when they please," etc.) were clearly not the rights envisioned by most Southern poets who, even in the darkest hours of the conflict, maintained that the "right" of a Southerner lay in his opportunity for martyrdom in a cause which, since it was God-inspired, could never in the larger sense be lost.

Secession is one of two poems which Nelson published together in one volume, the full title of the book being *Secession or Prose in Rhyme and East Tennessee a Poem by an East Tennessean* (Philadelphia, 1864).

SECESSION

What pen can trace, with just impression,
The glowing wonders of Secession,—
So peaceful once, so warlike now,
With ghastly form and frowning brow? (1)
Once holding out, by way of suction,
The principle of reconstruction;
Now branding all as traitors, who
Would past alliances renew; (2)
At home, arousing States to fear
That Abolition's sway was near;
Abroad, denying that such cause
Made States and men defy the laws;
Here, charging home, like cunning knaves,
That "Lincoln's War" would free the slaves;
There, beginning England's cash and aid,
To speed the progress of "Free Trade;" [3?]
Here, fighting for the right *to* man,
There, offering Abolition plan;
Now, claiming Cotton as the King
Of all the world—the magic spring
To press crowned monarchs to their knees,
And make them do just as we please;
But, finding dull *that* cotton phasis,
Proclaiming it a specie basis;
Then, teaching that all men should spurn it,
And, with religious fervor, burn it; (4)
Inviting foreign intervention
To stop, at once, a fierce contention;
But foiled, denying recognition
As needful, in our strong condition; (5)
With Protean shape, chameleon hue,
Forever changing, ever new—
A thing of magic and of might,
Ne'er warmed to wrong, but always right!

THE GLOWING WONDERS OF SECESSION

Who hath not heard that WASHINGTON,
With all its wealth, would soon be won? (6)
That one brave bee, of Southern hive,
From Northern swarms, could vanquish five?
That craven Yankees would not fight,
And, seeing us, must take to flight?
That war *their* fields might desolate,
But dare not visit Southern State?
Tho', if it came, then glory's blaze
Should burn it out in sixty days?
While Southern men need have no fears,
As none might fight but Volunteers? (7)

Who doth not know that WASHINGTON
Has not been reached, will ne'er be won;
That one live Yankee is as much
As Southern knight may safely touch;
And that to tread on Northern soil
Somehow produces strange recoil?
Who hath not seen the fierce conscription—
In all its moods, beyond description—
Compel the twelve months' Volunteers,
Against their will, to serve three years? (8)
Hunt Union sympathizers down,
And, handcuffed, bring them into town?
Who doth not feel that War, defied,
Has sadly humbled Southern pride,
When conquering legions come at will,
Our lands and harbors all to fill?
Who now can Northern courage doubt
When promised victory proved a rout?

If tidings of their fame you seek,
Go view the flight at Fishing Creek;
If useful truth not prone to shun,
Behold the fall of Donelson;
If falsehood, trained to scorn and hate,
Of many a stronghold read the fate,
And learn that every place which fell
Was heralded—impregnable!
No foeman's face should e'er be seen
To frown, or smile, at Bowling Green;

Columbus, Island Number Ten,
Could never yield to Yankee men;
While Norfolk, New Orleans, Shiloh,
Would each inflict a fatal blow,
And Vicksburg, as a fortress stand,
The pride and boast of Dixie land! (9)

The people drank the bitter cup
As, one by one, they all "went up;"
But, in their grief, were blandly told
That neither place was—*fit to hold!*

If Lee, with cannon, sword, and lance,
On northern soil makes proud advance,
His aim will thousand tongues unfold
To conquer towns with daring bold;
To seize their Railroads, burn their cars,
And wave o'er cities "Stars and Bars;"
But if, perchance, each nobler deed
Is baffled by the impetuous MEADE—
If, with a routed army, LEE,
O'er swollen streams, is forced to flee,
He never purposed to remain;
His object was—*to save his train;*
And, tho' he retrogrades his track,
'Tis no retreat, but—"*falling back!!*" (10)

Ere war began, a wordy flood
Of eloquence, belittled blood,
And Orators, ere war should stop,
Would spill their last and reddest drop;
But, since they raised the awful flame,
Their best performances, how tame!
The tattered Southern army view,
Dragged out by an ambitious crew
Of selfish leaders, 'gainst the right
And their own native land to fight.
How few of those who strove to fire
The Southern heart with war and ire,
Among their guilty, naughty pranks,
E'er deemed it safe to join the ranks!

How many of the selfish brutes
Were swift to hire substitutes,
Themselves from all exposure shield,
But others urge to take the field,
While they could stay at home and make
Whatever gains they chose to take:
Or, if provoked by pride or shame,
On tented field to win a name,
They, from their firesides ventured out,
To share in victory or rout,
'Twas only that as officers,
With gilded coats and brazen spurs,
They might the soldier's duties shun,
And snatch the fame that he had won!

What useful lessons spur our sense,
When taught by sour experience!
We've learned "Virginia's sacred soil,"
Like common earth, may bleed and toil; (11)
That Tennessee in zeal may flag
To witness the dismay of Bragg,
And that our Floyd was taught to dance,
In reels, by master Rosencrans—
An active, flying Dutchman, who
Our straggling armies *will* pursue;
Or, if outnumbered, hold his own
With all the masses round him thrown.
But what of these? Bring Conscripts out;
The men of fifty oft are stout,
And, should they strive to hide or fly,
The lash and ball you may apply—
No Volunteer so freely fights
As one who's *forced* to seek his rights. (12)

Old Union never gazed upon
Such piebald rights as have been won;
By valor gained, in open day;
These let Secession proud display—
A motley group of great and small,
But, in hotch pot, behold them all.

The right to have our ports blockaded,
And our own paradise invaded;
To be, at once, sublimely roasted
With "*that same*" fire of which we boasted.

The right of Preachers, who inherit,
From ancient Seers, "a lying spirit," (13)
To prophesy that we, in battle,
Should slay our brethren just like cattle;
But, when the fiery tide was turning,
With hell-born inspiration burning,
Besetting heaven that war should cease,
And wrestling lustily for peace,
As if THE JUST would deign to hear
Prayers meant alone for human ear. (14)

The right to banish silver, gold,
And paper promises unfold,
Printed and paid, amidst duress,
In every shape of ugliness; (15)
To laud each petty corporation
That labors to build up a nation;
To fill your pockets with "shin-plasters,"
Prolific fruits of cash disasters,
And take as good, all free from stricture,
Whatever rags display a picture.

The right to force your hay and oats (16)
With, or without, Confederate notes;
To have your mules and horses prest,
And swear that you have been caressed;
To see your treasured wheat and flour
Consumed by military power;
To part with fodder, corn, and bacon,
At arbitrary value taken;
And feel that farmers freely bleed
'Neath prices stamped by lawyer Sneed— (17)
A man whose mind alone enlarges
When pondering o'er his own huge charges.

The right to let rude soldiers seize
Your milk and poultry when they please;

Grab all your bed-clothes, sugar, honey,
And think your murmurs very funny;
The right to have your country take
Your leather for the army's sake;
In one of patriotism's fits,
To make your harness of oak splits, (18)
And let your wives and children go
Barefooted through the mud and snow,
While some young stripling, whom it suits,
Struts, high and dry, in seven-leagued boots!

The right to have your stills destroyed
That liquors may be well employed—
For common soldiers all "*go dry,*"
That officers may frolic high— (19)
The right to make your coffee, tea,
Of rye, or roots, and boast you're free;
To learn the art of breeches thatching,
Grow skilled in many-colored patching;
Wear faded clothes till old and rotten,
And make the new of Dixie cotton. (20)

The right to close all business doors,
And do without the shops and stores;
To see your loving wife grow mad
When pins and needles can't be had;
Heave sighs for silks and calico,
And wonder where the sugars go;
To grasp you sternly by the throat,
With rents in her last petticoat,
Or wear some hideous hat or bonnet
And scream a threadbare rebel sonnet!

The right to travel as first-class,
But, like a negro, show your pass; (21)
Large hires to pay for substitutes,
Then be compelled to "go it, boots;" (22)
And, when Secession cuts a caper,
The news to read—on wrapping paper.

The right to pay the heaviest tax (23)
That ever broke a people's backs—

(In vain the sturdiest Southern writhes
At thoughts of paying cash and tithes)—
The right to hear of sons well-fed,
In distant armies, bravely led;
To be assured they get relief
Against the climate, with mule beef,
And that 'tis glorious when they die,—
They know not where, and care not why. (24)

The right to disarm Union men
By dash of ZOLLICOFFER's pen; (25)
With tents and blankets to dispense,
And burn their cheap or costly fence;
Their houses search, their persons seize,
With hostile bands of Cherokees;
Then "devilish Yankees" to abuse
Who negroes in their service use.

The right to dream that all's impartial
Which may be done by Provost Marshal;
To view the scum of all the nation
Promoted to official station; (26)
By drumhead law, to hang bridge burners,
In terror to Secession spurners; (27)
To murder men and boys unarmed,
Who are not with its beauties charmed;
When startled renegades evanish,
Their goods to steal, their wives to banish, (28)
And give your safety the eclat
Of bayonet courts and martial law. (29)

Such priceless rights he never felt,
Who, at the Union altar, knelt;
Such blessings ne'er were seen or sent
In our "old, rotten government;"
They came—so willed the smiling fates—
From our beloved Confederate States!

Let these, and other changes prove,
How their whole country all should love;
How WASHINGTON's Farewell Address
May every noble mind impress;

How wise and just his sage reflections
On party names and wars of sections;
What madness has controlled the hour,
And wildly led with demon power!

Oh! Union, born in throes and blood,
Well nurtured by the wise and good,
What wickedness has sought thy life,
'Mid civil broils and party strife!
'T was thine to crown with happiness
A land that Heaven rejoiced to bless;
Extend to all a parent's care,
With poor and rich thy bounties share;
Whate'er was wrong, subdue, correct,
Nor smallest privilege neglect;
'Twas thine to give the exile home,
Guard well thy people should they roam;
Shield citizens in desert sands,
Or wandering o'er the prairie lands;
Exact from Savages and Kings
The homage that from power springs;
Of Liberty the guide to be
In newborn States begot of thee,
And see thy children thrive and grow
With active limbs and healthful glow;
Wealth springing up at their command,
From mines of ore and teeming land,
With naught to fear or emulate
Save progress in a rival State!
With thee, religion, equal law,
Went, hand in hand, the vile to awe;
Thy youth were taught, and hoary age,
In safety, spoke its counsels sage;
The humblest man in power or place
Might boldly his accuser face,
And from the courts of right demand
A speedy trial in native land;
No hidden foe could have him borne
Away, in distant jail to mourn;
No myrmidon could keep him there,
For Justice reached him everywhere,

And Law's great writ of common right
Flashed o'er him its resplendent light; (31)
No coward fears, no false alarms
The people robbed of safety's arms;
Long-cherished charters did assure
Their property and lives secure;
No fetters chained the free-born mind,
No prisons innocence confined;
The ruffian's search, the assassin's tread,
Ne'er filled the land with silent dread; (32)
The tyrant's power, unfelt, unknown,
By patriot fathers overthrown,
Existed, in the dreamy past,
Like memory of a thunder blast,
And, in the sunshine of the day,
The horrid phantom fled away!
Where'er thy flag disturbed the breeze,
On oceans wide or distant seas,
Already had thy matchless name
Aroused the trumpet blast of fame;
O'er all the earth down-trodden man
Revered the word—AMERICAN;
And panting to be great and free,
His fondest wishes turned to thee—
The despot's foe, the living light
To guide the struggling nations right!

Shades of our country's champions! where
Dwell ye amid the ambient air?
Are ye allowed to see or know
All that occurs on earth below?
Are Freedom's heroes, when they die,
Wafted above the deep blue sky?
Their thronging spirits! may they tell
How conflict rages like a hell?
And can ye yet exert a power
To lull the storms that darkly lower?

It cannot be—or WASHINGTON
Would sternly censure what we've done,
And hush the cannon that declare
Our slight of his paternal care!

It cannot be—or JACKSON fierce,
The grave's dark gloom would boldly pierce,
And back to earth, in wrath return,
"With thoughts that breathe, and words that burn!"
It cannot be—or WEBSTER, great
In all the lore that forms a State,
Would, for the Constitution, plead,
And shout—of Anarchy take heed!
It cannot be—or matchless CLAY
The veil that hides would tear away,
And his tall form erect display
Arrayed in dazzling robe of white,
And, flashing with angelic light,
Upon an arching rainbow stand,
Viewed by a torn and bleeding land;
And, with an eloquence new-born,
A maddened people loudly warn;
Bid War's infernal carnage cease,
And million's voices cry for peace!

What hissing curse, or crushing blast,
Shall be o'er perjured traitors cast,
Who swore their country to sustain,
But gladly give that country pain? (33)
Who can atone for all the blood
That deluges, like angry flood,
And fills a land with groans and tears,
That happiest stood among her peers?

The orphan child, the widowed wife,
The soldier ruined, maimed for life;
The patriot scourged, the prisoner freed,
All who have suffered, all who bleed;
The thousands who in lies believed,
The millions in their hopes deceived;
The cheerless homes, the ruins black,
The fields thrown out to War's wild track;
The very horses, starved and thin,
With ghosts of murdered men, begin,
In bitterest strains, to chant, rehearse,
The traitor's doom, the tory's curse!

Where'er they go, let withering scorn
Against their coming quickly warn;
Whate'er they say, let shy distrust,
In doubt, deny their statements just;
Whate'er they do, let jealous eyes
Their best performances despise;
From their vile presence turn away,
Trust not the miscreants who betray;
Do not their callous conscience mock
With oaths that cannot bind or shock;
Withhold the honors they may seek
With brazen front or bearing meek;
Imbue your children with a dread
Of all who in Rebellion led;
And, while its gay, deluded fair,
And misled votaries you spare,
Let every proud, detested name,
Be "damned to everlasting fame!"

NOTES

(1) PREVIOUSLY to the war, and with the view of creating the belief that such an event was impossible, there was an incessant cant, among Southern leaders, in favor of "peaceable secession." [This and the following notes to *Secession* are Nelson's. Editor's note.]

(2) The doctrine of "Reconstruction" was freely promulgated until all the seceding States "went out;" but afterwards it was regarded as treason to speak of it.

(3) The Southern Commissioners, who were sent to England, knowing the hostility of that country to slavery, argued *there* that Abolition was not the cause of the war, and referred to Mr. Lincoln's inaugural to prove it. It was said that, after lashing the whole South into fury on the slavery question, they offered a plan for the gradual abolition of slavery; and represented opposition to Free Trade as the cause of the war!

(4) Southern leaders boasted that "Cotton was King," until they began to believe themselves monarchs of all the earth. Their boasts, as to European dependence, have not been fulfilled. Cotton has not been made a specie basis to sustain the Confederate currency, as they promised; and Confederate notes, even among themselves, are 1500 per cent. below par.

(5) In the hope of keeping up the spirits of the people, Southern papers have published articles, *ad nauseam,* upon foreign intervention, ever since the war began. But, of late, they argue it would be of no service. See the fable of the Fox and the Grapes.

(6) Mr. Secretary Walker declared, in his speech at Montgomery, on the 12th of April, 1861, that "the flag which now flaunts the breeze here, would float over the old Capitol at Washington before the first of May;" and many a deluded soldier believed him.

(7) It was a stereotyped expression that "one Southerner could whip five Yankees;" yet, ages ago, it was said: "Let not him that girdeth on his harness boast himself as he that putteth it off."

(8) The Conscript Law was passed to keep the Southern army together. Thousands, who had volunteered to serve twelve months, were forced into the three years' service. In executing the law, in East Tennessee, Union men and women were whipped, and the latter sometimes hung, to make them tell where the Conscripts were secreted. Many were shot, and nothing was more common than to bring them tied and handcuffed into the little towns. At Knoxville, conscripts were whipped, compelled to wear the ball and chain, and, in some instances, hung for desertion. CAPTAIN HARRIS, a respectable young man, of Jefferson County, was sentenced to be hung, although he was never in the Confederate service, on the technical ground that, as his name had been enrolled, he was to be regarded as a soldier. It was with the utmost difficulty that his numerous relations and friends obtained a commutation of the punishment to imprisonment for life.

(9) Before the capture of the places named, they were each represented as of great consequence and impregnable. Afterwards, it was said they were not good strategic positions, and had been badly fortified!

(10) Southern papers never admit that an army is defeated. They modestly call it—"*falling back!*"

(11) Poor old Virginia! Land of politics and pride, and victim of traitors! The cotton States were too smart for her, and transferred the war to her sacred soil. She rushed into it without cause, and her fields are desolate; her bosom, a graveyard! She has nothing left but the Resolutions of '98.

(12) The phrase most popular among Southern men, was that they were "*going out of the Union to get their rights.*" The enumeration which follows, if not poetical, is, at least, true, and drawn from actual occurrences.

(13) Once upon a time, the question was put:—"Who shall entice Ahab, king of Israel, that he may go up and fall at Ramoth Gilead?" And a spirit said: "I will entice him and be a lying spirit in the mouth of all his prophets." There were 400 against one; yet Ahab fell, as Micaiah predicted; and our Parsons may learn that it is not always right to "follow a multitude to do evil."

(14) The clergy—whose proper business it is to declare "on earth peace, good will towards men"—with a few honorable exceptions, forgot their calling and clamored for war, when no man in the United States could truthfully say that he had ever been oppressed by his government. After a few defeats, and after thousands of widows and orphans had been made in the land, in a great measure through their influence over the public mind, they began to "walk softly" before their Maker, and to

pray for peace. Let them now, in good faith, practice that repentance which they preach to others.

(15) Never, since the world began—no, not in the days of Continental money, or of the French assignats—was there such a currency! States, Counties, Banks, Corporations, Companies, and individuals, have issued their notes by the bale, printed in the meanest style and on the meanest paper. Oh! for the tongue of old Bullion, to lash the Southern States-rights-hard-money-Democratic leaders!

(16) No pen can describe the pilfering and stealing depradations of the Southern cavalry in East Tennessee. The Impressment Law was a farce. The property of Union men was generally taken in the same manner, but certificates were generally issued to them; and, in order to obtain payment, they had to run the gauntlet of the "Circumlocution Office," and then received about half-price in Confederate notes.

(17) W. H. Sneed and W. E. Travis, grand commissioners of valuation under the impressment law, fixed the price of corn, in their Schedule No. 1, at $1.85 and $2 per bushel, when it was selling at $5, and other articles in proportion. These gentlemen, of profound erudition and limitless knowledge, actually valued bacon at 35 and 40 cents, and country-made soap at 50 cents, per pound; thus presenting, although the army was half starved, a strong temptation to manufacture all the bacon into soap!

(18) Sixty per cent. of all leather is taken by the rapacious and unscrupulous government; and, as a consequence, hundreds—not to say thousands—of women and children have been compelled to go barefooted through all the inclemency of winter. The "Lynchburg Republican" recommended the oak substitute, as stated in the text, and his [*sic*] article was extensively copied by the Southern papers.

(19) The orders and acts of the military authorities in East Tennessee, prohibiting the manufacture of liquors, closing groceries, and destroying stills, were palpable violations of the license laws of Tennessee; but, notwithstanding the stringency of these measures, many of the officers contrived to have the article manufactured, under the pretence that it was needed for the hospitals, and were often gloriously drunk.

(20) It has been, and is impossible to procure anything like an adequate supply of the most common articles, and the "*makeshifts*" are legion.

(21) Martial law was declared and has been kept up in East Tennessee, in defiance of all law. The passport system has been exceedingly oppressive. Under it, some of the Provost Marshals refused to grant passports to Union men to go for salt, with their wagons, to the Salt Works, the only place where it could be had!

(22) Conscripts were called out, first, to the age of 40; then to 45; and the militia, under the State law, to 55. A person who hired a substitute under the first call, who was over 40, but under 55, is now required to serve himself.

(23) The Confederate tax law takes one-tenth of all grain and other agricultural productions, in kind, and provides for the appointment of Tithing-men to collect it. It taxes the same person and the same thing in a great variety of forms. It beats anything that ever was passed in

America; and, in many respects, is equal to England. But what are our new-fledged rights worth, if they cost us nothing? By the time we are fully overrun by the two opposing armies, we shall begin to appreciate their value, and to learn that war ought never to be resorted to, except in cases of absolute and imperious necessity, and is not to be justified on the ground of theoretical and imaginary injuries.

(24) Remember Vicksburg and mule beef.

(25) Among the papers of General Zollicoffer, found after his death at Fishing Creek, was an order to Major Wood, directing that the tories—*i.e.*, the Union men—should be disarmed. This was done under his order, and an unconstitutional law passed by the State Legislature. It was pretended that the arms were needed by the Southern army. They consisted chiefly of old rifles, shot-guns, and pistols, and were never used, but were boxed up. The real object was to deprive Union men of all power of resistance. Southern leaders "prepared the Southern heart, and fired the Southern mind" with the idea that the object of Mr. Lincoln was to SUBJUGATE the South; yet, in their own practice, they subjugated the people of East Tennessee, so far as it was possible for them to do, and attempted the same thing in Kentucky and Missouri; thus showing that this, as well as all other pretexts for the disruption of the government, were false and unfounded.

(26) Some of the Provost Marshals and Enrolling Officers, not to speak of others, were the grandest rascals the Confederacy could produce. In the boiling of the political cauldron it was natural that the scum should rise to the surface!

(27) If the bridge burners acted under the authority of the United States, they were guilty of no offence. If they acted without such authority, they were amenable, for a penitentiary offence, to the State laws. In either view, their execution was a murder, for which all concerned may be lawfully indicted and punished—if the people will take care not to elect Secessionists to the offices of Judge and Attorney-General; but especially the latter.

(28) The Confederate soldiery have, in a vast number of instances, stolen the property of Union men, sold it at public sale, and divided the proceeds. The Confederate court has shown equal rapacity, in the numerous cases in which the confiscation law has been enforced, and its Judge solemnly declared, in open court, that an alien—that is, a Union man who had fled to Kentucky—had no rights in his court. On the 23d of April, 1862, an order was promulgated from headquarters, at Knoxville, by the Provost Marshal, to the effect that those who had fled might return within thirty days; but that, if they did not do so, their wives and children in East Tennessee "should be sent to their care in Kentucky, or beyond the Confederate lines, at their own expense," it being declared that "the women and children must be taken care of by husbands and fathers, either in East Tennessee or in the Lincoln government."

(29) In September, 1861, Hon. West H. Humphreys—who was impeached as a Federal Judge before the United States Senate, but contrived to hold a similar position in the Confederate government—held his high court of Star Chamber at Knoxville, having the court house

filled with armed soldiers, who prevented the entrance of any one who had not express permission. Such a scene was never before witnessed in Tennessee. Some foolish circuit Judge, whose name was not published, afterwards imitated the example at Athens, but was admirably rebuked by the Athens Post.

(30) In view of the thousands who have been sent to prison in this and other States, without accuser and without trial, let the people read again and love more than ever the Bills of Rights in every American Constitution!

(31) General Buckner informed the State Judges, in East Tennessee, that he would not obey their writs of habeas corpus, and that such process, to be respected, must emanate from a Confederate Judge. As the proper residence of the Confederate Judge was at Nashville, and his ambulatory domicile was everywhere, it was thus rendered impossible for a soldier, or other person wrongfully held in military custody, to obtain a legal release.

(32) Confederate soldiers, directly in the teeth of all our constitutions and laws, were constantly in the habit of searching and robbing the houses of Union men by day and by night; but none of them were ever punished, or, if they were, the public journals did not state it, lest it should fill their own description of the Yankees.

(33) Let it never be forgotten that governors, members of Congress, judges, clerks, lawyers, sheriffs, justices, and all other officers, were sworn to support the Constitution of the United States. Those of them who inaugurated or advocated secession before the State "went out," were guilty at least of moral perjury. But those who acquiesced in or supported it, after a government *de facto* was established, stand on a very different footing. They, and also the vast numbers who, by means of actual or apprehended force, were compelled to take the oath, are certainly excusable, and perhaps justifiable.

Chapter Four: Slavery

I. SINCE MERCY FELL BY TYRANNY

Poets North and South were convinced that the Civil War resulted from clearly defined forces over which man had, or should have had, control. From this attitude grew an intensely vitriolic verse. And, since vitriol is vitriol, wherever one finds it, it is not surprising that Northern and Southern poets employed identical epithets. A favorite label of opprobrium, knowing no geographical boundaries, was *Tyranny.* The Northern poet Dexter Smith, and the Southern poet Cornelia J. M. Jordan, similarly charge the opposition with Tyranny in the poems which follow. Smith's poem is from *Poems* (Boston, 1868); Jordan's poem is from *Corinth and Other Poems of the War* (Lynchburg, 1865).

IN MEMORIAM (ABRAHAM LINCOLN)

Columbia weeps! Her cherished son,
  Who struck her fetters to the ground,
Who saved the land of Washington,
  Has passed from earth's most distant bound.

His spirit went to realms on high;
  His dust, alone, the earth could claim;
His memory will never die
  While freemen live to bless his name.

Columbia swears anew her vow
  To guard the birthright of the free;
Unsheathed, her sword of Justice now
  Since Mercy fell by Tyranny.

Our nation's hopes and fears alike
  Are with the land our fathers trod,

And while for Freedom now we strike,
  Our future is alone with God.

—Dexter Smith

OUR FALLEN BRAVE

They fell! in Freedom's cause they fell,
  The noble patriot band,
And Freedom for their sakes, becomes
  A mourner through the Land.
They rushed to Victory or Death,
  They struck for Liberty,
And Victory's tears now gild their swords—
  Our fallen and our free!

They met the Tyrant's vassal-hordes;
  No faltering hearts were there—
Our Country's truth their battle-cry,
  Our Country's weal, their care.
They marched into the jaws of Death;
  No wavering pulse they knew,
And minions crouched before their blades,
  Our valiant and our true!

They fought as patriots, fearless, bold,
  As patriots too they fell,
And struggling nations yet to be
  Their daring deeds shall tell.
Aye, nations yet unborn shall smile,
  To learn that Victory
Embalmed with tears their shattered shields,
  Our faithful and our free!

They sleep—no wail of sorrowing Love
  May break their deep repose,
Nor blast of bugle, fife or drum
  Their dull cold ear unclose.

They sleep—they are not dead the while,
  Though funeral banners wave—
They live in Memory's holy place,
  Our beautiful, our brave!

They live in hearts that fondly prize,
  The proud immortal trust,
And Fame's unfading chaplet crowns,
  Pale slumberers in the dust.
Their story shall but nerve our arms,
  Their names our War-cry be,
And Glory's star shall light their graves,
  Our fallen and our free.

—Cornelia J. M. Jordan

II. GAUNT TREASON

The North, if anything, had the edge on the South in vitriolic language, in part because the alleged treasonableness of the South rankled in the hearts of Northern poets with such peculiar bitterness. Along with the charge of Tyranny, which they were obliged to share with Southern poets, Northern poets frequently added the charge of Treason, particularly in their call-to-arms poems. In its use of the charge of Treason, in its invocation of the Revolutionary War, in its assertion that God is on the side of the North, and in its plea for a preservation of the Union, the following poem by J. A. Nunes is typical. The poem is from *Day Dreams* (Philadelphia, 1863).

FREEDOM'S RALLY

Wake, Freedom, with thy trumpet tongue,
  Each echo in the land,
Till, at the sound, both old and young
  In arms before thee stand!
Gaunt Treason, stalking in the light,
  Uprears its hydra head,
And thy bright hosts must prove their might,
  And strike the monster dead!

Form, freemen, as the snow-flakes form
  Upon the mountain side,
And onward move, as moves the storm
  In its relentless pride!
Let traitors learn that treason's woe,
  And, while their cheeks still blanche,
Impel yourselves upon the foe,
  A living avalanche!

Shall it be said that Lexington
  In vain gave freedom birth;
In vain was seen by Yorktown's sun
  Oppression crushed to earth?
Shall it be said the wise, the good,
  The brave, who've been our pride,
Poured forth in vain their precious blood;
  In vain have fought and died?

No! By our sacred sires, and Him
  Who nerved their hearts with fire!
Their godlike deeds shall ne'er grow dim,
  Nor shall their names expire!
We'll bear the glorious flag they gave
  To our protecting hand,
Until its folds again shall wave
  Triumphant through the land!

Until each star upon its field
  Shall blaze with meteor light,
And till each foe is seen to yield
  A captive to its might;
Aye, till the continent pours out
  The war-cry of the free,
And joins in one exultant shout,
  For God and Liberty!

III. ON NONE DEPENDENT, SOVEREIGN, FREE

Since Treason was so logically equated with Secession, Southern poets seldom added the word to their stock-in-trade of epithets.

Another word, however, was more in demand by Northern poets even than Treason, and this word was not their prerogative, but was equally the property of the South. This word was *Freedom*. Northern and Southern poets, understandably, used different dictionaries in defining this word. Claudian Bird Northrop suggests the Southern definition in his "The South Carolina Hymn of Independence," where, after characterizing Northern soldiers as ruffians, slaves of mammon, a hateful horde, Northrop declares that they are waging "a ruthless, robber war," and expresses the hope that they will find a final resting place "in Southern soil, to freedom dear." Freedom to Northrop, as to Southern poets generally, meant the opportunity to pursue an established way of life. Note that Northrop, uncharacteristically for a Southern poet, charges the North with "foul treason," although, significantly, he leaves the exact nature of the charge undefined.

The poem is from *Southern Odes, by the Outcast, a Gentleman of South Carolina. Published for the Benefit of the Ladies Fuel Society* (Charleston, 1861).

THE SOUTH CAROLINA HYMN OF INDEPENDENCE

AIR—*The Marseillais* [*sic*]

South Carolinians! proudly see,
  Our State proclaimed to all the world,
On none dependent, sovereign, free.
  Foul treason has its flag unfurled.
  Foul treason has its flag unfurled.
From the plains, and from the mountains,
  From the ocean's far resounding shore,
  Rushing to war, our people pour,
Like a torrent from its fountains.
Arm! Carolinians, arm!
Our country shield from harm.
March on! march on! our banners wave.
The drum has beat th' alarm.

Ruffians bought,—to Mammon, slave,—
  With treach'rous chief,—a hateful horde!
Onward they swarm, and fiercely rave.
The tyrant comes with fire and sword,
The tyrant comes with fire and sword.

Our altars, and homes to profane;
  Mean of heart, and false to their word,
  By malice driven, and discord;
With blood, our peaceful land to stain.
Arm, Carolinians, &c.

No sacred standard do they bear,
  A ruthless, robber war they wage;
And, howling, from their wolfish lair,
  Rush on, with anarchy and rage,
  Rush on, with anarchy and rage.
Let them find dishonored graves,
  In Southern soil, to freedom dear;
  From Southern heroes, fighting where
Our own Palmetto banner waves.
Arm, Carolinians, &c.

Independent, with Sovereign right,
  Our soldiers, courageous and Free,
Will valiantly press to the fight,
  On to death, or to victory,
  On to death, or to victory.
Closing their ranks, in battle's shock,
  Breasting firm, the billows of death,
  The bayonet's charge, the cannon's breath,
Like breakers on the solid rock.
Arm, Carolinians, &c.

Remember our great English sire!
  How Alfred drove the Danish horde;
Saint Andrew's cross, and Erin's lyre;
  Marion's swamps, and Sumter's sword,
  Marion's swamps, and Sumter's sword.
Of brave DeKalb, the bloody grave;
  Our hero Rutledge's great soul;
  That awful cannonade,—whose roll,
Fame, to our lov'd Palmetto gave.
Arm, Carolinians, &c.

The God of Justice, and of Right!
  Oppression's sinful hosts disarms:

When, with Christian faith, we fight,
  Heaven blesses patriot's arms,
  Heaven blesses patriot's arms.
South Carolina's holy cause,
  Invites the brave of every land,
  Fighting in the glorious band,
For State, for Liberty and Laws.
  Arm, Carolinians, arm!
  Our country shield from harm.
March on! march on! our banners wave,
  The drum has beat th' alarm.

IV. THIS BROAD DOMAIN THAT FREEDOM CRAVES

According to Southern poets, Freedom meant the right to be let alone. Northern poets possessed an equally circumscribed, if very different, definition. In the minds of Northern poets, Freedom meant one thing: Emancipation of the Slaves. Short lyric outbursts against the evils of slavery, equating Freedom and Emancipation, were common in the North. Typical is A. J. H. Duganne's "The House of Bondage." The poem is from *Utterances* (New York, 1865).

THE HOUSE OF BONDAGE

From mossy woods and cypress bolls [*sic*],
The swimming snakes have sought their holes;
On heavy wing the night-owl flits,
With drooping head the vulture sits,
And down the bayou's sultry tide
I hear the stealthy cayman glide.

I weary of these orange-blooms,
And tuneless birds with gorgeous plumes,
And white magnolia's sweet attaint,
Whereof the honeyed air grows faint;
I weary of this golden cane,
This silvery cotton—and this chain!

The iron chain—the rusted chain,
That manacles each fruitful plain;
That binds the woodland and the sward—
That binds the laborer and the lord!—
It wearies soul—it wearies strength:
I think it wearies Heaven, at length!

Dear Heaven! this green and fertile mead—
These fields, that swell with pregnant seed;
These orchards ripe and gardens rare,
And sunlit skies and fragrant air;
This broad domain that Freedom craves—
Why must it be the House of Slaves?

The red oaks lift their vernal sheen—
The cypress waves in lustrous green;
But underneath lies withering bark,
Where creeps the swamp-moss, gray and stark,
And chokes the sweet life where it hangs—
Fit type of Slavery's deathful fangs!

I marvel oft, if shames distil
From lands that nurse no rippling rill;
If wrongs must still oppress these leas,
Because they feel no upland breeze;
If slaves must breed in swamp and fen,
While hill-tops suckle freeborn men!

No, Freedom! no!—thy generous veins
Can flood with life these sluggish plains;
Thy breath, that lifts our flags to God,
Shall quicken all this servile sod:
All dead things shall thy voice obey,
And rise, like Lazarus, from decay!

From Texas and to Hampshire snow,
Five hundred thousand bayonets glow!
I cannot think these Northern knives
Can e'er be forged to Southern gyves;
Or they that wield them—freeborn men—
Will build the House of Slaves again!

I draw my sword, and poise the blade—
I feel no manly strength decayed:
I swing it through yon palmy sedge—
It smites—it bites—with warlike edge!
It cuts as well—this freedom-brand—
In Southern as in Northern land!

I kiss my sword, and gripe [*sic*] the hilt—
I think of blood for Union spilt:
Beneath my flag of stars I stand—
I lift this steel blade in my hand,
And swear that all this land is free!—
O God! break not mine oath for me!

V. THE THIRSTY LASH, WITH SHARP, STEEL-POINTED THONG

Slavery constituted the chief battle-ground on which poets of the Eighteen-Sixties fought. Northern poets took the offensive quickly over the slavery issue, asserting almost without exception that anyone in league with slavery was a henchman of Satan. While short lyric outbursts against the general evils of slavery were common in the North, the opportunities slavery offered for melodrama lured Northern poets far beyond the confines of generalized protests. The real or imagined cruelty afforded slaves by both slavers and slave owners clearly invited dramatization. One of the fiercest indictments of slave owners published during the war was T. H. Underwood's *Our Flag. A Poem in Four Cantos* (New York, 1862).

from OUR FLAG

[At the beginning of the narrative a Negro slave fleeing to the North pauses to tell a poet how his mother had been beaten to death by their master. Apparently the slave's mother has been guilty of some slight misdemeanor, which brings on the following scene.]

"I heard the furious stamping of a heel,
  And saw the brute, with unrelenting air,
Assault his wife with force that made her reel,[1]
  And clutch my mother rudely by the hair;
With violence he dragged her to the door,
And thence his victim to the stable bore.

"He stript her naked, bound her to a stall,
  Tied ropes about her hands, her feet, her hair,
Then locked the door. I heard my mistress call:
  'Jeff! Jeff!' In haste I mounted up the stair,
But sudden stopt—there rose the wildest cry
That ever startled hell or shocked the sky.

"More like a corpse than anything of life,
  Save in her moanings and her face of fear,
Prone on a pallet lay the shivering wife,
  Her nervous palm pressed vainly to her ear;
She vainly strove to stop the dreadful sound—
It pierced her soul, as arrows pierce a wound.

" 'O master! master!—God! O *God!* O God!
  O! O! O!—help me, missus!—help me, do!
Do spare me, master! mercy! mercy! God!'
  The fearful cries went stinging through and through
Her frightened soul. She started from her bed,
And, wildly screaming, down the stairway fled.

* * *

"Enough of this: I leave the rest with God,
  Who then beheld and suffered this great sin.
These crimson spots are my poor mother's blood;
  This was the winding sheet I wrapt her in,
When, in the night, I stole her corpse away
To give it rest within its house of clay.[2]

* * *

[The slave subsequently is sold farther south to another master, who one day unexpectedly promises that on the morrow the Negro and his wife shall be free. Elated, the Negro goes to tell his wife the good news.]

"With eager haste I opened wide the door
  And called to her. She neither moved nor spoke.
I called again; I thumped upon the floor—
  No other sound upon the stillness broke.
With quick impatience to her side I flew—
Saw!—sickened and appalled, I backward drew!

"Ah, God! a chill of horror seized my joints!
I stood stone-still, blood oozing from my lips—
I dimly saw a hundred wiry points
Play round my wife, on bloody, spectral whips,
And each fell point plowed deep into my heart
With anguish such as no flesh-wounds impart.

"O'er all her face I saw great ridges rise;
Like fiery snakes they coiled about her throat—
They strangled me, they darted at my eyes,
And with their fangs the burning eyeballs smote.
Large, quivering welts were creeping, red and black,
With bloody scales, along her naked back.

"The deep-cut furrows of the steel-thong'd whips,
Red-rimmed and raw and open to the air,
Plowed through her bosom and along her hips,
Unfleshed the sinews, and the bones laid bare.
No word she uttered, neither curse nor prayer,
Nor wept, nor moaned, nor seemed to heed me there.

"Then through my brain, with hot, impatient heels,
Trooped the damned brotherhood of tyranny!
I heard blasphemous shouts and laughter peals
In mockery of Freedom. Sneeringly
The scoffers taunted me with chain and rod,
And bade me call upon the Negro's God!

"In trembling eagerness I drew a stool
Close to my dying wife, some water brought
To bathe her bleeding wounds, and strove to cool
The deadly fever that the whips had wrought.
But all my efforts and my tears were vain
To soothe the body's or the spirit's pain.

"She suffered much, but did not suffer long—
The murd'rous hands had done their work too well;
The thirsty lash, with sharp, steel-pointed thong,
Too skillfully had opened that deep cell
Where Life, imprisoned, waits the coming time,
Nor asks who knocks—disease, or age, or crime.

"Her face was lovely as she turned to me,
The light of heaven beaming in her eye;
She faintly said, 'Rejoice, for I am free!'
Her life went out. Oh! do not ask me why
I shouted 'Joy!' I felt sublimely brave,
For she I clasped was mine, and no man's slave.

"And thus my master kept his word with me—
His fiendish promise given yesterday—
'Your wife is feeble, I will set her free;'
And mine, of course, will come without delay.
I know not how, nor care I to inquire—
Enough! 'tis welcome, be it rope or fire.

"A bruiséd corse now lay upon my bed,
In bloody garments, torn of brutal hands.
More beautiful to me my mangled dead
Than in the morning of our nuptial bands,
For now my darling in her slumber lay
As royally as lies the noblest clay.

* * *

[The poem closes by showing the slave's pursuers catching him and burning him alive.]

NOTES

[1] Underwood, in a chivalric bow to Southern Womanhood, pictures the master's wife as having tried to assuage his wrath.

[2] The slave here displays to the poet an American flag which he is carrying with him.

John Burke's "Chivalry and Slavery" constitutes a peculiarly fierce indictment of slavery. According to Burke, the devilish slave-holder united vocation and avocation by torturing, maiming, and wantonly killing his property. All of the instances which Burke relates are, he states, founded upon well-authenticated facts. Following are some excerpts from Canto II. The poem is from *Chivalry, Slavery, and Young America* (New York, 1866).

from CHIVALRY AND SLAVERY

II

It chanced that in a Southern State,
Which one 'twere bootless to relate,
Two slaves were, under the pretense
Of some—by no means grave—offense,
Pinned down and fastened to the ground,
Their backs by scourging made one wound;
Then on the bleeding, mangled flesh
Were knots of pitch-pine, cut afresh,
Ignited: each to each was near,
The bubbling blood-streams to ensear;
Nor till the tortured victims died,
Were wrath and vengeance satisfied.
The overseer, and not the master,
Was the foul cause of this disaster;
In *sham arrest,* he broke *parole!*
The guilt lies still upon his soul,
His body safe: for Alabama,
Or for the coast of the Grand Lama,
For aught we know, he left; we leave him.
Can he repent, so Heaven forgive him! !
What the unpardonable sin is,
Not very easy to explain is:
Some say the callousness of Pharaoh,
And some the cruelty of Nero,
Some one thing say, and some another;
But though the point excite such pother,
The sin, we think, is found in *both*—
In *Rome* and *Egypt, will* and *oath*—
Cause and *effect, combined* in *one,*
A cruel will, a heart of stone!

III

Bound down and pinioned, as we've stated,
Another (so *authenticated*)
O'er the stark bodies of his slaves
With threats and furious vengeance raves;
Flatways a saw descending hacks
And lacerates their subject backs,
By atmospheric pressure denting
The stricken part; thence raised by force,
It scatters in its upward course,
A mince of dripping flesh and blood!
Can such atrocities, O God!
Begin, thy *lightning* not *preventing?*
The wretch who thus his negroes treated,
Had all such chattels sequestrated,
And by an act of legislation
Condemned, disfranchised, by the nation
Or State (we rather should have said),
Is now *politically dead!*

IV

Two hands beneath a cotton-press
Were placed; the *martyr*—was he less?—
Thus left all night to writhe in pain,
Lived till the morning dawned again.
Enters the master: his poor slave
Now turns his head, relief to crave.
"What! damn you! grin," the tyrant cries,
"*In* with him; *press!*" The victim sighs
His last brief litany, and dies!

V

We knew a youth, his name was Daves,
His father owned a score of slaves—
It may be more, it may be less;
We might in either acquiesce,
Although to have them *overrated*
Gives less offense than *understated.*

No man of property so proud as
He who of slaves a numerous crowd has;
So true it is men often *boast*
Of that which ought to shame them most.
Our youth was graduate of a college,
And had, 'twas thought, imbibed some knowledge—
Not a great deal, we may presume,
Nor think it too much to assume
That graduating is no test
Infallible of what is best,
Or for the body of the Soul,
As evidenced in self-control,
Or rather *want* of it, in schools
Where rods ne'er reach the backs of fools!

VI

By power, licentiousness and drink,
This hopeful heir had, we think,
His head and heart alike corrupted.
One act of his is here reported:
He tutored thus his overseer,
His negroes' flesh with whips to tear:
"Rise on your feet, as I on mine—
You so a better purchase gain—
Then, jerking, bring the thong toward you;
The practice soon will well reward you!"

VII

On whisky-cask, bound down with rope,
And *taut* as any iron hoop,
He rolled a hapless slave around,
His back one wide and ghastly wound,
His blood fast streaming to the ground.
The tyrant's dogs, without control,
Lap fiercely up the crimson pool,
While bellowing cattle spurn the gutter
Infuriate, as from scent of slaughter.
The beardless Nero sank exhausted,
So long the sickening torture lasted:

He sank, we said, but soon upstarted,
And to the whisky-bottle darted.
Thence, quick returning, he renewed
His work of blood; but what ensued?
How long the victim lived we know not,
And what we know not, we avow not;
But *this* we know, that, bending double,
His after life was pain and trouble;
He rather crawled than walked as man,
Till death released him from his pain.
And *this* we *know,* his wicked master,
  Or urged by drink or something worse,
From crime to crime went fast and faster,
  Till *suicide* cut short his course.
Thy snow-white cotton, Carolina,
Was blood-stained by this fell hyena!

* * *

VI. THE FESTAL MARCH OF IRON

Southern poets had no recourse against the Northern indictment of slavery as cruel and barbarous except to show the other side of the ledger, and depict slaves whose loyalty and happiness, quite obviously, grew out of loving treatment. But the South, in the years prior to Fort Sumter, was not content simply to picture the happiness of slaves. As early as 1854 William J. Grayson's *The Hireling and the Slave* had instructed the South that the idyllic nature of Southern slave life might be exhibited to better advantage if contrasted with the limitations of Northern industrialism. Grayson's argument, interestingly enough, had found its way into the North by the year the war began. An anonymous poet who used the memorable pen name of Jehu Geeup of Jackass Alley published, in 1861, his *North and South, or, What Is Slavery?,* in which the degradation of Northern industrialism comes out second best when compared with the mild evils of Southern slavery. Although the imprint of Geeup's poem omits the place of publication, Geeup makes it clear in his poem that he is a Northerner who has had more than enough of "slave" labor at the hands of Northern industrialists.

Although Southern poets during the war were too busy commenting on the war itself to bother carrying on Grayson's tradition, the memory of this earlier argument appears to have made a particularly deep impression on at least one Northern poet, who rather elaborately took up the gauntlet of industrial degradation. In a pair of complementary poems, "The Song of Iron" and "The Song of Slaves," Kane O'Donnel sang the praises of iron and industrialism on the one hand and, on the other, hymned a dirge in which slaves bewailed their lot. It is difficult to believe that O'Donnel's poems represent anything except a direct reply to the Jehu Geeups and William Graysons, whether they resided in Northern Jackass Alleys or down on the Old Plantation.

The poems are from *The Song of Iron and the Song of Slaves; with Other Poems* (Philadelphia, 1863).

from THE SONG OF IRON

O'er flaming, roaring forges,
  The dingy rafters are,
Black with a sooty midnight,
  And red with sun nor star,
Where toil the iron-workers
  In leathern guise and grim;
As bounds the heavy hammer
  Resounds their sturdy hymn:
Hurrah! this world of ours,
  Of fire, cloud and power!
Thus, iron beats on iron
  And shapes the serious hour.

Into the hungry fire
  This rusty lever throw;
That wheezing windy whisp'rer
  The stout-lunged bellows blow.
Red-hot upon the anvil
  The angry barrier glows,
Crowned in a flying splendor
  As down the hammer goes.

Hurrah! this hour's creation,
The iron hand, hurrah!
Thus down on good unshapen
Strikes the almighty law!

Beneath the chimney blazing,
The canopy so murk,
The gnomes with zeal amazing
Are sweating at their work.
See, how like Etna's giants
With rage their sinews swell;
Angels of use and power
Are hard at work in hell!
Hail! hail, ye sacred children
That sing in heat thrice-hot,
Toil on, ye faithful Shadrachs,
The fire shall harm ye not!

Hark! in the blasty hollows
The savage, suffering ore,
Molt-white with heat infernal
Groans from the open door
Where swarm the devil choirs
With all the breath of doom—
Ply well, thou nude-black monger;
Gold issues from the tomb!
Ho! for this gold of iron!
Hurrah! the wonder-glow
These stalwart sons of fury
Wrought from the fiends below.

To strain of iron fibres
The molten glories swing,
Earth-sprites of fire and darkness
The lumpy meteors bring.
Fate, with the weighty rollers,
Moves on in fear nor ruth,
So, into form and wisdom
Is crushed the truth of truth.
Hurrah! the light of labor!
Hurrah! the task of grime;

THE FESTAL MARCH OF IRON

Earth brightened out of chaos
And grew to use and prime.

Loud, loud, at shop and foundry
The echoing hammers clank,
From swart mechanics busy
At boiler, pipe and tank.
Grows 'neath the dark creator
The iron life of towns,
The arteries of empires,
The civil links and bounds
The quick and breathing iron
That leads and rules with fate;
Nor hero were more noble,
Nor tyrant e'er so great.

Out from your dungeon stithies,
And potent, wise and tame,
With beam of pond'rous order,
The massy engine came,
And so, to throb of duty
The merry factories go,
Chase not away the fairies
But bring the gods below.
So, came the great steam-being
With fiery breath upcurled,
A rude alarum angel
To waken up the world!

Behold the heavy limber
Of this Cyclopean jade,
Its fast, huge-moving muscles,
Its organs monster-made.
Stands there a brawny rider
With iron rein and curb,
Who'll match this smoky Arab
His likeless iron barb?
Hurrah! the courier iron!
And lo! the courser bold
The godlike man-creator
Hath fashioned out of mould.

On, in intrepid action,
  Light-speed and thunder-rune,
The festal march of iron
  With missionary boon!
Strong-winged o'er flood, thro' mountain,
  This stern evangel true
Runs thro' the life and ages
  A golden deed to do!
Then blessing crown the iron
  That still doth blessing bring;
Naught but a crown of iron
  Shall crown the iron-king.

Thro' forests old, tenebrous,
  In dense and dead of night,
And with the tread of earthquake,
  And with the speed of fright,
The indomitable iron
  Fierce life in death doth seem,
With one large eye of fire,
  And with a voice of steam!
Lo, mail-arrayed and hostile
  The iron vikings shine,
The adamantine navies,
  The bulwarks of the brine.

O iron benediction!
  The happy village gleams!
Ay, laurelled be the iron—
  See how the furrow teems!
Glad be the eager darling,
  Her manly brothers come,
And husbandmen and sire
  Sing in the harvest-home.
And iron cheereth iron
  And rules forevermore,
Bright be its wake on river,
  Its journey on the shore.

Yes! 'twas for this the miners
  Like grave truth-seekers dug,

Brought up the ore so ugly
  With many a wrench and tug;
But 'tis an honest goblin,
  Tho' rust its russet mood,
And thus 'twas all unhandsome
  The first-discovered good,
Till kindling education
  Made all its beauty bright—
Put truth into the furnace
  And sure, 'twill come to light!

For this, on ferrial mountains,
  The trite and dusty elves,
By moon and tree incanting
  Danced where the digger delves;
With nick and pix eccentric,
  And imp or lurikeen,
These earthen-queer wiseacres,
  The little eld, were seen;
With abra and cadabra
  Their merry sorcery spelled—
Ha! ha! the magic iron!
  Oho! with witching weld!

And so, this daedal iron
  With skilled endeavor wrought,
In intricate wild cunning
  Confirms the curious thought;
Deep-hearted and far-minded,
  For evil and for good,
Gleams in the soul of purpose
  And rises in the blood.
But honest be thine iron
  And still its temper new,
Love mingle in thy daring
  And keep its valor true!

In weird human nature
  The mineral virtue lies;
It chains us unto labor,
  It links us to the skies.

For heat and toil and travail
  Our iron fate decreed,
And from the fiery trial
  We enter use and deed.
So grew the sombre epochs,
  The battle-life of clay,
Man's path and course historic,
  A devious iron way.

* * *

Hark! hark! the mortal clangor!
  In devastating breath
The thunder-crash of cannon
  Rolls on the ears of death.
Descends on good and evil
  God's awful iron rain,
And blows thro' gloom of havoc
  The leaden hurricane;
The demons forge in earnest
  And fight with rage sublime,
Rapt, in Plutonic chaos
  Lit up with lurid crime!

Ho! sons of Mars and thunder,
  Of Vulcan and of flame,
Shall Slavery chain the ages
  And link the time to shame?
What! lacks this stubborn iron?
  And have ye vainly bled?
Oh, there's a taint of iron
  Within the tears we shed.
Ho! for an iron leader,
  An aim for men and braves,
Or smites a robber's weapon
  To brand us slaves of slaves!

On! on! our iron armies,
  And oh! diviner blood
Work in the work of iron,
  Ye toiling slaves of good.

THE FESTAL MARCH OF IRON

Down on your myriad anvils
  Let all the hammers light,
Crush out the monstrous treason
  And shape the wrong to right.
Clank! clank! on chain and rivet,
  Upon the limbs of thrall,
At work are all the hammers—
  Hurrah! the shackles fall!

Rise! yet undying Freedom
  And lead our failing van,
O strong shall be the battle
  When man appeals for man!
Bear down on banded darkness
  The legions of the light,
Then build immortal empire
  Upon eternal night.
Yea! blest shall be the struggle,
  And sacred be the sod,
Hurrah! the brand of Freedom,
  The iron arm of God!

---

from THE SONG OF SLAVES

Hang thy sword upon the wall,
  And let it rust for shame;
There is no longer right or truth,
  Nor honor is nor fame.
Since love hath lost its faith,
  And justice is a lie,
What matters it to live?
  Yet what avails to die?
We are shackled unto graves,
  And unto life are thrall;
We are knaves, and less than knaves—
  We are slaves, slaves, all.

Hang thy gauntlet on the wall
  For a challenge to thy shame;
Life is not life when life is base,
  And death hath lost its fame.
For we are bond to each,
  And unto none are brave,
And life and death together find
  A prison and a grave.
This is the end of shame;
  This is the fate of thrall:
We are knaves, and worse than knaves,
  And slaves, slaves all.

Hang thy shield upon the wall,
  And let it rust for shame;
A canker waste a noble mind
  And blot a father's fame.
In the rack of old emprise,
  With the dregs of joy and wine,
Thy gross retainers feast—
  But the castle is not thine;
And the soldier's soul is scorn,
  The minstrel's heart is gall—
We are freemen nevermore,
  But slaves, slaves, all.

Lord! by a foe's caprice;
  Bankrupt, with greed for gold;
And bargainer, with sword in hand,
  Of birthright bought and sold!
What's won?—a servile rest;
  What's lost?—the world and sun!
Thy gains are needs; so count them o'er
  And curse them one by one.
We are driven unto wrong;
  We are fools in hut and hall;
We were tyrants—we are slaves—
  We are knaves, knaves all.

What is thy house?—a jail;
  Thy banner, but a rag?

The cormorant by thy standard sits
  Where the bailiff drives his fag;
And cormorant to raven croaks,
  Thief unto thief replies:
"Not long we wait who prey on state,
  For he is dead, or dies."
Then call thy crows to feast
  In carrion festival,
Corpse and ghost of what thou wert,
  Slave, slave for all.

There's crime by fear caressed,
  And intrigue, keen and neat,
And heartless ignominy dull
  By bolder sin browbeat;
To politicians' wit
  The hypocritic laugh;
And, winking by thine elbow, Fraud
  Writes down thine epitaph.
Thine inventory's made,
  And for a pledge they call!
Slave of a thousand slaves,
  And lord and fool of all!

Who's friend? and who is foe?
  For each one wears a mask;
Who cringes most? who cheats the most?
  The foolish riddle ask.
True foe were better friend,
  True friend were better foe;
Since thunder cannot shake,
  And lightning cannot show,
Thyself to fate and thee!
  Ourselves to woe and thrall;
Thou worst, and we accurst,
  Slaves, slaves all!

* * *

"Place shackles on the heart,
  And fetters on the mind,

Till we become the things we loathe,
And man shall lose his kind;
Be sold as slaves of state,
As lambs of church be slain,
And let the things of night and death
Usurp the dawn again.
We are shackled unto graves,
And unto life are thrall;
What is the world that God hath made,
And what is man at all?"

Something more than church
And better than the state,
Moulds the commonwealth of man,
And turns the wheel of fate.
'Tis freedom, man, and God,
And nature, kin-allied;
Lose this, and lose thy soul—
What is the world beside?
'Tis the outlaw Truth that guards
State and city, fane and wall,
More than statesman, more than priest,
More than chief or general.

And when revolution comes,
Crisis in the roll of fate,
Let the outlaw be thy law,
And the battle shall be great.
Take all the right thou hast
For all that wrong can be,
Advance, advance, and live with truth,
Or truth shall bury thee.
For must wing the cherubim,
Must the reptile crawl;
From progression's righteous law
Who would lapse must fall.

Can'st thou stay God's hand?
The eternal purpose stay?
Can'st thou kill the immortal mind?
Blot out the trial day?

The sacrifice of self
  To wrong or right must be;
'Tis life or death!—come, choose for God,
  He'll give it back to thee.
Thou canst not nature 'scape,
  Thou canst not keep her thrall;
By God's revenge, and man's desire,
  Thyself alone shall fall!

Who binds shall thus be bound;
  The slaves shall be slaved;
Who raises, shall himself arise;
  The saver shall be saved.
For man is one with man,
  And man by man must gain,
And his best self's his brother's own,
  Or else the creeds are vain;
And the gospel true is man,
  Else is not God at all,
Else are we knaves, and worse than knaves,
  And slaves, slaves all!

O People! see and hear;
  The letters are of fire,
The words are thunder, and the voice
  God's want and man's desire.
It vexeth the just Heaven,
  To hear the tory prate;
It vexeth the high Truth
  To hear the traitor rate—
Peace! hypocritic peace!
  They bate with evil breath!
Peace! 'tis the serpent's hiss,
  And the sting is death.

Arise, O God! Arise, O God,
  And let thy judgment fall,
Ere *we* be babes, ere *we* be knaves,
  Ere stand the innumerable braves
As cowards on their fathers' graves,
  And slaves, slaves all!

VII. MOST GLORIOUS SOUTHERN LAND

Southern poets delighted in picturing the South as a gracious, idyllic land, a latter-day Garden of Eden. It was difficult, in fact, for a Southern poet to write for very long about any aspect of the war without pointing out that the land which the Northern barbarians were desecrating had been rapturously beautiful. Southern poets never drew any direct connection between this idyllic environment and the condition of the slaves, but the implication was clear that here was a setting which could scarcely help spreading its benediction over White and Black alike. Typical is the description of the South given in the title poem of Charles T. Daniel's *William and Annie: or, a Tale of Love and War and Other Poems* (Guelph, 1864). This long narrative poem by a Kentuckian who fought for the Confederacy relates how William married Annie, only to be obliged to go to war. Annie characteristically dies of a broken heart, at news of which William recklessly throws himself into battle and is killed. At the beginning of the poem, after invoking "my harp," and assuring it that "No school-boy's fancies wait upon thee now," Daniel launches a typical encomium on the South. It must be admitted that Daniel's representative picture of Southern Womanhood, which he works into the encomium, does much to adorn the landscape; but even without these "maidens, beauteous as the blush of morn," the Southern environment Daniel describes is highly reminiscent of the state of things before the Fall.

from WILLIAM AND ANNIE: OR, A TALE OF LOVE AND WAR

Most glorious Southern land, of thee I sing,
  Thou art the clime of chivalry and song,
Where virtue blooms in one eternal spring,
  And beauty, with her chains, sweet, fair and strong,
Fetters the heart and senses fast and long.
  To thee the soul's best tributes, richly due,
Shall ever haste in an increasing throng,
  Whilst birds shall sing, or cloudless skies be blue,
  To cheer thy brave and generous sons, thy daughters true.

* * *

Where the Kentucky's bright and peerless stream
Glides smoothly as the fancies of a dream,

* * *

Oft in the silent eve my thoughts will roam,
As memory wakes the joys I felt at home.
There flowers bloom fairest, and the birds are fair;
There flocks sport freely in the genial air;
There younglings of those flocks skip light and gay,
And roses cling around those cliffs of grey.
There childhood laughs and shouts with boundless glee;
There mirth spreads broadly as a shoreless sea;
There youth are manly, honest, handsome, brave:
No other wealth than as they have they crave.
They walk God's footstool with an upright tread,
And view not tyrants with a thought of dread.
There maidens, beauteous as the blush of morn,
Their minds and hearts with virtuous thoughts adorn;
Coy, hard to win, yet knowing well to bless
With sweet confiding look and fond caress—
Simple, yet cunning—trusting, and yet shy—
With arts to please the heart and charm the eye;
Won but by honest deeds, they have at will
Glances to heal the heart—the same to kill;
Forms made complete, and features to surprise,
Brows fair, cheeks rosy, beaming, sunny eyes,
Lips dewy, tempting. Oh! what realms of bliss
There lie encompassed in one rapturous kiss!
And powers of earth and air who would not face
To gain the heaven of one warm embrace?

* * *

VIII. MAGICAL MESH, TO ENTANGLE A WORLD

Southern poets, after the fashion of Charles T. Daniel (see above), strongly implied in poem after poem that slaves could scarcely be other than ecstatically happy in the idyllic environment afforded by Southern plantation life. At least one Northern poet felt that Southerners were advancing altogether too many inaccurate implications with their Garden-of-Eden theme. Apparently acquiescing in the validity of such pictures as Charles T. Daniel drew of the Southern landscape, Volney Hickox decided that the best recourse was to turn the South's argument against itself. At the beginning of his *Palmetto Pictures* (New York, 1863), before presenting a series of highly eulogistic sketches of various Union generals, Hickox invokes a picture of the South from which the most ardent of Southern apologists could profitably have taken lessons. But Hickox is no Southern sympathizer, and invokes his lush description of the South in order to make more poignant his invocation of Cotton and the slaves who work it. Hickox's lament that a potential paradise should harbor slavery is clearly not the implication which Daniel and other Southern apologists had in mind when they drew their pictures of gracious agrarianism.

from PALMETTO PICTURES

Beautiful Land, where the bountiful sun
    Blessed the bond of savannah and sea,
Neither so lovely till blended in one
    Each to the other shall complement be,
Magical dews that the tropical day
    Kisses to rapturous odor and hue,
Myrtle and laurel and orange and bay,
    Purple and emerald, golden and blue.

Yonder indigenous endogens wave
    Banner-like blades on a mystical bole,
And, with a vigor perennial, brave
    Boreal blasts from the alien pole,
Over the plaited palmettos, abroad
    Brawned like Briareus, century-old,
Grimly magnificent evergreen god
    Realm of the greenwood the live-oak doth hold.

Tempests the thunderous foliage toss,
    Locks of the Deity wizard and hoar,
Awfully sighs the oracular moss,
    Art thou incarnate Dodona of yore?

Dead generations rejoiced at thy birth,
  Peoples have flourished to power with thee,
Cities have leaped from thy generous girth,
  Art of the shore and the ark of the sea.

O these soft Isles of the summery sea!
  Angels their daintiest prisms composing,
Turn the kaleidoscope watching with glee,
  Every moment new glorious disclosing.
Land of the Beautiful, Bountiful Land!
  Sweet is the blossom, but sweeter the boon,
Flowers are bright and their odors are bland,
  O but the *fruits* of the tropical noon!

And the delirious chorusses [*sic*]—hush!
  Mockingbird, whippoorwill, nonpareil,
Nightingale, killdeer, and passionate thrush,
  Fringed by the petrel's tempestuous peal?
Tribes of the sea, how ye cherish these shores,
  Meeting in wild multitudinous play,
Muscles rejoice in the succulent pores,
  Crabs and soft shrimps, Epicurean prey.

What do the elves of the sun and the sea,
  Cunningly comb from the glistening sands?
Is it the fleece of a sorcery
  Weirder than wildered the Argonaut bands?
Magical mesh, to entangle a world—
  Commerce, religion, philosophy, art,
Liberty, peace, from their pedestal hurled—
  Cotton, the tyrant of manor and mart.

Ominous plant! thou shalt never again,
  Ghost of the tears and the blood of the slave,
Phantom of knout-welted corpses of men,
  Stalk like a ghole [*sic*], with the gust of the grave,
For there's a judgment, wherever hath trod
  Blistering foot of the bondman, and earth
Gapes to develope the vengeance of God,
  Ruin and rapine, and ravage and dearth.

This is the Land of divinest Delight,
  Riches of rapture in every ray,
Gold of the morning and amber of night—
  Passionate peace, nought to take it away.
This is the Land, that the Serpent of Sin
  Seeks to beguile of a generous God,
This is the Land that His servants shall win—
  Liberty's Eden from Slavery's rod.

* * *

IX. THE BOOK OF BOOKS WE CONFIDENTLY QUOTE

To both the North and the South the Civil War was a Holy War, poets on both sides maintaining God's partiality with equal conviction. But, fortunately for Southerners, unfortunately for Northerners, the Civil War was fought at a time when an intensely literal interpretation of the Bible prevailed throughout America. Both Northern and Southern poets were aware of the apparent acceptance of slavery as a normal condition of things in the Scriptures, and more than one Southern poet exploited this knowledge. In the year prior to Fort Sumter, Mary Sophie Shaw Homes, writing under the pen name of Millie Mayfield, brought the twin arguments of biblical authority and evolutionary doctrine to the aid of the South in a long poem, written mostly in heroic couplets, entitled *Progression; or, the South Defended* (Cincinnati, 1860). Mrs. Homes divided her poem into seven sections: "Introduction"; "Creation"; "The Earth"; "Man"; "Slavery"; "The South"; "Valedictory." In the "Introduction," the poet tells what the work is to accomplish: Mrs. Homes proposes to justify the ways of Southern Man to God, or at least to any Northerners who may be broadminded enough to give ear. "Creation" recounts the creation of the world according to the Nebular Hypothesis, for knowledge of which, the author tells us in an extended note, she is chiefly indebted to Mantell's *Vestiges of the Natural History of Creation.* "The Earth" tells how the world was formed, advancing the evolutionary doctrine and asserting that this concept redounds much more to God's glory than the idea that God reached down and created man in an instant of time. The author insists throughout on the validity of spontaneous generation, another evidence of her reading in early evolutionary and geologic materials. The chapter entitled "Man" argues that differing races have evolved differing distances: the Caucasian most, the Negroid least. Thus the Whites are doing the Blacks a favor to keep them in bondage in their present benighted condition. A time may conceivably come when the Black will have evolved sufficiently to be able to handle Freedom, and when that time comes he will be free, but should not, for the good of society, be turned loose until then. "The South" presents the usual idyllic picture of a region whose topography, geography, and climate combine to produce peace on earth and good will toward the Black Man. "Valedictory" closes the poem with a generalized plea for understanding of the Southern position.

Below are excerpts from "Slavery," the fifth chapter of the poem. A reader will do well not to expect entire consistency in Mrs. Homes' reasoning. The poet can confidently open the chapter by citing various instances of slavery in the Bible, and a few lines farther along rejoice that we have outlived a time when slavery is accompanied by the cruelty so often mentioned in Holy Writ. There seems to have been no thought on the poet's part that any contradiction exists between this justification of slavery on biblical grounds, and the argument that evolution may one day make slavery a thing of the past. At a time when biblical scholars as well as scientists were seriously disturbed by contradictions between orthodox biblical Christianity and the New Science, Mrs. Homes confidently eats her Southern cake and has it too. But Mrs. Homes, by reminding the North that Abolition was contrary to the thinking of the biblical patriarchs, was advancing an argument which gave the North trouble, and which it was unable, or unwilling, directly to answer.

from PROGRESSION; OR, THE SOUTH DEFENDED

Slavery

The Book of books we confidently quote
In reference to the past, doth plainly note
The fact, that slavery existed when
Good Noah (he who found above all men,
Grace in the eyes of God) dwelt in the land
Deluged, 'tis said, by the Divine command;
For in the malediction breathed upon
His younger and his most irreverent son,
These words he used: "Accursed shall Canaan be,
A servant's servant ever shall be he
Unto his brethren,"—and by this, 't is shown,

That servitude 'mong men is fairly known
To have existed ere the floods of heaven
Poured forth, we're told, upon an unforgiven,
Corrupt, and wicked generation; for,
'Twas shortly after that fierce watery war
Was said to have been waged, that Ham provoked
His parent's ire, who vengeance dire invoked
On him and all his progeny—and hence
We've ground for the belief, that Slavery thence
Has progressed 'mong the nations of the earth,
And claims this far-removed and ancient birth.
  Nimrod's the first that dealt in slaves, that we
Can trace such dealings to. We're told, that he
Became a mighty one upon the earth—
"A mighty hunter before the Lord!" Now, worth
Is given by commentators, to this clause,
Proportionate to all translations' flaws—
They give the literal meaning thus: "Of *men*
A mighty hunter he became;" for then,
By Scripture it appears, his conquests were
Immense, the territories of Ashur
Invaded were by him—he seized upon
That far-famed city, Ancient Babylon,
And made it what it was, the capital
Of the first kingdom in the world! And shall
We err in saying, that the captives ta'en
In war by him, were forced to remain
Bond-servants to the conqueror!
                                        And 't is seen
'Twas so—for seventy years scarce rolled between
The death of Nimrod and good Abraham's birth,
Yet in that Patriarch's age there was no dearth
Of servitude—in his own house were born
Three hundred and eighteen slaves; and on that morn
When Siddam's vale rang with the din of war,
And battle's issues, on the "Four Kings' " car
Of triumph, captive placed his brother's son—
He armed his "trained servants," every one,
Pursued the conquerors unto Dan—by night
Smote them, and still pursued to Hobah quite,

Nor ceased till he'd recaptured all the spoil
(He and his servants) of the bloody toil,
And brought back women, goods, and *people,* too,
To Sodom's king—who generously, in view
To reward him, said: "The *persons* give to me,
And take the goods to thyself." By this, we see
That each one thought the conqueror had a right
To hold as slaves all captives ta'en in fight.
And many other scriptural texts will show
How valued then all bondsmen were; for so,
The sacred writer Abraham's wealth describes—
He says, that he had of men-servants, tribes,
And sheep and oxen, and he-asses, and
Maid-servants, and she-asses, to command;
And camels. Such was also Jacob's dower,
And Isaac's estimated wealth and power.
  That Slavery was authorized by law
Among the Israelites, we find no flaw
In Holy Writ to contradict; we see
There, also, how all servants were to be
Treated. First: They were to be bought alone
Of heathen—for, if a poor Jew was known
To sell himself either for food, or debt,
The limits of his servitude were set
To expire upon the year of Jubilee,
If after six years' bondage he would be
Considered still a servant—then, to show
That from this service he declined to go,
The master, with an awl, bored fast his ear
To the door-post, to show that he would here
Remain a slave till jubilee's blest year.
But slaves for life, those bought and sold again,
Or which as fixed inheritance remain
In families forever, were of those
Taken in war, the heathen, strangers, foes.
Says Moses: "Both thy bondmen and bondmaids
Shall be of the heathen." And he further adds:
"And ye shall take them as inheritance
For your children after you." And if (as chance
Might be), a master beat a slave to death,

He was not doomed by the unswerving breath
Of justice stern, to pay the penalty
Such crime exacts from high and low degree
In human courts to-day—but simply was
Punished proportionate unto the cause,
As this was deemed sufficient. Such was then
The power that man held o'er his fellows, men.
  Ah! happy we to have outlived the time,
And reached the borders of a milder clime,
Where mercy and compassion's wreaths entwine,
And justice and humanity combine
To lighten fetters forged by direst need,
Pour balm on wounds destined so long to bleed,
Till bondage sweet sympathy made light,
Sees not its shackles, unless thrust in sight
By self-styled friends! who rattle loud the chains,
And the poor victim writhes 'neath fancied pains;
The while these wolves clothed in their sheepskin garbs,
Sink deep their fangs, their sharp and poisoned barbs,
Which with their victim's life-blood mingles, and
The tares of discontent on every hand
Spring up, and choke the better fruit whose bloom
Was lighting the dark passage to the tomb,
Till these rank weeds o'erspread the kindly soil
And crushed the produce of a better toil;
Planting a bitter enmity 'twixt those—
Master and slave—who never should be foes;
Tightening the latter's bonds and locking up
The former's sympathies. And this, the cup
Of bitterness, these meddlers mix for those
Poor idiots, who know not friends from foes!
  Ah well! there is a proverb old, doth say
That mighty "Rome was not built in a day."
And let us hope these bigots yet will see
How false the path they've chosen. If to free
The Negro is their *only* end and aim—
And such the generous purpose they would claim—
We'll trust to time's all-powerful, potent test,
To prove their error, leaving God the rest!
How laws unceasing will work out their end,
However men may strive or fools contend;
And when they cry, "A lion's at the door,"

Before we fly we'll wait to hear him roar,
Nor conjure beat [*sic*] with *longer ears* to be
The king at whose loud voice all creatures flee;
And go unflinching on our path, with faith
That sober second thought will lay the wraith
Of troubled Abolitionism low—
That wandering spirit with perturbed brow!
 Now turn we to that land by classic song
And Homer's verse, immortal made among
The lands of earth! We find, that Slavery there,
Despite its orators and heroes fair,
Existed, and atrocities most foul
Were perpetrated; while the victim's howl
Of anguish, music was most sweet to hear,
To the ferocious conqueror's bestial ear.
Such were the habits of the Greeks of old.
And even in Alexander's time, we're told,
That when he had rased [*sic*] Thebes, he seized and sold
Men, women, children, all for slaves. But still,
The Spartans were most cruel—for with skill
They trained the Lacedemonian youth
To practice all achievements void of truth,
Purposely to deceive and butcher those
Poor captives seized as slaves from out their foes.
And this was but to show their progress in
The strategems of massacre, and win
A base applause for deeds of wantonness
'Gainst those who had no means of just redress.
 Even Rome, imperial city of the East!
Could boast but little over these—at least
Till Christianity's mild rays shed holier light
To turn brute force and question wrong and right.
For the blood-stained arena's gory flow,
The dark, inhuman, gladiatorial show;
The stiffened corpse dragged thro' the circus' round
(First scourged to death the slave was, and then bound
In his hand a fork in gibbet form); the dread
And brutal Vedius Pollio's conduct; still must shed
A nameless horror o'er those barbarous times
And cause us bless the ring of happier chimes.
 In Sicily, during the commonwealth,
Masters, to keep their slaves from march of stealth,

Branded their foreheads with an iron hot;
And one slaveholder (Damophilus), not
Content with this security, shut fast
His slaves at night in prisons close, then pass'd
Them out like beasts to daily work at morn.
Thank Heaven, we now can hail a brighter dawn,
Tho' fleecy clouds *may* hang upon its brow,
Their silver edges tell how bright the glow
Behind them—a radiance which shall pierce
The farthest limits of the universe,
When rolling time shall reach the point at last
Where misty doubts, into Faith's ocean cast,
Resolve themselves to pearls of truth and love,
To gleam and scintillate in courts above!
  A milder form of Slavery prevailed
Among the ancient Germans. This assailed
Not wantonly its subjects, nor imposed
Undue exactions; slaves were not exposed
To cruel treatment. Attached to the soil,
And working and improving it their toil,
With tending cattle, they could neither be
Made articles of commerce nor yet free.
The only ones that could be bought and sold,
Were freemen who had lost themselves for gold;
For it was no uncommon thing to see
An ardent gamester stake his liberty
Upon a dice's turn; the victor then
Could sell his property to other men.
But the condition of the slave still seems
To have been much better than the savage gleams
Thrown from the annals of the polished Greeks
And Romans.
  Then, by one of those strange freaks
Of retrogression, which sometimes exist
'Mong nations of this "island in the mist;"
The Anglo-Saxons seem not to have been
So honorable in this traffic as we've seen
Were their Teutonic forefathers. As when
Alfred (he, surnamed "the Great") pass'd 'mong men
A law forbidding purchase of a *man,*
A *horse,* an *ox,* without a voucher: can

We doubt, the statute was but to prevent
The *stealing* of such property? This bent
Must have prevailed to have called forth the law.
And, to apply an almost worn-out "saw:"
" 'T is a poor rule that will not work both ways,"
Men must have been property in those days,
Otherwise, why steal them?
A species too
Of slavery, alike to that which thro'
The German States held sway, existed in
The Kingdom of Great Britain, till within
The last three centuries. And this is seen
From a commission issued by the Queen,
The famous Queen Elizabeth of yore,
In fifteen hundred and seventy-four,
Inquiring 'bout the lands and goods of all
Her *bondmen* and *bondwomen* in Cornwall,
Devon, Somerset, and Gloucester,
In order that they might compound with her
For manumission, and enjoy their lands
And goods as freemen. So, the matter stands
Till now. A work of later years has been
To free the Colliers, Salters—who were seen
To have endured a wretched serfdom, worse
Than negro-slavery's much quoted curse.
Doomed in dark mines, to wear life's threads away,
Robbed of God's precious gift, the light of day!
And even their wretched children born to share
The curse, which shut them from sunshine and air,
Till little better than the grub, they crept
Thro' their dark holes in mother earth, or slept
A sort of waking sleep—for intellect,
Crushed by the nightmare, darkness, can't reflect
The hues prismatic which life-giving light
Calls forth victorious o'er the brooding night,
And in an apathetic torpor run
Their race, destined to end where it begun!
So far, so good; and England acted well
In freeing those poor wretches doomed to dwell
In earth's dark bowels—for, of the same race
These sons of toil held with her equal place

In human grade—but stepped she not too far
In leaving her West India door ajar,
And vesting savages with powers and rights,
To equal sway with more enlightened Whites?
And what's the result, this vaunted labor free
Has brought her? Where once there used to be
Most ample stores of tropical produce,
The soil, from dire neglect and rank misuse,
Scarce yields supplies for home consumption—while
Fair Cuba's sugar-fields prolific smile;
Her green tobacco waves in fragrance sweet,
And fills the holds of many a noble fleet.
And why? Because *right* management and toil
Bring out the richness of the generous soil—
The White man's intellect, the Negro's strength,
Are brought to bear, and harvest comes at length.
  But, as the Negro will not work unless
Compelled why lay such monstrous, direful stress
Upon his slavery, which brings to him
Comforts he'd never have the will to win
If left to himself? This, England knows full well,
And free Jamaica's sterile fields now tell,
The world would suffer for supplies of those
Commodities, on which it vainly throws
The obloquy of "slavery's products;" *while*
The want of them would hardly cause a smile,
If on "free labor" we'd depend, to give
These necessaries by which millions live.
For *White men* can not stand a tropic sun,
And *Blacks, by nature fitted for it,* won
Can never be by *hire* to do more work
Than will keep off starvation; they will *shirk*
(To use a Yankee phrase) all that they can,
Are naturally lazy to a man.
Why is it sinful, then, to take them from
The barbarous wilds of Afric [*sic*], where they roam
But little else than brutes—and give them homes,
And turn to *men* these dark ungainly gnomes?
Will any other means ere [*sic*] civilize
These savages, beneath our Christian skies?
Or, setting that aside—must these fair lands

Remain as deserts 'neath our helpless hands,
When means are known on earth, if well employed,
To cause them yield what we've so long enjoyed?
Nor only us—the workers have their share;
Well fed, well clad, and taught both praise and prayer—
Saved from the darker horrors that await
Less fortunate companions in a state
Of barbarism still in their own land,
Stamped as it's always been with savage brand,
And made their being's aim to understand.
That Africa at any time was free
From the most horrid forms of slavery,
All history forbids us to suppose.
There, tribe 'gainst tribe, arrayed as mortal foes,
Enslave each other. 'Mong the ancient race
As far back as we've records left to trace,
Even to the era of the Trojan war,
We find Phoenicia trading with Lybia [*sic*] for
Her slaves; and Carthage, which was known to be
No more than a Phoenician colony,
Following the customs of its parent state,
Still carried on the traffic with the great
Interior tribes of that wild, desert land,
Where burning sunbeams flow o'er parched sand,
And the tall palm-tree with its high plumed head,
Scarce deigns a strip of grateful shade to shed;
But miles of sterile, unproductive land
Stretch far and wide around on every hand,
With only here and there a little dot
Of verdure, a grass-grown and welcome spot
That marks a water-course; and which the cry
Of thirsty camel tells, ere man can spy,
That 'tis the blest oasis which they near
To yield their worn-out strength its grateful cheer.
  And still in modern times her sons are seen
Subjected unto bondage. They had been
Made slaves of by the nations of the earth
Of European slavery of the race.
'Tis proved beyond a doubt, that we can trace
A trade in slaves to have been carried on
By Arabs wild, previous to this, upon

The coast of Guinea—e'en some hundred years
Before the incursive Portuguese appears
Upon the western coast, or e'er had seen
A woolly-headed Negro. 'Twas between
The war of the Crusaders in the year
Eleven hundred (when it doth appear
That Europeans first obtained a sight
Of Africans, which caused their army quite
A burst of merriment), and that fierce time—
Some cycles back in rolling centuries' chime—
When Nubia's king, sore harassed by the host
Of bold Egyptian Arabs, who did boast
Mohammed as their God, agreed to send
By way of tribute—and also, to tend
Toward lessening these annoyances—a vast
Number of Nubian slaves to Egypt. Fast
To this covenant held, each year was he
Then forced to drain on neighboring bands; we see,
He bought the Blacks of Guinea, whom he paid
In tribute to the Calif—thus the trade
May have been said to have commenced abroad,
Tho' long prevailing 'mong each native horde
In the interior.

That this was so,
To prove, we need no farther backward go
Than the last century. The Dahomans,
One of the wild interior's warlike clans,
Had never seen a White man till the year
Seventeen hundred and twenty-seven; and here,
Their prince and army met some travelers
In Sabi, and were so shocked, it appears,
At their complexion and their dress, they were
Afraid to approach them, and were heard demur
As to their being *men* until they spoke;
Then satisfied that it was not a joke,
They yet were much astonished when informed
That *these* were buyers of the slaves that swarmed
For purchasers upon the Guinea coast.
Yet these Dahomans, most inhuman, boast
Such horrid cruelties to such poor slaves
As chance they hold, that a wretch freely braves

The unknown good that may in foreign chains
Be found, to native bondage with its stains
Of cannibalism, its most monstrous rites,
Unholy usages and shocking sights!
Such is, we find, the present state of things
In Africa; and this conviction brings
Us to the inquiry: Where will we see
In the world's annals, a community
Composed of Negroes, that have ever been
So well off as our slaves? Better ('tis seen
By the distress and want that wide prevailed
In late disastrous times, and fierce assailed
The working classes of the North) by far,
Is their condition, than nine-tenths that are
Compelled to earn their all by labor free;
For, let a "panic" stop the wheels, and see,
The *poor* man is the sufferer; no right
Has he to "daily bread," unless his mite
Of work is added to the general stock.
And, as "retrenchment" bids the master lock
His coffers, and reduce his working hands,
Minus employment, the poor laborer stands
But little chance of shutting his slight door
On wolf-like hunger's fierce and maddening roar.
Not so our well-fed Negroes. Housed and warm,
They, unconcerned, abide the wildest storm
That shakes the base of the commercial world,
Nor heed the rudest tempest ever hurled
From speculation's giddy hights [*sic*]. For them
Decline of stocks no terror has; they stem
The tide of life, sure of a hand to save
From every 'whelming billow and each wave
Of want that o'er the working White man rolls.
Their bodily requirements met—their souls,
Exhumed from the foul rubbish and neglect
Of savage ignorance, can full reflect
The beams of Christianity's bright sun;
Showing how well the work that was begun
Long years ago for their advancement, is
Progressing to its end of future bliss!
"O Shame! where is thy blush," that in such cause

Wild fanatics should, 'spite their country's laws,
And in the face of verdict just, see flaws
To cavil at? Such men would, doubtless, see
Motes in the eyes of Truth? A class, a flea
Would choke, but who, without grimace or gag,
Can swallow camels whole! For loud they brag
Of tireless efforts in behalf of those
Who're well protected from privation's woes,
While brothers round them starve for want of work,
And sisters, under master fierce as Turk,
Stitch, for a pittance, their life-threads away,
Yet mourn they for the slave, more blest than they,
Who, free from care, with childlike confidence
Looks for protection, comfort (*competence,*
Compared to those poor creatures' ill supplies),
To him who seldom want or wish denies.
For the "good servant" knows his lord will yield
Increase to him whose talent in the field
Lies buried not—the laborer will find
He's worthy of his hire; and master kind
Supplies the mental force that can direct
The Negro's muscle. Thus, our land is decked
With the rich crops by which we want defy,
And White and Black have plentiful supply.

* * *

That slavery of the African will last
While Cotton's King, analogy must cast
The crowning vote to; for have we not seen
All things on earth subservient have been
To human needs, by wise, Almighty plan?
God's laws assisting the advance of man
Along the steep hill of progression. See
How useful by this means the Black can be
Toward beautifying and adorning this
Fair earthly temple, to the praise of His
Omniscient name, the Architect supreme
Of the whole universe! who deigns a gleam
Of radiance to cast o'er savage man,
To rescue him from barbarism's ban,

And place him where his attributes will show
To best advantage, where his part below
He may act out, and thus assist the whole
Great human mass, whose bulk will ceaseless roll,
Till grain by grain it loses all its dross,
And rarifying with supernal gloss
'Twill shine, the embodiment of truth and love,
And fitted for a higher march above
Dull matter—'twill, expanding, soar away,
To realms of glowing light and endless day!

* * *

What
But sheer infatuation, e'er could plot
So wild a scheme as it would prove to be,
If e'er effected, all our Blacks to free?
Why, such a gang of paupers, or, still worse,
Of thieves and villains, would our country curse,
That even Europe's gipsy hordes could not
Compare with; for the Negro is a sot
Of beastial [*sic*] description, and when free
Spends most his time in low debauchery.
And this the population that would spread,
In vagrant swarms, and in their vileness, shed
A merited opprobrium on the head
That first conceived the wondrous plan that set
The ball in motion!

* * *

My pen indites
These truths, not that I would decry the North—
I state but simple facts for what they're worth—
For *all* this land my country is, and wrong
Or right, is still MY NATIVE LAND! O! strong
The ties forged by those magic words, to bind
The human heart, to link it to its kind;
And dastard he who'd seek to set a stain
Upon the sod that gave him birth, or gain
A doubtful reputation at the shrine

That immolates all that is most divine
Or sacred held by man! Not this, not this
The paltry motive whose base prompting is
The lever which calls forth what I indite;
But when a people willfully invite
Contention, as the Northern mass has done
By heaping slanders and abuse upon
That section of our land known as "The South,"
And using for this means the ready mouth
Of pulpit, press, and rostrum, to create
A furore false 'gainst each slaveholding State—
It is but natural that this should cause
Some refutation of our outraged laws
To be attempted; tho' the arm that wields
The defensive armor, boasts not manhood's shields
Of confidence and liberty of speech;
Yet once, *a little child was brought to teach*
Wise men, and sat down in their midst!
And 'tis this simple thought aroused, that bids
Me lift my feeble voice to quell the storm,
And call on God to aid the motive warm
And sincere, that from my heart of hearts
Leaps into words, and its own strength imparts
To what my pen, without that motive true,
Could never fashion or do justice to.

* * *

Come with me, one and all, unto this land
I'll lead you gently, with a loving hand,
And point out all its beauties, if I can,
Until, for very shame, you'll to a man
Exclaim: "Is this the people, these the laws
We've sought to crush? O! surely, we must pause
In our mad judgment of an upright cause
That wide disseminates its blessings, and
With peace and plenty crowns a happy land,
Where each the station holds by Providence
Assigned him—and where broad diverging thence

The bounteous streams of industry glide on
To beautify our common country."
Gone
Will be all prejudice, if with the eye
Of truth you seek our merits to descry,
And, with the tongue of probity, send forth
Your firm convictions for just what they're worth,
When you have fairly weighed us and our cause
'Gainst wild fanaticism's fickle laws.

X. ALL SCRIPTURE IS USEFUL IN ITS PLACE

In the main, Northern poets were content simply to assert the partiality of God in the cause of Emancipation, and let it go at that. Indeed, the relative absence of any direct reply to the Southern defense of slavery on Scriptural grounds attests eloquently to the literal interpretation of the Bible which prevailed in the North as well as in the South. One of the very few, and by far the most ambitious, attempts to refute the Southern biblical defense was P. J. Randolph's *The Slave-Mongers' Convention: a Satire on American Despotism, and Men-Stealing Religion* (Sauk Co., Wis., 1861). Randolph's poem is in six cantos, consisting of speeches by the Hon. Mr. Avarice, the Right Reverend Bishop Blindleader, the Hon. Judge Lawless, Colonel Hatework, the Hon. Mr. Freeman, followed by a conclusion. The Preamble to Canto I introduces the work, and makes clear Randolph's intention:

> Agreeable with a preconcerted arrangement in secret conclave, and with a following public announcement, the abettors and leaders of human slavery met at the Old Castle to devise and adopt measures suitable to the progress, profit and safety of the institution. A majority of the delegates seen there, if an exterior finish were a safe guaranty of honor, might have been mistaken for gentlemen; but under their garments and their polish, were the dispositions and tools of robbers. Mingling and familiar with them were to be seen a class of strangers, whose hideous and hateful features carried positive proof that they were neither of earth nor Heaven. Conspicuous among the latter class, was to be seen a personage, whose commanding appearance seemed to sway the multitude at will; and when the house was called to order, he was elected President of the convention, as the Hon. Mr. Avarice.

The Right Reverend Bishop Blindleader being in attendance was elected Vice President, and Toucey and Lickboot from the North were chosen Secretaries.

Avarice, Blindleader, Lawless, and Hatework, in turn, address the assemblage, each urging the perpetuation of slavery, using arguments which Randolph confidently hopes will portray these advocates of slavery in an unfavorable light. These speeches are followed by that of a nominal slaveholder, the Hon. Mr. Freeman, spokesman for a small faction at the convention which wants speedy or immediate emancipation. Randolph's "Conclusion," in which he speaks in his own person, re-enforces the arguments of Freeman.

Following are excerpts from Canto II, in which the Right Reverend Bishop Blindleader advocates the perpetuation of slavery on biblical and other grounds. Randolph's idea, obviously, is to make Blindleader's arguments so specious that readers will unhesitatingly desire the opposite of whatever Blindleader advocates. Randolph's intention recalls James Russell Lowell's portrayal of Birdofredum Sawin in the first and second series of the *Biglow Papers*. But Randolph is not Lowell, and succeeds only in causing Blindleader to defame himself in a blatant and quite unbelievable manner. At the end of the canto, for all of Randolph's pains, the Bible and its apparent condonation of slavery stand as firmly as ever, probably because Randolph himself, incensed though he was by the Southern biblical defense, believed as firmly in the literal truth of the Bible as the fictitious Blindleader himself.

from THE SLAVE-MONGERS' CONVENTION

Canto II

And there shall be like people like priests, and I will punish them for their ways, and reward them their doings.—*Hosea.*

When the presiding spirit of the nation and of this Convention had concluded his speech, and sat down amidst the usual amount of cheering that ever attends such demagogues, the Right Reverend Bishop Blindleader was loudly called for. The Old Chairman introduced His Worship to the Convention as one of his old and particular friends, and requested the Bishop, in behalf of the friends and of the cause of men-stealing, to give his views of Bible slavery, and to show how foolish and daring mankind may be in the commission of crime and yet be good christians [*sic*]. To which the worthy Reverend responded as follows:

SPEECH OF THE RIGHT REVEREND BISHOP BLINDLEADER

My brethren, most beloved and dear,
Right glad am I to meet you here;
And as I now begin would say,
We'll just omit to sing and pray,
For 't is not often that I mix
In mud and filth of politics.
We preachers should not stoop so low,
Our calling is too high, you know,
Except when politics will pay,
We do not mind them any way.
I bless my Lord, that by his grace
We meet our brethren in this place,
By slavery's telegraphic wires,
Well advertised of our desires,
Have each arrived, dressed like esquires;
And like the Spartan band we meet,
Each sworn to each, and no retreat.
And though our foes, like Persians old,
Outnumber us a thousand fold,
Each like Leonidas can die,
But never from the cause can fly.
Like Spartans, too, when forced to yield,
Each one will wear the victor's wreath,
Each one a conqueror unto death,
When borne away upon the shield.

But best of all, dear friends, it happens
We priests fight not with carnal weapons;
But mightier far than tempered steel,
They conquer while they may not kill.
'Gainst spiritual wickedness we fight,
That teaches "slavery is not right."

* * *

Brethren, our church has sent me here
Some great objections now to clear;
Some Bible matters that seem strange
To minds within a narrower range.
You may expect that I shall spare
No pains to treat its wishes fair.
The church has always paid me well
For my well-known pro-slavery zeal;
They know I never quarrel, either,
With different views of men together;
That by my learning I can settle
The filth and scum on any kettle;
For charity, though sometimes thin,
Can cover any monster sin.

Some stumbling stones brought in of late
By preachers from each northern state,
Such great objections stir up strife,
And dangerous to some men's belief.
Yet, bless your souls, they're lighter far
Than chaff or puffs of empty air.
Dear brethren, you that love my Lord,
Each well acquainted with his word,
Know that our Bible makes it right
To steal and sell men, black or white;
While rulers in our supreme court,
Of modern democratic sort,
With each court-puppy through the states,
Elected by whisky democrats,
Bow to our laws and creeds, you see,
That human beings are "property."

Now we will look at one objection,
And see if it will pass inspection.
Great bug-bear to some men indeed,
Not well informed in southern creed,
But easy of an explanation,
By great divines of southern fashion.
'T is James, fifth chapter and first verse,
Which seems the meanest and the worst.

ALL SCRIPTURE IS USEFUL IN ITS PLACE

"Go to ye rich men weep and howl
For miseries coming on each soul;
Your riches are corrupted, through,
The moth consumes your garments, too,
Your gold and silver gathers rust,
Cankered the Gods in which you trust;
While such decaying things ye crave,
Shall witness against you to the grave.
The wealth ye trust in and desire,
Shall eat your flesh, as if 't were fire;
Your treasured heaps, your joy and praise,
Laid up for use in future days,
Is not your own. Your ill-gotten gain,
Withheld where due, makes want and pain.
Those that have reaped down your fields,
Should share their part that nature yields;
Their hire you thus keep back by fraud,
Comes with their prayers and tears to God;
The Lord of Sabaoth sees and knows
Your avarice and your bondmen's woes,
And fearful will be your last reward,
Standing in judgment before the Lord."

Ha, ha, just see what sheer pretence,
For modern learning and common sense;
For steam and lightning democrats,
With printed piety in our hats.
This text, no doubt you all have seen it,
Can have no reference to slavery in it.
This speaks of those who work'd for hire,
Whose wages were kept back unfair;
Do we hire slaves, or do we buy them?
Or, do we owe them and not pay them?
It seems to me that those who read
Will no such strange delusions heed.

Another, too, that we often see,
From Jeremiah's old prophesy,
Much quoted by the insane few
That unchristainize [*sic*] both me and you.
Hear how it reads, dear friends, and see
How sinful we appear to be.

"Wo unto him that builds his house
By any unrighteous means for use,
And finish his chambers tight and strong,
Yet does the work entire by wrong,
Using the service of his neighbor,
But pays him nothing for the labor.
Such house or owner cannot stand;
Mountains may turn to flying sand,
Sin overthrows in every land."

I think just so, for when we hire
Our neighbors, we should pay them fair.
But neighbors are equals, all may know,
And when they work for me or you,
Justice requires we pay them too.
But what has this to do, we pray,
With Christian slavery any way?
Our "goods and chattels" are not neighbors,
Nor do we owe them for their labors.
We buy them as we do a horse;
They and their work are ours of course.

There's many other scripture rules
Quoted by abolition schools,
Which, left to their interpretation,
Would curse each man-thief in our nation.
"David and Solomon both," they say,
"Were abolitionists in their day;
And all the prophets in those times
Pronounced oppression the worst of crimes."
Bless your dear souls, old brother David,
Like many of us sometimes behaved.
We often fancy some man's wife,
Yet seldom take the husband's life,
But use the most pacific means,
And send the husband to New Orleans.

Objections by hundreds we might read
Against our piety and our trade,
From visionary phantoms wrought,
As baseless as a painted thought,

If it were any use to name them.
Most cheerfully we might proclaim them;
To answer some men 't is not fit,
Notice but flatters their conceit;
To meet such little things, you see,
Like loading guns to shoot a flea,
Might do for sport with little minds,
But would not pay as great divines.

All scripture is useful in its place,
Like every other means of grace,
Where we great Doctors, wise and holy,
May give interpretations truly;
But ignorant men, with Bible laws,
Learn to dispise [*sic*] our righteous cause;
They do not see the reason why
Some men may rob, and steal, and lie,
Yet be so full of piety.

Just let me say to this convention,
To which all men may give attention,
That our belief is as we preach;
To all that come within our reach,
We priests are "all things to all men,"
That each some proselytes may gain
Each charitable, kind, and loving,
To keep the gospel wagon moving,
When we're with those that lie and cheat,
We mingle with this and mix with that,
Each like the chamelion colored be,
To suit the color of its tree.
In whisky shops, midst fumes of gin,
We sip and sagely talk of sin;
Preach of repentance at the bar,
But touch not on the practice there;
In gambling dens are not so nice
To spurn the billiards, cards or dice,
But serve our god and praise his name,
While studying deeply at the game.
A game with publicans and sinners
May save their souls and get their shiners.

* * *

Brethren, please notice as we pass
How each example suits our case;
We'll prove each case by scripture text,
And now will turn to Abram next.
His servant Hagar had a son,
A stubborn boy, much like our own.
Sarah, you know, was jealous of Hagar,
As our wives are toward fancy niggers,
Compell'd the girl to leave, you know,
As southern ladies often do,
And good old Abram, rich enough,
Just let the girl and boy go off.
He might have sold them if he would,
But he was very kind and good,
And Christains [*sic*] had better suffer loss
Than chase their slaves and make such fuss.

* * *

One more important text appears,
Where slaves were bored through the ears,
Which act enthralled them during life,
Parents and children, man and wife,
They volunteered thus to remain,
And toil through life for other's gain.
Their masters, too, were grand and rich,
And some of them did often preach,
Great patriarchs with vast estates,
With servants bought of Canaanites,
Founders of our grand institution,
Men that obeyed the constitution.

Some tell us that the Jubilee
Would every human being free,
That this great law oft violated,
The worst of consequence created.
"Foretold by* Prophets long before,
The fearful woe impending came,

* Jeremiah 34:17. [Randolph's note.]

When scattered from shore to shore,
That rebel race returns no more,
Their idol-homes no more to claim."

Mistakes are frequently committed,
By those that with mistakes are suited,
The jubilee to none was given,
But Hebrews, the favored ones of Heaven,
While all their chattels, all the 'ites,
From Canaanites to Jebusites,
Were slaves for life, and made to toil,
While sons of Jacob shared the spoil.

The heathen nations round about,
Served wooden gods, from trees hewn out,
And had no psalms or sermons printed,
And would not read them when presented;
They cared for no religious order,
Like Mexicans upon our border,
Like us, the Hebrews Polk'd them over
When wanting wider fields of clover.

For this same cause can men deny us
Our servants, when we are so pious.
The Hebrews kindly did invite them,
Tried every way to proselyte them.
When nought availed by preaching talkers,
Sent in thier [*sic*] fiilibuster [*sic*] Walkers;
As they make slaves of stubborn pagans,
We'll do the same with Nicaraguans.

Yes, universal, equal rights
Are but imaginary flights,
Will-o'-the-wisps of insane minds,
Or goblin voices in the winds,
Of different race, and varied caste,
Men have remained from first to last.
Adam was head of the favored race,
With Anglo-Saxon form and face.
Others there were, of meaner blood,
Where Cain took wife in land of Nod.

* * *

Now here's one more great scripture text,
Much quoted by slave breeding sects,
Supporting merchandise in men
As lawful worthy means of gain,
The sons of Jacob sold their brother,
Then why not Christains [*sic*] sell each other;
And lo, what an interesting tale
Follows the history of that sale.
Old Jacob's starving sons forlorn
Soon had enough of Egypt's corn.
Whole loads of corn, that cost them nothing,
With silver cups, and richest clothing,
Old Jacob's family then could eat
Of Egypt's mutton, beef and wheat,

And what of Jo? just think of him,
Poor little boy, so lean and slim;
'T was luck for him they sold him so,
(The boys had pocket money, too,)
No more obliged to fetch their dinner.
And then be called a little sinner,
Swap'd of his coat, patched up with colors,
For royal robes of Egypt's rulers,
And soon in Phario's court could stand,
And Egypt's millions could command.

Methinks the boy must had high times,
Enough to eat, enough of dimes,
And plenty of leisure time for sport
In that great monarch's golden court.
The boy was lucky, I confess,
When dreams could bring him so much bliss.
If dreams could make me half so rich,
I'd dream, and let my brethren preach;
Indeed, I'd willingly be sold,
If I were sure of so much gold.

* * *

ALL SCRIPTURE IS USEFUL IN ITS PLACE

[With a low bow the reverend worthy took his seat, amidst immense applause; and as soon as the old Bishop was fairly down, some one ironically asked his worship to oblige the convention with some familiar hymn. He seemed very willing to comply, and as he was about making up his mouth to commence, a fine musical voice was heard ringing through the long coridors [*sic*] and arches of the old castle, and while all eyes were turned in that direction, the songster struck up as follows:]

The night was black
On the mountain track,
As the lightning-lantern danced,
And the pelting rain
Shot down amain,
Which but my flight advanced.

I heard the sounds
Of baying hounds,
'Twixt peals of thunder jarring,
And hounds on pegs
With less of legs,
And less of brains, were swearing!

Hope smiled ahead,
And with me fled,
Kept watch and ward around me;
Some had their fun
With dog and gun,
And sought, but never found me.

Wise men of state,
That legislate,
Wove legal snares to catch me,
Some swore to find,
And shoot or bind,
Dead or alive to fetch me.

One paid a price
To advertise,
And said he was my owner;
With money spent,
And wrath had vent,
He found I was a goner.

And here will I
Your power defy,
Your statute laws, or lawyers,
Your judging coons,
And priestly clowns,
And pious thief employers.

Let bears and wolves
Pass their resolves,
To stop the eagle flying,
But when such things
Will clip his wings,
Is better know [*sic*] by trying.

Go forge your chain
For the boiling main,
Tie up the tossing fountain,
And cram your laws
In the frothy jaws
Of the grinning cat-o'-the-mountain.

Go sing and preach,
Persuade and teach
All those who wish to hear you;
Seek not to blind
One of my kind,
I neither love nor fear you.

Your preaching knaves
Would starve their slaves
To buy a clean shirt collar,
Your judges fell
Would rake out hell,
To find a red-hot dollar.

I'm not you [*sic*] slave;
God never gave
My flesh to bear your lashing;
Your whips—

[Here the song ended, amidst the confusion occasioned by it, but the songster could not be found; and when order was partly restored, a motion prevailed to adjourn.]

XI. YOUR FATHER, BOY, WAS EAGER

Northern poets were probably more content to let the Southern biblical defense of slavery go unanswered than they otherwise would have been had they not possessed such an adequate substitute argument of their own. In the American past Northern poets found a usable answer to the Judaean culture in which the South found refuge. For after all, had not America been founded because of a desire for freedom on the part of the Pilgrim fathers? The analogy between the desire of the Pilgrims for religious freedom and the desire of the North for freedom of the slaves seemed to poets unmistakable, logical, and clear in its implications. But the motivation of the Pilgrims counted for little beside the Spirit of '76. Again and again Northern poets asserted that the impulse which had called into being the Civil War to free the slaves was closely akin to the impulse which had called into being the Revolutionary War to free America from the yoke of Britain. Poets drew this analogy most often in the call-to-arms poems which they manufactured in such prolific quantity. It was difficult for any Northern poet to call on his countrymen to arm against the foe without reminding them that in so doing they would be emulating their forebears.

Moses Owen's "The Call to Freemen" is typical in its invocation of the Revolutionary War as an incentive for present action. The poem is from *Fragments* (New York, 1868).

THE CALL TO FREEMEN
1862

But for three hundred thousand of freemen true and brave,
To crush the serpent Treason—a bleeding land to save?
To raise the starry banner o'er Freedom's sacred soil,
To keep intact our father's gift gained with such ceaseless toil?
We know our brothers, marshalled, are panting for the fray,
Not great in force but great in heart they wait the coming day;
The foe, exultant, presses and boasts that right is low [*sic*],
Up every Freeman of the North, and show them 'tis not so!

Young man, arise! each southern breeze is fraught with dire alarm,
Your country calls!—you can but hear!—she needs your stalwart arm;
Your brothers call!—full well they've borne the the [*sic*] burden of
the day,
Gird on your armor—meet them South, and rout the foe away.
Obey the call and hurry on—three hundred thousand strong,
And when you're gone—we'll follow on—we hope it won't be long;
Come from the workshop and the bench, send up the deaf'ning cry,
"For Freedom, happy, we will live, or happier still will die."

Three hundred thousand, well we know, with those before us gone,
Must make it lighten all around and show the coming morn;
But for the mid-day panting, our souls await your call,
But give it "Father Abram" we'll "push them to the wall!"
This is no baby's pastime, no sight nor grand review,
A bleeding country, groaning, calls; we all have work to do;
Why stop at home deriding the Southron's skill and power,
And boasting of the conq'ring North, when dark the tempests lower?
For Right must have her champions—and strength decides the fray,
Trust in your powder—in your men, and God will give the day.

List to that wail on Southern breeze! your brother's tones are there!
They speak and urge you now to come on every breath of air;
And can ye now forsake them—the fearless and the brave?
No! Freemen, No!—they've gone before—if needs we'll share their grave!
Go ask that Spartan mother, though all her sons have gone,
If she'd one more—for Freedom's cause she would not urge him on?
I see her dark eye kindle—I hear her stern reply,
"Go forth my boy, I give you up, there is a God on high!
"And living, is but dying, if with a coward's fear,
"You dare not face your country's foe, howe'er he may appear.
"Your father, boy, was eager to smite the Briton's pride;
"You are his son—I know you'll stand firm by your brother's side;
"He gave his life for Freedom and, 'mid the cannon's roar
"He only mourned he could not live to give it o'er and o'er!
"His spirit now is present—his voice is breathing low,
"Go forth my boy, your father bids, your father bids you go!"

Then give the call!—the Eastern States will hurl their legions on,
The noble West bear on the cry,—Maine join with Oregon;
Atlantic to Pacific speak, and scorning Nations see
That Freedom's fires shall brighter glow—that men can yet be free.

Chapter Five: Stories of the War

I. SHE GAVE A SHRIEK AND CRIED ALOUD

The long verse narrative—sentimental, melodramatic, moralistic—constituted one of the mid-century's most popular poetic genres. These poetic counterparts of the sentimental novel frequently conformed, as did their sisters in prose, to a rather inflexible formula. Most came equipped with spotless hero, virtuous heroine, and consummate villain, all of whom were expected to move according to established patterns of conduct. The hero and heroine, desperately in love, were allowed to discuss that love only in Platonic terms. The duty of the villain was to separate hero and heroine and to keep them apart. Unless the villain happened to be the heroine's father, he was required to attempt, unsuccessfully, to seduce or ravish the heroine. The hero and heroine, kept apart during most of the story, were always reunited. Only in the final disposition of their characters did poets indulge in the luxury of choosing from among alternatives, although these alternatives were few, and themselves stereotyped. The hero and heroine might live happily ever after or, as was more frequent, might die in one another's arms. The villain might repent, although he was not required to do so; he might meet death at the hands of the hero or, if that worthy happened to be particularly magnanimous, the villain might be allowed simply to disappear. The villain functioned as something of a *deus-ex-machina*. The important characters were the hero and heroine; the important objective, to dramatize their highly emotional, highly moral reactions to the vicissitudes of life. The villain was not indispensable for achieving this end; crass coincidence could serve. But Evil most often took the form of an unregenerate.

The view of life reflected by nineteenth century heroes, heroines, and villains constituted melodrama, rather than tragedy. Mid-nineteenth century poets were unprepared to present a character so complex as that of the tragic protagonist. Denying as they did the existence of both good and evil within the same individual, poets wielded only black and white brushes in drawing their characters. The mixed propensities toward good and evil which the tragic view sees within the same individual were thus separated, hero and heroine becoming a distillation of virtue, the villain a distillation of vice.

This division of metaphysical labor caused verse narratives to dwell exclusively on the externalities of existence. Sudden reversals of fortune, the buffeting of coincidence, cases of mistaken identity: these experiences reveal the shallows, not the depths, of human personality. The heroes and heroines, despite their authors' lavishing care, remain static creations. They constitute, however, exact replicas of the way mid-nineteenth century Americans regarded themselves: they are creatures of sensibility, whose lives are guided by the twin poles of emotionalism and fervent love for God. The villain, although scarcely more than a two-dimensional abstraction, frequently presents a more attractive appearance than the characteristically colorless hero and heroine, by virtue of his adamant, albeit stereotyped, will.

In working out their basic formula poets chose settings indiscriminately: the America or Europe of the present, the aboriginal frontier, the Revolutionary War period, the Middle Ages, Fairy Land. It was in the nature of things that, come the Civil War, poets should appropriate the conflict as a scenic backdrop against which their heroes, heroines, and villains might work out their predetermined fates. The war, after all, provided a natural, and convenient, method of separating hero and heroine. In fact, the war more than once found itself playing the rôle of the villain of the piece, the hero's obligation to battle the archenemy being cause enough for the heroine to die of a broken heart. But whether war proved the villain, or whether villainy came clad in the despised blue or gray of the enemy, hero, heroine, and villain worked out their destinies in Civil War narratives exactly as they had been doing all along.

Shortly after the close of the war a Northern poet, John M. Dagnall, published *Daisy Swain, the Flower of Shenandoah. A Tale of the Rebellion* (Brooklyn, 1866). The publishers, Nathaniel Mayfair & Co., labelled *Daisy Swain* an "admirable work," a "great American poem." Mid-twentieth century readers may accuse Nathaniel Mayfair & Co. of an inexact use of language; however, the contents of the publisher's brochure advertising the poem suggest why such labels were deemed not extravagant:

> The story of DAISY SWAIN most vividly and truthfully portrays the incidents in the life of a young maiden, who from the day of her birth to her sixteenth summer, bloomed as fresh as a rose, fragrant, sweet and pure, in her childhood's home in the Shenandoah Valley, where her contented father lived in peace. It tells of her pious mother who cradled her infant form. Depicts intensely, the fanatic and the demagogue. Describes how freemen were made foes; how they fought and bled, and died mingling their blood upon the gory field. Paints in glowing terms the youthful volunteer; how his soldier heart beat high with pride at the

sound of martial drum and fife; and why he left his northern home, the spot where his ancestors slept, and in his youth and strength bore, amid the roar of cannon on the battle-field, the flag of freedom through the thickest of the fight. It details, minutely, his thoughts of home and distant friends as he wounded lay upon the margin of a stream, bleeding out his patriot blood and musing in the despair of death. Tells how Daisy, fair and tender, like an angel clothed in white, found him in the twilight all helpless and dying, wrapt up in the riven standard which he had borne through blood and fire. Describes how the light of heaven in her face, so fine in beauty, cheered him, and how beside his sick couch she ministered to his pains. It tells of the hopes she cherished in her young heart's love for him; how those blissful hopes on earth were blighted in her bloom when her soul was in its pride of freshness; and of her faith and tears, her wailings and weary watchings, after a gang of bold guerillas who had in their despotic pride came [*sic*] to her peaceful home, and with their traitor hands conveyed her lover and her aged father far away. It states how she was made an orphan, and how within her desolate home, during many hours of solitude, she would mourn her lover dead. Narrates the trials and hardships she endured; how in her adversity she never faltered while searching for her lover, who had escaped from his vile prison and was then once more fighting the battles of his country: setting forth how strangely they met and how upon the battle plain her lover fell; but not until he had with strength of valiant arm and Union bullet killed the bold guerilla chief, who no mercy showed the innocent, whose agony could wring no tear of pity from out his callous heart. Finally recounting how Daisy and her patriot lover, enshrined in death upon the battle field, sleep the peaceful sleep that knows no waking.

No tongue has spoken nor pen recorded a moral story so touching in its incidents, which from the beginning never flags an instant, but holds the reader spell-bound to the end.

The publishers obviously are relying heavily on the domestically-angelic person of Daisy to interest readers in the volume. A review from the *Boston Transcript* reflects just how attractive the period found its stereotyped, Platonically-beautiful heroines. The reviewer begins by declaring: "If any Englishman should contemptuously ask now 'who writes an American Poem,' we should triumphantly answer 'John M. Dagnall.' We have just received a volume bearing his name, entitled 'DAISY SWAIN, the Flower of Shenandoah. A Tale of the Rebellion.' The versification of this poem is its great originality." The reviewer then quotes the opening eight lines of the poem to illustrate just how great Dagnall's originality could be. But, lest there be readers to whom Dagnall's excruciatingly rough iambs may not seem greatly original, the reviewer assures the poem of enormous sales by continuing: "If this specimen does not sell a thousand copies of the volume, the following description of Daisy herself certainly will," after which he quotes in full the description of Daisy from Chapter I.

The content of Dagnall's poem shows yet another reason why the long verse narrative proved a popular genre. Its loose form and flexibility allowed poets to range broadly through their repertoires, and to treat any subject to which they felt inclined. Dagnall thus succeeds in working into his poem almost every attitude toward the war which his fellow poets expressed throughout the entire body of their lyric verse.

from DAISY SWAIN, THE FLOWER OF SHENANDOAH. A TALE OF THE REBELLION

CHAPTER I

Reuben Swain—His Character—The Birth of Daisy

[Three elements typical of mid-nineteenth century verse narratives appear in Dagnall's opening chapter. One is the rustic and idyllic rural setting. In the wake of earlier nineteenth century Romanticism, American poets of the Sixties unanimously suggested the beneficence of the rural, as contrasted to the corruption of the urban. More than one poet re-enforced Dagnall's suggestion that America was a sort of latter-day Garden of Eden, invaded by the Serpent in the guise of the Rebellion.

The strong moral tone provides a second familiar element. Poets passed by few opportunities to drive home a lesson. In this instance, knowledge that the heroine's father is abstemious appears tenuously, if at all, connected with the course of the narrative, but Dagnall does not let this stand in the way of striking home a temperance lesson.

A third, and indispensable, element in verse narratives is the beautiful, albeit rather colorless heroine. Daisy, a member of a vast sisterhood, is a curious blend of homespun domesticity and Platonic idealism. Dagnall's description of his heroine provides insight into the period's ideal of Womanhood, as that ideal reflected itself in literature. If Daisy strikes readers a century removed as two-dimensional, those two dimensions were deemed entirely adequate by poetry readers of the Eighteen-Sixties.]

Long ere ruthless civil war laid waste
The fertile Shenandoah Valley, there dwelt,

In all his rustic nature true, and free
As the wind, contented Reuben Swain. On
A green mound, close by a stream, zigzagging
Like an eel on sandy bed around the vale,
Reuben's lovely home, a neat white cot, stood
Raised on cedar spiles. This marked his prudent mind;
As ague poisons lurk in meadow damp
And spring freshets had inundate the plain.
No cupola his cottage roof adorned,
Nor did paintings decorate its inner walls [.]
All such ornate pride he left to autocrats,
To tilted [*sic*] lords, and traffic's purse-proud kings.
For, truly, Reuben's nature was too simple
And full of the most gentle virtues as
To even think of such vain, showy things;
No, his pride was only that of self-respect.
Being one of God's true creatures, Reuben,
Ere each morning sun arose, would upon
His bended knees, at matin prayer, offer
Up his humble thanks to the Giver of all good
For blessings which he hourly conferred,
Of health and vigor, with their many joys,
Cheering his path through life to ripe old age.

* * *

But the numbing hand of time had scarcely
Affected Reuben's senses; for his ear
Was then as quick to catch faint sounds, as when
A boy, hunting squirrels in the wild woods;
And therefore sounds of friendly footsteps knew
From the stealthy tread of a sneaking foe.
Nor was his the sluggard's leaden sleep, who
Will, even when his eyes are open, lie
In supine lethargy dozing, peering
Through a misty veil of film; and blinking
In the light of day, soon again drop off
Unconsciously to sleep. But no such languor
Blurred the light of Reuben's eyes: once their lids
Were raised, their lamps would brightly burn renewed
With vigor's oil, by which he'd soon discern

Strange visions, should they near him flit at night;
Which as soon as seen about, his hand
Would on his gun, already primed to kill
The prowling wolf and panther sly, that sometimes
From their lairs in forests wild came, and raised
Nocturnal havoc 'mong his sheep, be clasped.
Then, as to his neighbors of the plain, Reuben
Knew their habits, tastes, and pedigrees too well
To fear his gold would jaundice their eyes. They
Reuben's gentle, upright nature also knew;
Knew that the beam of divine justice shone
In his heart to every one alike within
The valley; and blending theirs with his, lived
In peace and harmony together:
For each one's sense of equity was just.
Honor was kind Reuben's guide; probity
Their counsellor; nothing foul corrupted
Reuben's mind; nor was his taste depraved;
His bev'rage was the same that Adam drank:
Water pure from clear springs and rocky founts.
This he knew would poison nought within, nor
Thrill his nerves awhile with spurious ecstacy,
To deaden the keen sensibility
Of body, heart, and soul, like alcohol,
The demon, that fires with delirium
The drunkard's brain, and fills the minds of men
With dark designs and treason's treach'rous guilt,
Angry quarrels, murder; then remorse which
Struggles hard with sleep. No, Reuben would shrink
With loathing from the devil's nectared bane,
And aught which tended to engender heat
Of blood, burning thirst, and gusts of passions vile.
Temperate wishes only were in his soul.

The fleecy fabric shorn from his own sheep,
Woven on his own loom, sufficed to guard
His body 'gainst inclement gales, and warm
Him in the fiercest wintry blow; and in
This simple raiment clad, Reuben felt
As great as any Eastern nabob proud,

Bedecked with royal robes; as nature's lord
Was he, and reigned supreme in his neat cot,
His castle proud on nature's realms built,
On a green lawn, within a bounteous plain,
Where creation was prolific with her products.

To Reuben 'twas the loveliest spot on earth,
Where many sunny years of bliss he passed,
Sharing the joys of dear domestic life
With the partner of his soul, his Nancy dear,
More faithful, fair, and kind than half of those
Who blaze in vain, proud, ostentatious show:
One who knew her duties well, her womanly sphere,
And the sweet pleasures of the virtuous heart;
Which was the only bliss her husband sought.

There, in the quiet place wherein the happy pair
Found shelter, food, and rest, reason ruled
Their minds and guided them with judgment; for
Too well they understood the sacred bond,
By which their two dear souls were bound as one,
To mar their wedded bliss with household jars,
Knowing angry breath in ears young is baneful:
And in sweet connubial union their love
Long ago had multiplied itself. The seed
From vigorous stem was cull'd, and free from
Withering blight; kind nature undertook
The task imposed; and time brought forth a bud
Of grace, all tenderness, which doubly blest
Their yoke, and crowned with joy their nuptial couch.

The germ in beauty's mould was cast, budded
Forth, and blossomed; in sacred soil grew up
To vernal morn of life, fresh as a rose
In unmolested shade, or violet chaste
In all its virgin freshness, unassuming,
Modest, all rural grace, and simple charms.

The joy of her pure heart, all smiles, all cheer,
Like rising sunlight on a dewy lawn, shone
On her dimpling cheeks; rouged with tincture from

Vermeil meads: health's purpling flood that coursed in
Her azure veins.
                                        The vital essence glowed
In her eyes, radiant, pure, and mild, like two
Bright orbs fixed in the coronet of Heaven:
Endowed they seemed with photographic power
To print from blooming flowers certain shades;
As they one noon-time bright, while ardently
Fixed upon a variegated bed, drew
By some charmed affinity in their gaze,
Blended hues from both blue-bell and lily;
And so bright withal, that e'en a lover's glance might
Dim before their lustrous beaming, or be
Dazzled so his mind's eye would flashing see
Across his brain, a thousand stars glitt'ring
Resplendent with heavenly jewelry.

Enrobed in raiment woven plain upon
Her mother's loom, she, by broach or bracelet
Unadorned, looked with more attractive grace
Than if bedecked in fashion's gaudy finery.
Besides, her form was faultless as the Venus
Of Milo, as fair, as tender to the view;
Required no false blandishments to lure
The eye, nor stuffs to give herself proportion:
Her heart was void of all such guile, as truth,
Early to her God, had risen up her soul
To heaven, where her faith in Him reposed.

Thus arrayed in nature's simple beauty,
Daisy Swain, the flower of Shenandoah,
Since taken from her parent bed, was
Mildly nurtured with parental sway,
And prospered in her father's fostering hands,
Full sixteen years unconscious of a thorn;
Unstained by care and sorrow's withering sigh:
Nor had she felt the pangs of fickle love,
That sighs assent, then vanishes from sight.
She was her parents' joy; their dear pledge of
Reciprocal love; their pride of heart, whom
They idolized with fond, indulgent care.

* * *

CHAPTER II

The Comet—The Northern Fanatic—The Southern Demagogue—The First Shot at Sumpter [*sic*]—The Battle—The Wounded Federal

[In the first part of the chapter, here omitted, Dagnall decries the war as the work of demagogues and fanatics, North and South. This attitude, however much currency it may have had in society, enjoyed exceedingly small following in poetry. In adopting this approach, Dagnall may have been paving the way for the narrative's love story, which crosses sectional lines.

Chapter II also introduces the hero, wounded on the field of battle. Three characteristics marking Athol as hero immediately show themselves: the automatic way in which he thinks of home when misfortune strikes; his religious nature; his attitude that death in battle constitutes the noblest end of man.]

* * *

Sounds of trumpet, drum, and shrilling fife were
Heard through all the land, rousing men to arms,
Hurrying on the deadly conflict by
Parasites and cowards, both of North and South,
Who feared to stain their own right hands in
Human gore; and from window, pole, and peak,
Waved the civic garland of our liberties,
Inspiring chivalrous men to furious fight.

Then songs and bloody hymns were sung by sons
Undaunted, as they thro' the madden'd nation
March'd straight on to the red fields of slaughter, there
With dearest blood to fertilize the soil,
And earn, in righteous cause, a glorious name.
Soon war and rapine wild, both far and near, stalked
Madly o'er Virginia's soil. There, down in
The fertile valley of the Shenandoah,
Resounded loud red War's fierce rattle. There
Advancing hosts of bannered foemen met,
Emblazoned gay, in pride of fancy dress,
And charged each foremost line with musketry.

Alert, the rebels bold with desperate dash
Hurled, with all their ardor wild, their forces strong
Upon their Federal foes. Fiercely flashed
The red artillery. Swiftly shrieking shells
Burst in among the brave, and made their blood
In torrents flow. Then bayonets charged and clashed
Against each glitt'ring blade. Horse and rider
Plunged into the fray, and swelled the mortal strife
Of battle hot: while Death, through sulph'rous clouds
Of smoke, grinn'd and gloated as he eyes firm
Heroes, from their shattered lines and columns,
Fall and swell the slaughter; and where the maimed
Lay, here and there, upon the gory field,
Rending the air with fitful cries and groans,
Writhing, like wounded snakes, from horrid tortures.

So, in full retreat and loose array, down
The hill the Federals wildly rushed, o'erwhelm'd;
Rank and file, hard pressed by the rebels:
Through thickets dense, 'cross fertile fields and vales,
Dismayed their broken columns flew, leaving
On that bloody field many comrades brave,
Who now sleep in their trench-dug sepulchres.
Yet, one among the federal bands, wounded
And faint from loss of blood, footsore, halted
At a gurgling brook, where he, all smeared with
His life-blood, stooped down; and, in the hollow
Of his right hand, scoop'd drops of water few,
With which his burning thirst he quenched.

Then, from
The margin of the stream, he tried to raise himself,
Fearing, lest he there too tardy stayed, captured
He might be by some disloyal enemy
Prowling rampant round those parts, in hot pursuit
Of straggling and of ambushed foes: but irksome
Was the task. The sinews of his knees
Were void of strength. His tired limbs the burden
Of his body could not bear. A shudder
Shook his jaded frame: 'twas the harbinger
Of comfortless despair which soon darkened

His fevered brain; for, ere long, his head grew
So giddy, that the verdant landscape seemed
Unto his blurred eyes, just like a green mist
Risen from the ground. Then, round and round, his head
Reeled. Faint and sick at heart, he stagg'ring grasped,
With feeble hands, a willow twig dangling
Near him; and with its friendly aid lower'd
Himself down upon the damp grass, resolved
To abide the ordeal of strengthless fate.

* * *

But his fevered mind soon somnolent became.
In dreamy mood he thought of the home he'd left
Behind him, and of his aged mother
Far away: he fancied he saw her smile;
And with her arms outstretched in fullness of
Joy, ready to clasp to her fond bosom
Her soldier son. He, likewise, thought he heard
Her soft voice say, "Oh! Athol dear, how glad
Am I to see that you have home returned
From the rebellious, frantic scheme, with none
But honored scars." Then, thoughtful, he smiled; but
'Twas only a sickly gleam of joy,
As pale and transient as a streak of sunlight
Breaking through a rain-cloud, which shone upon
His wan face: for soon the past joys of home
And friends, his ardent fancy had conjured,
Quickly vanished before his reason's strength,
And left his mind in dark, despondent gloom.
Then he wept; for he keenly realized
The true condition of his hapless plight
And how fallacious was the hope, in such
A dying state, of ever sharing, with
His tender parent, her gladsome care again.

* * *

'Twas then twilight, yet no friendly succor
Came to his aid. Alone, the evening dew,
As 'twere, seemed to commiserate him, in

His hapless state, with tears compassionate
Shed on his languid form; and when he saw
The light of day fast fading from his view,
Hope's bright beam flickered in his panting heart.
Still, he'd judge it folly to repine 'gainst
What Heaven ordained, as his conscience told him
That man, soever good, and soldier brave,
Are sometimes in this checquered life destined
To suffer torturing ills, which often
Bring them, ere their lives have run the length of
The allotted span, down to early graves.

But it would, he thought, have been more honorable
If fate, with her unerring hand, had hurled
Upon the field, rebellion's missile swift
Through his brain; so that he could have fallen
'Mong many warring hosts unknown, but brave,
And mingled his with their courageous blood,
Than there, with feelings sore, linger and waste
Away by fever; be flesh-conquered; die
And rot: his body fill no hallowed vault
Nor soldier's grave, but lie exposed, where
Buzzards sought their prey: he shudder'd at the thought,
And gasping, shrieked aloud, they soon would
Fly around his bier and riot on
His lifeless flesh.

CHAPTER III

Reuben's Alarm at the Sound of Battle—Daisy's Absence from the Cot—Her Return Home with the Wounded Soldier

[This chapter, while it advances the plot by bringing together the hero and heroine, is noteworthy chiefly in that it allows the author to throw into relief an additional characteristic of hero and heroine: piety on the part of the hero, innate sympathy on the part of the heroine. Poets used these two aspects of personality to differentiate the hero and heroine, on the one hand, from the villain on the other. The villain could match hero and heroine down the line so far as intrepidity was concerned, but he was powerless to pray, possessing a heart of stone.]

SHE GAVE A SHRIEK AND CRIED ALOUD

Upon the balmy breeze of that same morning
Reuben, the peasant, from his smiling cot,
Heard the battle's horrid din resound,
And saw, afar, thick, sulphurous smoke dimly
Rear in black wreaths to'ards the glaring sun.
'Twas but an hour before the valley rang
With war's alarm, that in the morning ray, he
O'er his neat fields trod; nor feared to meet
Friend or enemy of the warring bands.
Both were foes to him.

For when the roar of
Booming cannon echoed on his startled ear,
He thought that ere the evening came, he'd look
Upon his burning cot and wander round
A homeless man. But twilight came. Long since
The battle's warlike blasts had died away;
And glad he was to find his fields were still
Adorned with waving grain.

But when he saw
His beloved child was not at home to cheer
Him with her pleasing smile, and bless him at
The evening board, a poignant pang went straight
To his heart, that some mishap his daughter
Had befallen.

For no tidings of her had
Arrived, since, in the gleam of morning's sunshine,
Her father's cot she quit, to saunter through
Her native vale; and blithe and jocund wind
Amid its green retreats; joyously scent
The woodbine wild, and quaff the balmy air;
And to let the zephyr of fragrant meads
Mellow in deeper tints her beamy face.

But as she gayly tripp'd with fawn-like steps,
Through green paths, observing with enraptured eye,
The varied landscape o'er—her soul's delight—
And breathing sylvan sweets with spirits gay,
War's infernal gong through the surrounding hills,

Reverbrated [*sic*] loud and pierced her ears.
The dread shocks her heart's blood stagnated. Fear
Forced its livid pallor o'er her roseate cheeks,
Which marred awhile the lustre of their bloom.
But the rose ne'er drooped. The shock was but
A passing gust, which chilled awhile her warm blood,
As she soon revived and glowed again in
All her fullness of sweet budding charms.

* * *

At length the din of battle paused upon
Her ears. Twilight shadows round her gathered;
And setting sun-beams faintly gleamed upon
A rolling cloud, whose ruffled crest, bright plumed
With crimson tints, passed o'er her. Thus forewarned
Of night approaching the shadowy rock,
On which she sat, up she quickly rose, and
Down through the hillside's winding paths she ran
Towards the cot.

Scarce had she neared a glade,
Ere she heard, upon the evening wind, screams
Of woe. Bewildered quite, she quickly turned
Around and gazed about, above, below;
Peeped through the murky glare of eve, but nothing
Saw of life. Then she wondered whence the sound
Arose, and what it could have been: listen'd
Like a hare startled by game-dogs on the scent:
Still, all was silent round, save the rustling
Of leaves, the barking of tree-toads, whimp'ring
Of bats, and the incessant buzz of insects,
Holding their nocturnal jubilees.

So, she fancied that the wail she heard was
Perhaps a catbird's woful [*sic*] mew, and hasten'd
On again along her woodland way. But ere
Her nimble feet had measured paces few,
The groan again, more agonizing still,
Burst on her ears. Appalled at the sound, she shrank,
Like the tendrils of a fragile flower

In a chill autumnal gust of wind, still.
Soon her doubting fears were gone; as, she knew
Full well that such a sad lament could only
From a human soul distressed issue.

Then, soon,
Compassion moved her. Through a willow copse
She hied, slow pacing cautiously, and reached
The margin of the stream where lay half dead,
The wounded soldier. Soon the tender fair one
Tremblingly bent o'er him and closely scann'd
Him with her pity-gleaming eyes. She saw
The light of life still flickered in his heart;
But wav'ring on the balance side of death
Whose shadow glimly danced upon his features,
Which in their livid aspect seemed to her
So beautiful, so mild. Then, with mute surprise,
She viewed his anguished mien, and wound all bare:
And dropt in cleansing tears, the limpid chlorine
Of her soul, upon his bleeding scar.
A transitory smart he felt. He muttered
"Oh!" and casting up his glassy eyes, he saw,
Low bending o'er him, so grateful in the gloom,
And all compassionate, the maiden fair in
White robe meekly clad.

"O Heavenly Father!
What angel from thy throne of glory hath
Fled, to chant the sad requiem o'er my cold clay?"
He cried. "One whom a ruling Providence
Hath hither sent, the friendless to befriend,
The helpless to save," she cried: saying which,
She brushed the matted locks back from his brow.
Then, she from her side a napkin took,
Saturated o'er with dew, and with it laved
His pallid brow; his parched lips moistened; plucked
A plantain leaf which on the streamlet's margin
Grew, and with its cooling texture improvised
A bandage for his wound; then tied it with
A ringlet of her auburn hair.

Meanwhile,
She made his prospects of recovery bright;
Told him, that not far from thence safe, nestled
In a grove, he would within her father's cot
A refuge find. This cheering hope his soul
Elated. Forthwith his glad heart urged his hand
To be extended to the gentle maid.
She took it kindly in her own and raised,
With all the strength her fragile structure had,
Him from the blood-stained ground. Faltering,
He leaned his right arm on her shoulder. Halting
At alternate steps to breathe. Well she bore
The burden of his weight, without a murmur,
With maidenly resolution all the way
Thro' thicket paths, 'cross glades; guided only
By the light which faintly glimmer'd from the cot.

Then, soon before its wicket gate they stood.
Quick the maiden pushed it open; as quick
Upon its thongs elastic back it swung,
And grated harshly on the latch. The pointer
Barked and quickly scented the stranger; while
The father to his feet started up, grasped
His gun, and to the door ran just as she knocked.
The gentle tap he knew came from his daughter.
Quick the door flew back, creaking on its hinges,
Upon the threshold stood the anxious father,
With extended arms to clasp his daughter;
But back a pace he bounded, as his eyes
In started sockets stared upon his child,
All fagged, all faint, with the feeble soldier.

Soon the mute appeal of Athol's wound went
To the parents' hearts. Warm commiseration
Thawed from out their breasts the icy chill of fear,
As they soon placed him on a mattress near
Some hick'ry faggots blazing, a helpless,
But a welcome guest beneath their roof.

* * *

CHAPTER IV

Athol tells the Cottagers the Story of his Life—His Convalescence and his Love of Daisy

[In this chapter Athol and Daisy fall in love, a feat accomplished by hero and heroine from the time of Homer. What demands commentary is the manner in which falling in love, at least in literature, was accomplished during the mid-nineteenth century. At this period in America's cultural past idealization of Womanhood reached its zenith. Neither before nor since in America have so many extravagant things been said about Woman. As hero, Athol is obliged to respect this idealization, and therefore cannot look upon Daisy as an object of sexual attraction. To look on a woman to lust after her was the province of the villain. Daisy, to be sure, possesses more than sufficient attractiveness to suggest sub-Platonic thoughts, but Athol, even though his intentions are honorable, must look for what almost amounts to an excuse for falling in love. Hence Dagnall's insistence that it is Daisy's angelic sympathy with which Athol is in love.]

At early dawn the wounded Federal,
Much improved in health and quite refreshed in
Spirits from his night's repose, awoke; and glad
Was he to find himself so near kind friends.
Especially his frail rescuer, who
Then stooped o'er him, with helping hands and raised
Him on his pallet soft. He knew no balsam
For his pains and aches more sanative than
The soothing office in which she was
Engaged, and thanked her for the kind attention
She had rendered. Daisy curtseyed low and said:
That both her mother dear and father had
Taught her, long since, the divine injunction,
"To do good to others forget not;"
And never, when want and suff'ring implored
Her kind assistance, to withhold relief.

As the impressive tones on Athol's ears
Fell from her lips, his head reclined, entranced
With dreamy thought, which Daisy soon observed:
But she knew not what was passing through his mind,
Nor why hope's inward beam his count'nance brighten'd;

For her gladsome gaze was too intently
Fixed upon his handsome face, admiring
The graceful contour of its features, which,
In his pride of youth, show'd her that scarce had
Twenty summers' blooms their roseate honors shed
Upon his head.

* * *

So, as
Time roll'd on, Athol's frame evinced contempt
Of death; and, ere a month elapsed, the tide of
Life, full high, in the crooked channels of his veins,
Return'd its purple flood. Restored at last,
He from his ailing couch arose, renewed
In lease of days and years, quite sound in health,
In spirits buoyant; but with a sensation
In his heart unfelt ere he became thus
Convalescent. A sacred charm it was;
Supremely divine; so soul entrancing;
But quite mysterious in its strange effects
Thro' all his being: but especially,
Did young Athol, when his benefactress
Stood, so kind, so fair and pure before him,
With her brow serene as the effulgent moon
Beaming down thro' Heaven's blue dome, keenly
Feel, in his warm heart, that inward pleasure.

Was it the grateful services, which in
His hours of sickness, her gentle hand had
Render'd? that which, day after day, he blest?
The one, which from the cold damp ground, had raised
His drooping head and bound with fingers fair
His wound? which smoothed his pillow? which prescribed,
In that propitious hour, the remedy
Whose potent agency within his frame,
Made his soul feel loath to leave its feeble house
Of clay, that caused the glow within his breast?

Was it her graceful form and beauty rare?
Her dulcet voice that softly syllabled

Sweet Bible stories, and sang in accents
Toned divinely, choice psalmody, which had
In Athol's hours of fevered sleeplessness lull'd
His throbbing brain to rest? or was it the power
Of Daisy's pity, that in Athol's heart,
Had softly struck the mute accord of
Sympathy divine?

Such, in truth, it was;
For the compassion of his cherubim had
In his heart enkindled the pure flame of
Love: for gratitude begets love; and when both
Are happily in women's [*sic*] heart combined,
What panacea so potent to remove
The anguish'd bosom's pain, to raise the head weigh'd
Down with cares, and solace give unto life's woes?

Athol, then, the more he saw the maid, became
Enamored with her sprightly comeliness;
With her spirit beneficent, and with
The beam celestial which sparkled brightly
In the light blue eyes of Daisy: for he saw
The beam of truth in her heart illumed
Her cheeks with virtue's flame. In her presence
He would quite forget his past disaster,
And seldom thought that he had peril'd death
Upon the field of slaughter, so overjoyed
Was he, that he felt he could in seas of
Carnage wade, aye, a thousand dangers brave,
To pin so fair a jewel to his heart,
And keep the precious treasure there for life.

So, thus, while the maid in Athol's bosom
Was the only bliss; the only vision that
Beguiled his mind; the sole angel who came
To cheer him in death's dread hour: his treasure
Rarest that moved his bosom with the throb
Of fond affection. Daisy, herself, felt swayed
By some resistless influence in his soul.
'Twas the same power which she'd infused in his heart,

That in her own rebounded, and there found
Its sweet abiding place; strange affinity
That tied their two souls with dearest amity:
For the more he amended, the more she droop'd.
Alternate gay and pensive were her looks.
Her languishing mien evinced her heart was
Fraught with love, which Athol saw and heard breathe
In her tender sighs; and knew her condolement
Was the purest emblem of a constant mind;
That her modest sweetness showed her virgin soul:
And that, although her tongue was then too coy
To breathe the tender vow, yet her silence
Was but the dumb rhetoric of her heart,
More eloquent of love than her sweet tones could lisp.
His fond gaze likewise made her looks obey
Her passion's impulse, burning in her heart,
So fervently; as it summoned the blush,
Which her chaste bosom wore, to carminate,
As like a peach's rind, her modest cheeks.

'Twas thus that her affection for Athol
Her affliction became; for, when he had
Recovered to that normal state which makes
Health laugh at death, she leaner grew, and proved,
By her pallor and sigh spontaneous,
The hidden pow'r which he exerted o'er her.
To him, in short, a thousand nameless actions,
Spoke the evidence of a tender wound
In her breast. Thus did the dominant passion
That sways the world entire, enchain the hearts
Of both the rescued and the rescuer.

CHAPTER V

The Lovers—The Vow—The Adieu—The Storm—The Guerillas—The Altercation

[After the neo-Platonic approach to romance afforded thus far, the love-making which Dagnall now permits between hero and heroine may come as something of a surprise. Daisy and Athol, however, are acting according to a perfectly acceptable mode of conduct. Daisy joins a vast literary sisterhood in being free with kisses and caresses, once she, and the reader, are assured that the hero has not professed love for her merely in order to attain them. There is scarcely a verse narrative of the period, regardless of whether or not it possessed a war background, in which the hero did not draw the heroine to his breast, in which the heroine did not fling her arms around the hero's neck and cling to him, in which troth was not plighted and sealed by an extravagant number of kisses. Poets consistently employed hackneyed phraseology in describing this lovemaking, however, and it is likely that poets and readers alike looked on these outward signs of endearment as something of a convention to be gone through with by hero and heroine, rather than as a manifestation of unbridled passion.

Chapter V also introduces the villain. Not all of the villain's stock-in-trade of characteristics come to light in this chapter, but his pride and hardness of heart are too thoroughly ingrained not to show themselves immediately. Although this pride and hardness of heart cause the villain to assume a stately and impressively dignified manner, such pseudo-stateliness and dignity are pictured not as potentially favorable attributes, but rather as stumbling blocks prohibiting the villain from attaining what the poet regards as the ultimate goal in life: a warm, sympathetic heart and Christian humility.

The rebel chief, who will prove the villain, comes equipped with the standard supply of henchmen to do his bidding (as contrasted with the hero, who characteristically plays a lone hand), and effects the inevitable separation of hero and heroine.]

One bright morn as the lovers near the cot
Breathed forth their vows, Athol, in his own, took
Daisy's hand, and pressed it tenderly; drew
Her to his breast and sigh'd within her ear
The ardent nature of his love. Pallid
Spread her rosy cheeks. She trembled, and 'gainst
Her restraint, hung down her head in silence.
Athol, whose heart was full, stood mute awhile.
He scarce knew what to say, and deeply sigh'd:
But dared at length his passion to reveal.
He told her that he much admired her from
The time her eyes first on him gazed, and that
He then adored her fondly, so much so,
A king his bliss might envy; that, if she were
His own, a soldier's and a lover's soul
She'd crown; that when his term of service ended,
He'd hail her as his future bride; united,
Blest with her, in bitter winds of winter,

And in snow's incessant fall, in ev'ry
Vernal hour he'd with her live forever,
Her heart's true partner.

Now, what a shock was
That to one whose bosom was susceptible
And tender; soon her head reclined all
Pensive, which betrayed that something undefined
Was working in her mind. Some affliction
That spoke her sadden'd thoughts, tho' mute her voice.
In that still mood, she seem'd so like a bird
Allured, pent up in a cage with her captor
Near her, enamored, patiently gazing,
And awaiting its dulcet strains to hear.
As he then did the sanction of her smile.
So, in brief time, from his panting heart, she
Raised her drooping head, and with her face
Upturned, threw her radiant eyes, bedimm'd with tears,
Full on his own.

She told him that 'twere worse
Than death from him to part; that a prey she'd
Be to separation's pain and sorrow;
That none could comfort her but him; then said:
"Alas! when thou art gone, foul darkness will
Be seen where once thy lightsome footstep shone."
Then she hinted fears that, he now being well,
Would forever leave her in affliction,
And bade him, strenuously, to stay with her,
Where peace and undivided love reposed.

But when Athol heard her fear-fraught words, he
Swore he'd never from his plighted faith depart:
That sacred was his word: his mind too pure
And high: his heart too merciful and just;
In short, an honorable youth he was,
And loath'd the very name of infamy:
That naught within the wide world could seduce
Him from her, from truth, nor rectitude.
Then he told her that, although he'd suffer'd
From an outward wound—a bloody gash, that

He then suffer'd from an inward pang,
A heart-bruise deep, which naught could heal save but
Its kind:—"the tyrant god which thro' the world
Roams free, and robs its victims of their peace
And liberty."

Then Daisy looking up
With aspect mild, all inexpressive grace,
Her countenance beaming with approving smiles,
Which showed that Athol had with tones undaunted
Sued her not in vain, gladly promised
To commit her hand forever to his trust.
Athol then upon the head of his betrothed
Called Heaven's blessings down, and sealed his faith
With kisses on her dimpling cheek; gave her
From vest pocket, his own portrait color'd,
Which she kissed with ardor sweet, and said; "ah!
Thy much-loved image, Athol, in my heart shall
Be enshrined, by friendship guarded until
Life is gone, as I feel assured thou hast
Indeed an upright heart, a fervent soul,
And temper gen'rous—jewels which fame nor
Gold can buy."

So, when the sullen clouds of doubt
Flit from her mind, hope's bright sunshine Daisy's thoughts
Illumined and stamped its vignette bloom upon
Her cheeks. With unmixed ardor in her heart
She hailed the joyous day when hand in hand
Together she would with her Athol walk
On sunny paths, and rove in vernal meads,
Where birds and bees and flowers the light obey,
And to their happy sights their silken plumes
Disclose. For, then, no frowning clouds she thought
Were in the sky, ominous of fortune's wrath,
Would cause a tear of agony to start from
Out her gladsome bosom; that no lightning
Would flash and strike the bliss from out their barque
Of hope, while tossing to and fro on life's
Tempestuous billow.

'Twas then the noontide hour.
The fluid gold of light down from its throne
Of blue began to sickly gleam upon
The mountain's slope, as Athol stood prepared
Upon the cottage steps to take his leave.
In tearful eyes, the old folks held him by
The hands; and much regretted that they were,
So soon, deprived of their companion—
Their dear daughter's choice,—and welcomed him again,
If saved while warring with his brethren 'gainst
Traitors armed in his own country of birth.
Told him, too, that if he'd fall defending
His dear native land, they'd bless his name; but
Hoped that God would spare him.

Then Daisy flung
Her arms around his neck, and clinging to him
Prayed, as on he moved to go, that for the love
Of God and her he'd soon again return.
But, while Athol on the door-step stood wiping
From his humid eyes, the parting tear, he saw
The sunbeam from the casement faded fast,
And heard afar deep-noised rumbling thunder;
Saw the distant light grow faint and sombre;
And, hov'ring in the west, that thick, dark clouds
Announced a hostile sky; that a storm was
Gathering. Still his ardor was undaunted:
He cared not for the thunder's angry voice,
But wish'd to hasten thither on his journey,
To report at Washington for duty.

But just as he pronounced the farewell word
"Adieu," unusual darkness o'er the face
Of nature spread. A vivid flash lit up
The gloom. On through the immeasurable void
Of air, the war of elements roared and made
The welkin ring tremendously.—A flash—
A rattle,—down burst clouds of drenching rain.—
Fiercely howled the wind among the trees; they groan'd—
Strained heavily and rustled off their leafy pride:
But a gust still more powerful wrenched from

Its roots an agéd oak which grew hard by.
The crash, the old man startled to his feet.
Quickly he ran to the window to see
The damage done, when in a glaring sheet
Of vivid lightning which just then illumed
The dark profound, his quick eye saw, along
The hillside, a troop of mounted horsemen
All drenched unto the skin, slowly wending
Their way onward to'ards the cot.

Foremost in
The van, a stately creature tower'd, bedecked
Full proud in coat of grey all button'd up
But somewhat faded; for, its nap appeared
As if it had seen many dreary seasons.
Armed he was from the saddle to his teeth
With revolvers three, a sabre, carbine,
And a dirk, showing what a monster of
War and human blood was he; and the eye
That fiercely rolled beneath the knitted brow
Of this rough type of man, plainly showed
He was both bloody and remorseless
At his trade. His nag, likewise, looked mean, spare,
Not half fed; and its hide and harness was
With mud and grease and lather much befouled.

Soon at the cottage door the guerilla
Pranced his jaded steed, and deigned to knock. The noise
Of such a rap unusual startled all
The inmates to their feet at once. Quickly
The daughter to the door hasten'd, and with
A curt'sy low and smile serene, welcomed
From the fitful wind and rain, the stranger.

The inmates all, save Athol, looked amazed
Upon his gaudy form, from the knee-top boots
He wore, to his slouch hat by tassel girt.
Then soon, kind Reuben's liberal hand took
By the reins, the fellow's neighing palfrey,
And tied it to a hickory post close by.
As kindly, the matron spread before him

A meal, of which he heartily ate, eyeing,
In the meanwhile, the federal youth disguised,
Whom he pierced, as 'twere intuitively.

[In the section of the poem here omitted the rebel chieftain casts aspersions on Lincoln. Athol, as hero, is obliged to come to the defense of his head of state, delivering an impassioned oration which provokes the scene which follows.]

* * *

This roiled the rebel's temper. He, angry,
Made with his clench'd fist a thrust at Athol,
Who dext'rously warded off the blow;
Then to the door ran, with mouth all foaming
With rage, and shouted to his armed band, "Foes—
Enemy—hither hasten—quick." Soon they
The house surrounded, hooted, halloo'd, rushed
Through the door, and like hungry tigers, pounc'd
Quite furious on their prey.

Then all within
The cot was dire confusion. Bitterly
The mother and the daughter wailed. Morose,
The guerilla chief jerked the old man up
Off his knees, and "villain, traitor," term'd him.
While with abject mien and supplication low,
Reuben tried to melt the chieftain's callous heart,
And bade him listen ere he claim'd him: raised
His eyes up heav'nward, and told him he was
Innocent: implored his freedom to restore.
While, meantime, Daisy wrung her hands with anguish:
In mercy lifted up her voice on high:
Bent her knees, and murmuring, bade him spare
Her father's hoary head: to be merciful
And just for the sake of her dear mother,
Stricken down with age, who, if of her spouse
Bereft, wouldn't live to see the morrow's light,
As God would call her from life's checquered scenes.
"Thou hast the power to wound or heal, to blight
Or bless:" but all was dead and still about

The chieftain's heart—too callous and to all
The finer feelings cold. Nor even could
The nervous tremor of her hands, that clasp'd
His knees, vibrate soft pity to his heart.
Nor her sighs, nor tears, nor accents tender,
Nor e'en the melting sweetness of her eyes,
Nor their fascinating gaze, from which the heart
Of one less hard would sure destruction found.
All her pleadings were, alas! in vain; as
The bold ruffians, in the remnant of the storm,
Quickly bore their captives from the vale, and thrust
Them in a loathsome dungeon South.

CHAPTER VI

The Affliction of Daisy—The Death of both her Parents

[The death-bed scenes in this chapter, which leave Daisy an orphan, were a stock-in-trade of fabricators of verse narratives. If Dagnall's death scenes depart from the usual type of thing, it is by virtue of the relative restraint with which he portrays the demise of Daisy's parents. Writers of verse narratives were masters in the art of the death-bed scene, and frequently protracted the suffering of the dying individual insufferably.]

Down beside her senseless mother Daisy
Knelt, and loudly called to Heaven for justice;
Pour'd forth in fervent pray'r that mercy yet
Divine might smooth the captives' way—vain hope.
Bitterly, all that long and dreary night,
She wept her father's and her lover's hapless fates;
And when the next day serenely dawn'd,
It brought unto her mind no smiling light,
For, joyless all the live-long day, she thought
Of them o'erwhelm'd by tyranny:
Knelt, with her heart o'ercharged with woe, and pray'd
The right'ous soon would triumph o'er and sink,
To fathomless depths, their stern oppressors down;
Hop'd that they'd by divine vengeance be pursued;

That the wrath of Heaven would upon them
Hurl its thunderbolts and doom their overthrow;
Wish'd her aged father would again be
Free as the rolling cloud, enjoying once more
The blessings of liberty; and that the wind
From heaven, unconfined, would soon play round
Her lover's brow, to dare again the foe,
Till vict'ry crown'd his arms, and conquest, with
Renown, his freedom brought. For she knew her
Athol's noble heart was far too valiant
To shrink from treason-tainted foes; aye scorn'd
At danger; could hear taunts and wear his chains
In fetter's realms like a Christian martyr.

But such hopes her mother's mind relief denied:
Soon reason fled her fever'd brain; for when
By her injurious foes borne down, faint she
Lay outstretch'd, pale nigh breathless, upon
A bed of anguish.

Many nights Daisy
Watch'd with glistening eye around her couch;
And heard, in her mother's stifling moans, death,
In fullness of glee, with bony hands twang'd
At her heart-strings, the solemn tones which tell
Where the broken in spirit shall go. Yes,
The tale is told: hopeless of recovery
Was her state; for soon her weaken'd lungs closed
Their spongy cells against the air of life.
A sigh, a gasp, a rattle in her throat:
Her fitful struggles ceased, and all was still.
Her spirit fled its earthly confinement,
And soared far beyond life's narrow bounds.

If ever innocence knew distress 'twas when
Daisy, bending o'er her dying parent,
Heard her last breath, and felt her heart was reft
Of life's warm beat. In her deep despair she
Trembling knelt beside her deceased mother;
And from her weeping eyes she pour'd upon
Her cold remains many fond, filial tears.

Then she raised her sorrowing head on high,
And cried aloud: "To thee, Great God above, let
My imploring voice ascend. O Lord of
Mercy! hear my prayer. Thou hast the power
To raise or quell the storm. The struggling worm
Thou canst protect. Then, O Lord of Hosts! deign
To dispel the black'ning gloom which now o'ershades
The future of a helpless orphan just
Deprived of fond maternal care. Her voice
That once impressed celestial precepts on
My heart, is hush'd in death. Nor does my father
Hear his suppliant child beseeching Thy
Benign protection: for, far from me, alas!
He has been cruelly torn, and futile have,
I fear, his claims for mercy been; unfelt
On apathetic hearts his pleading soft:
Still hearing naught but insults vile, has sank
Beneath oppression's weight; and p'rhaps his soul
Has from its earthly cell been disencumber'd,
And upward wing'd its way to heaven for peace,
Leaving me an orphan here forlorn, the sole
Survivor of the wreck."

Too true, alas!
Was her prediction: for, unhappily,
In mouldy dungeon vilely smear'd with
Damps infectious, her father, hopeless, sleepless,
Many midnight hours, quickly pined beneath
His darksome prison roof; and while he droop'd
And lonely breath'd, despairing of each daylight's dawn,
He thought that safe, secure, tho' far away,
All whom he loved remain'd in sunshine bright.

He saw his white-washed cot, and the tall trees
Which rose above it proudly, tinted with
The beam. Heard the gurgling brook meand'ring
Past; and fancied, in its twirling eddies,
That he saw the trout disport: his daughter,
Too, quite fair; serene as mild mid-noon in
Mayday, sitting on its green bank twining

A wreath of flow'rets gay with which to crown
Her lover's honored brow, in token of
The laurel he might wear.

But yet, he knew,
The Fed'ral then with circling arms did not
Her slender bosom twine, as, like himself, he pined
In dungeon deep, in sad captivity,
Inly mourning the loss of her whom his soul
Loved best on earth.

Then forebodings sad soon
Banish'd from his mind the remember'd joys
That thronged upon his soul. He feared and wept
To think that both his wife and child suffer'd:
Yet still at intervals he felt consolement
In the thought that they unshared his woes. Hoped
And prayed that no dire ills hung o'er their heads,
And that his wife and lovely daughter solely
Mourn'd his loss of fondness. This 'twas that cheer'd
Him; for a degree of bliss he felt in
His heart that he might see them soon again.
'Twas but a mock'ry of joy, as forced was
The glow; ghastly the smile; his haggard cheeks
And hollow eyes that hope destroyed. For, fast
He sank: and, on the self-same night his wife's
Christian spirit fled into eternity,
Death freed Reuben from his clanking chains.

CHAPTER VII

The Funeral of Daisy's Mother—The Strange Visitor

[In the first part of the chapter, here omitted, Daisy's neighbors aid her in performing the last rites for her mother, following which she returns to her home. Dagnall then affords Daisy opportunity to reiterate her undying devotion to Athol. The sentimental heroine, even though she never gave the hero cause to doubt her utter fidelity, never lost an opportunity to insist anew on her faithfulness.

The arrival of the messenger also gives Dagnall opportunity to picture his heroine as a potential object of sexual attraction. The myth that our Victorian forefathers avoided the subject of sex does not hold up well in the light of what those of our forefathers who were poetizers actually wrote. The most—or the least, depending upon one's point of view—that can be said for the mid-nineteenth century treatment of sex in literature is that it assiduously avoided the use of what are generally called "certain words," and that it was not clinical. But what versifiers lacked in realistic detail, they compensated for by implication, suggestion, and innuendo. Thus, in the present chapter, Daisy's reaction to the stranger's encomium shows that Daisy herself is no such ingenue as the Victorian heroine is often thought to be. A Victorian heroine, although careful to use language which every member of the family might unblushingly read, was fully aware, undoubtedly as a result of experience, of her ability to raise lustful thoughts in the minds of the unregenerate. And what is more, versifiers became facile, if not artistic, in their ability to suggest this awareness without giving offense to the prudish.]

* * *

Soon upon the breeze she heard the tramp
Of horse—affright'd ran—reach'd the cot—turn'd round,
And saw a shadowy form hard by, hovering
Near. Quick the door she shut; but soon a rap
Vibrated on her startled ear. Trembling,
She thro' the window gazed alarmed, and thought
She saw the chieftain returned back to burn
The cot, as twilight shadows veil'd the man,
And made his garb appear like gray.

Now listen
To her mind by prudence temper'd, her caution
Spoke with earnest warmth. "Who in evening's mantle
Sombre wrapt comes here?" "A friend," was the response.
"A friend, forsooth! at such an hour! Perchance
A foe, as none but the intrusive would
Invade a lonely maiden's sanctuary:
None but the designing prowl about in
Gloomy shades of night, dark deeds to do,
In order that their evil work may the
Mortal eye elude, and you seemed fashioned
For no good intent."

"Call not suspicion
To your mind, lone maid; I'm not on mischief
Bound. Heaven is my witness. My mission
Is a holy one, and needs precaution.

To guard against impending ills I must
Shun the cheerful beam of day, and wander
Only when the night shrouds the world in gloom.
The letter which I carry in my vest
Declares the object of my visit, and will,
I'm sure, remove your doubts: it's from Athol."

When she heard the gentle name of Athol,
She felt conscious that the stranger's ends were
Right; and without further parley bade him
Enter. Then he proffer'd her the letter,
Which she gladly took, and turn'd it round and round.
Her bosom heaved convulsed with deep emotion,
The sullen chill of fear quit her blood,
And stay'd the with'ring grief that blanch'd her cheeks
With paly dye, and sooth'd her thorny pains.

Then while Daisy, in the dim twilight, cast
A joyous look upon its superscription,
The stranger saw how beauteous was the maid,
How serenely fair in ev'ry feature.
Then, with the light of new-born hope, she from
The folded letter raised her languid eyes,
And said: "Tho' the lines seem to have been penn'd
By a trembling hand, yet I can trace in
Then the ornate style of dear Athol; and may
Fate charter freedom's blessings to the brave
Who brought them. May ev'ry adversity
Give him renew'd courage, till his name shall
Be upon the rolls of fame enshrined, and
Honors, like his days, brighten full of years."
The stranger bow'd his grateful thanks.

"How was
Dear Athol when you saw him last," she said.
"In health and hope quite buoyant; for, to me,
His confidant, he often speaks of you
As being far above all mortal stars
That shine. My praises, too, with his can now
Be joined." Concluding which, Daisy look'd straight

At the stranger, and caught the quick glance of
His eye, but in it saw he was sincere:
Then, gently curtseyed at the flatt'ring words
Which he had spoken.

"Most loth am I, fair maid,
To bid you now farewell; but the pale star
Of eve shoots down its lustre, and shame might
Tinge your cheeks if here I tarried longer."
"O, sir," she said, "my tongue hath not power
Of words to tell the emotions that now
I feel: But give Athol this token of
My love, and murmur in his ear these vows
Of mine: Tell him that, 'so long as time shall
Last, his image will remain and still be
Cherish'd at my faithful heart, and that, like
The stream near which he's now encamp'd, my love
For him is deep and pure.' "

Delighted with
The kindly task enjoined, the courier
Promised faithfully her commands he would
Obey. Then both their hands in friendship's grasp
Were soon combined.

Hastily forth he sallied,
And nimbly mounted on his roan steed,
Which restlessly on the emerald sward paw'd
The deep green grass. "Adieu," he said. "Good bye"
"And may kind Providence guard you safely
On your way," was her response. Then quickly,
The horseman and his charger, to her sight
Were lost, in the gloom of night enshrouded deeply.

CHAPTER VIII

Athol's Letter to Daisy—She Quits her Place of Birth—Her Search of Athol—Her Despair—The Loyal Peasants—The Guerillas—The Burning Hut—Its Victims

[In Chapter VIII, here omitted, Daisy reads Athol's letter, which instructs her to flee from her home to avoid the rebel chief, who has formed a guerilla band, and is reported to be ravaging the countryside. Daisy quits her home and, after a period of harrowing and fruitless wandering in search of Athol, comes upon the home of peasants who tell her how they have been subjected to the plundering activities of a band of guerilla marauders. As Daisy is about to leave to continue her search for Athol, the guerilla band, led by the same chief who has previously disrupted Daisy's home, reappears. Accusing the peasants of harboring a spy, the band take Daisy captive and set fire to the peasants' hut, burning to death the inhabitants.

In keeping with most poets who used the Civil War as a backdrop for the action of their narratives, Dagnall concerns himself far less with depicting the war scene realistically than with dramatizing the perils of hero and heroine. The poet, however, is historically accurate in his portrait of the guerilla band, typical of those spawned by the war, particularly in the border states. Some of the most unsavory elements of the time composed these guerilla bands, which attracted soldiers-of-fortune for whom even the relatively lax discipline of regular army life proved too severe. Indiscriminate in composition, these outlaw bands preyed indiscriminately on the populace, paying small heed to the sectional allegiance of those who came in their way. Hence Dagnall, by depicting his villain as the leader of a guerilla band, rather than as a member of the regularly organized Confederate forces, is dyeing even deeper the conventionally sooty hue of villainy.]

CHAPTER IX

Daisy a Captive—The Bivouac—Daisy's Doom

[Dagnall's moralizing continues. The villain's "abject crew" are deep in their cups, an unmistakable earmark of unregeneracy. The story of the rebel chieftain's past, rather gratuitously given the reader, drives home the familiar lesson that inevitable ruin awaits those who dare desert native woods and templed hills for Sodom and Gomorrah. The set speech of Daisy's rescuer, at the close of the chapter, with its insistence that one may "fly from guilt's alarms," but not from a "wicked conscience," is presumably more for the edification of the reader than for the reform of the rebel chief, who probably is not listening anyway.

By this point in the narrative enough threads of plot have been unravelled to call for coincidence to help tie them together. It should come as no surprise that the guerilla chief whose clutches encompass Daisy is precisely the rebel chief who, earlier, had disrupted Reuben's sylvan home and carried Athol and Reuben to prison.

The villain's pride and hardness of heart have already appeared; in this chapter his lustfulness shows itself. Daisy, until relieved by the inevitable rescue, is confronted with a choice which she must face as heroine: she may yield to the advances of the villain or, by refusing, bring calamity on herself or on her loved ones. Daisy's choice is standard: death before dishonor!]

Not till their victims' charr'd remains exhaled,
Through murky wreathes of smoke, a pestilence
Most baleful, did the rebels quit the hut
In search of injured Daisy, whom they found
Much convulsed and with all her sense nigh fled.

Through dark desert ways and rugged paths they,
Unmindful of her piteous cries, her sobs,
Her plaints and bitter wailings, brought her to
A cavern deep, scoop'd out between two hills,
And laid her in a dark recess wherein
Her fate should be determin'd by their chief,
Who'd not, as yet return'd.

So, round a blazing fire,
The murd'ring crew caroused. Some the weed fum'd.
Some sang ribald songs by turns and smutty jokes
Got off, whilst others quaffed and pass'd around
A vile inebriant distillation.

"Drink, comrades, drink," more loquacious than
The rest, cried one. "Drain your canteens to the dregs.
'Tis the most potent of all drinks, to rouse
Our sluggish blood to life and fortify
Us 'gainst dangerous night damps. Besides, it is
Our chieftain's birthday night. Then let us all
Be merry, jocund, gay, and laugh at folly
As it flies on pleasure's wing. For, why should
We work our own annoy, when now we have
A chance to pass a lucid interval
From a life attended with so many
Dangers? True, to lead this wild course has been
Our own choice; or, rather, we were all forced
Into it by the roving propensities
Of our natures, and ungovernable wills
That could not bear restraints, nor drudgeries,
Nor the enervating dull routines of
The regular soldier. No, my comrades; among
These hills we are free to do what we please.
Here we can and do despise the outer world.
Where glaring vice and luxury prevail;

Where laws are made most stringently to force
City villains into decency.
But here, full of adventurous love, among
These mountain passes, we simply practise
The ancient virtues of our ancestors,
With a valiant chief whose freeborn soul nought
Can turn from perilous ways; aye, one who spurns
The niggard Yankees' selfish yoke and hates
Their clannish, over-jealous natures. Still,
Sometimes when he's not aware, I notice
That his high-toned spirits are much dejected,
So much so, in fact, he seems to struggle
Against some opposing fate, the cause of
Which I opine I know. So, if you'll cease
Your drowsy murmurs, and open your ears,
I'll breathe into them, the sad incident
Of his life which yet preys upon his mind.

"Two years have scarce elapsed since he was smitten
With the peerless charms of a Yankee maiden
Whose father, a Puritan born and bred,
Lavish'd on her with unsparing hands,
The wealth he'd gain'd running niggers from
Africa into the Isle of Cuba,
Hoping, thereby, that his gifts of fortune,
Along with her accomplishments, would add
Great dignity to his high lineage;
Grace the pious stock from which she sprang,
And draw around her swarms of wealthy suitors."

"Our noble chief, a Virginian by birth,
Was always at her father's house a welcome guest;
For he thither often went to interchange
With her father mutual thoughts concerning
Their clandestine interests in the slave trade.
So, whilst in social converse, the father learnt
That Agar was descended from one of the
Eldest and most distinguished families
Of old Virginia. Then coupling this news
With the proud notions of himself, he saw
That such high blood, with wealth united, would

Confer much honor on his house, and offer'd
Agar his daughter's hand in marriage,
With vested rights in estates as portion
Of her marriage dower. Agar consented,
And promised to solemnize the nuptials
When he'd returned from Paris, where he'd gone
Some months before the war broke out.

"But in
That gay city, where vice and shame strut round
Enrob'd in meek-sainted guise, wine and women
Soon his youthful bosom fired. Held spell-bound
By the charming witch'ries of the gay lorettes,
Who hold their bacchanals at the Chateaux
Des Fleurs and Mabille, soon his unthinking
And blind reason brought him down deep into
The gulf of dissipation, which soon made
Him needy; for, amid his orgies, he thought
Not of the ruin he was bringing
On himself, but, to relieve his pressing wants,
Continued to make frequent demands
For means from her father, and gave his lands
In Virginia to him as surety
For supplies.

"At last the day of reck'ning
Came. The Yankee complain'd of tardy payment;
Felt touch'd to the quick in consequence,
And vouchsafed to lend our chief no more funds.

"So, one bright morning, the captain awoke
To the consciousness that shadowy ills
Obscur'd his stores at home; and once more steer'd
His shatter'd barque across the ocean wave.
On arriving home he found his domains
Were laid waste by the war which fiercely raged
Upon his native soil, his slaves set free;
In short, his happy home, and what remain'd
Of his once fair realms, confiscated were
By the Federal jackals.

"But yet his cup of
Mis'ry was not full: one drop it lack'd
More turgid still. Adverse fate deign'd to add
Poignancy to his misfortunes: for with
Harsh disdain the maiden's father on him
Fix'd an eye malignant, and with anger
Bade him never more to cross his threshold.

"Struck with such unkindness, our chieftain took
It in his heart to loath forever more
The Yankees, and swore he'd hold dread reverence
O'er their heads, joined our cause, then took these hills
To—"

Awe-struck, they him beheld. He came with
Hurried tread. Amazed, he stood awhile as
If some boding ill gleam'd through his eyes.
Soon his abject crew bent to his pride, and quit
The bivouac his wishes to fulfill:
To forage round and ransack spots, which, in
Open day, their footsteps fear'd to tread.

When gone, the ingrate bold the weak maid eyed
O'er and o'er; gave her many a wishful look;
And urg'd by lust, the leafy couch approach'd
On which she slumbering lay. She started up
As from a trance, with hair dishevell'd much,
And features fix'd in stern expression wild,
And on him threw the keenest dart of scorn.

Barb'rously severe he her accused of
Trait'rous complicity, and, indignant,
Said: "Haughty fair one, now thy doom's decreed.
Thou shalt have but one hour more to linger here,
If now thou dost not to my wishes lend
A gracious ear."

Down on her knees Daisy
Look'd up at him with mild, imploring eyes,
And with anguish in her bosom, wailing,
Said: "Alas! he's thought severe who thus condemns

The innocent and unhappy. Hast thou
Not one friend to whom the sacred heart relies
For truth and honor? If not, then such have
I—one ardent, noble, kind: In faith and hope
Unfaltering we are bound."

But her soft pleadings
Could not move his harden'd heart: It was bereft
Of all that's meek and tender. He heeded not
Her tears, her firm faith, nor virtue proud,
But said: "You'll never see your lover more.
In prison he now wears his chains. P'rhaps ere
Now, the Yankee's rotten carcase has been
To the buzzards thrown." "Then if Athol is
To me forever lost," she cried, "God bless
His soul. His image so dear to my sight shall
In my heart be firmly fixed, nor ever
From my cherish'd memory fade. But thou,
Vile minion of all that's mean and great,
The willing tool of that vain man whose pride
Is phrenzy, whose ambition's but despair,
Whose heart is void of ev'ry spark divine,
The curse of orphans and the cause of
Many a widow's tear, know that you may
Glitter in your infamy awhile;
But the potent grasp of might shall be soon
Wrested from you: The majesty of pow'r
Is in the avenging sword held in the hand
Of Heav'n: 'twill yet descend upon and burst
Your vaunted bubble to the sun, aye, blast
Your lauded greatness: Deeds of retribution
Deal unto the mean and base ambitious fools
Upon the gibbet; and righteous justice
Yet shall hurl upon thee its avenging ire,
For the wrongs which thou hast cruelly brought
Upon my Athol's hapless head: Aye, you
Who came into that happy home where dwelt
In blessed peace the innocent whose ears
Were strangers to the blast and din of war,
And vilely brought, therein, much misery,
Wretchedness and mourning. My father's name

Blasphem'd with curses foul, then reft him from
Me, and in a dungeon dire, him thrust, to pine,
To starve, and die: my aged mother caused
Through pining grief to sink into her grave
Ere she'd time to don a widow's mourning weeds;
And me an outcast orphan made for life.
But remember, yours is but a weak boast
Of transitory power. Successful guilt
Can but triumph awhile: For soon before
The keen, relentless weapons of the North,
Both your stuck-up pride and cause shall
Tumble: 'tis to them alone revenge is
Given. Beware."

At this, in drunken fury,
The chieftain laugh'd outright, and said: "Murmur
Not, my dear, fond bird. Do you think I'd injure
A bosom so fair. Beauty like thine was
Form'd for joy; and you must own I'm now
Your lawful lord."

Then he strove with eager arms
To grasp her. As quick she from his touch recoil'd.
"Shrink not," he angrily cried. "Succumb
To my power thou must, or, in this dense wood
Unseen by mortal eye, from life to death
Thou soon shalt pass; for, longer my mind
Thy indiff'rence can't bear, thy peevish censures
Endure: nought but thy consent to be my bride
Can satisfy my burning soul." Saying which,
He grasped her by her long dishevell'd hair.
"Swear," he cried, "ere this dagger's keen edge shall
In your heart's blood be imbrued."

"No, no," she said,
"Fate will ne'er permit me to touch thy hand,
It hath the stain of murder'd blood; and such love
As thine, the tender-hearted would defile:
Forever unhappy she'd be whose bosom
Hath therein sincere passion glowing. No,
My honor lives for one most dear to my heart.

Therefore, if my ardent troth for him I love
Can't kindle in thy breast compassion's warmth,
Why longer the sacrifice delay? Why
Tantalize your victim like a cat ere
You destroy? or like the venom'd adder
Coil your folds around ere you sting to death
Your prey? For well I know he who would not
Spare my father's life will not spare my own;
And death would end the tortures which now rack
My beating heart. But beware. He yet lives
For whom my soul with sacred fervor burns.
He whom thy bold hands hath sway'd with cruelty,
But who will yet thy proud triumph guilt
Avenge."

Then reviving wrath the chieftain's soul
Inflam'd. The name of Athol moved his heart
To hate; and black as night he frown'd and spent
His rage on helpless Daisy, who struggled
At his feet. Her clasp'd hands clinging round his knees;
With dripping eyes to Heav'n raised and crying,
"Oh! God of mercy! is there no friend nigh?"
"There is a friend," a deep gruff voice behind
A rock exclaim'd. "Arrogant knave, forbear."
The rebel heard the voice. It rived his heart.
His stern determined look he took from off
The mortal place, and quick with fright he started
Back, recoil'd and dropt unstain'd upon the ground
His sheathless dirk, which high above her head
He held.

Again he heard the voice upon
The midnight blast exclaim, "Outcast of earth
Is searching among these hills, to ravish
Helpless women, then to thrust them from you
As in scorn, to murder in cold blood
Thy vaunted chivalry? The crimes which you've
Already done, now cry aloud to Heaven
For vengeance. Therefore, thou rebel reprobate!
Beware. If you murder her nigh strangled
At your feet, hell's furies, that now thirst

Unceasing for your blood, will pursue you
Everywhere. Horrid sounds will rise on
Ev'ry wind and in your blood-stained conscience
Howl these words: 'Seducer, coward, murderer.' "

Pale turned the chieftain's cheeks: His joints trembled
As if by an intermittent ague shook.
Then he quickly, like a fleeting shadow,
Vanish'd through the gloom, whilst the voice, meantime,
Hard on his trail, cried: "Thou curst, abandon'd wretch,
Well may'st thou fly from guilt's alarms,
But never from your wicked conscience.[")]

CHAPTER X

Daisy's Rescue—Her Deliverer—Her Meeting with Athol—The Battle—Death of the Lovers

[Having reacted throughout as befits a heroine, Daisy sees her part through to its close. She evinces open-eyed surprise that her rescuer should be none other than Athol; she reiterates her constant and undying love, only to die of a broken heart. The villain is sacrificed on the altar of poetic justice. The hero is, arbitrarily, killed. Nothing in Athol's past makes death a particularly fitting climax to his career. Dagnall has been faced with the problem common to all writers of sentimental, melodramatic verse narratives: shall the ending be happy or sad? Dagnall chose the sad, and one may be certain that many a pair of eyes a century ago blurred with tears on reading how Daisy "kissed his bloodless lips/And on his mangled bosom died."]

When the chieftain deep into the forest shade
Had fled, the stranger from his covert hied
To the gloomy spot where Daisy's cries for
Mercy had arisen, and found her there
Half dead by fear, murmuring in despair.

Soon he from the ground her faint form raised,
And in her livid cheeks beheld how much,
Alas! her inmost heart was wounded. Then
From the rocky cell along a vernal path
He bore his fragile trust in safety,
Until a hazel glade he reached, where obscur'd
From curious sight, he halted near
A tinkling rill, which down a pebbly steep

Slow trickling ran, and with its ice-cool water
Daisy's fevered temples lav'd.

Soon with
Open eyes she hailed the breaking morn's gray light;
Her ears caught the plaintive murmur of the rill;
Her low voice muttered, "Where am I? By whom
Thus held hand bound? Who's my deliverer?"

'Twas then the stranger read with glad surprise
Her brighten'd looks, and thro' her gleaming eyes
Saw her life was safe; but yet a symbol
There reveal'd some hidden secret in her heart,
Which, altho' her charms had been by the keen blight
Of sorrow faded, still show'd that the soft tinge
Of beauty lingered on her care-worn cheeks.

"Oh, Sir," she said, "to you I owe my life,
To you my grateful thanks are due. Never
Can my heart renounce thy hallow'd friendship's claim."
Then she told him all about her hard fate:
What wrongs she'd from the rebels borne, and how
Of father, mother, friends bereft; and one,
Also, who found her young, torn from her fair.
"Ah!" she sigh'd, "oft together we have form'd
Our mutual faiths with fondest truths, and sealed,
With true love sighs, our promised hymen vow.
But being then of him and friends bereft
By that pamper'd son of vice and tyranny,
No one was left who could my griefs assuage;
And oft I've visited the blissful bowers
Where we were wont to meet, and wander'd often
O'er and o'er again our fiel[ds] of cheerful love;
But all those once bright scenes were clouded;
Nor sun, nor moon, nor stars had light for me.
Each hour his absence wrung my heart. Many
Long, sad days I heard no tidings of him;
And feared I was, alas! forever doom'd
His friendship's bitter loss to taste, when—" Here
She paused to wipe away the tears that dimm'd
Her eyes.

"Alas!" her friend then cried, "how strange
Do secret sympathies human souls pervade!
The hardest heart in grief like thine would feel
A share; and even now to see thee weep,
Connects with thine my own remember'd joys
Unto thy wretchedness; for thy plight afflicts
My heart, and, like me, I learn thou art to love
And keen despair a prey,—a victim of
The self same ruffian vile who thrust me in
A dungeon dark, where many weary days
And nights I, caged up like an untamed beast,
Imprison'd sat, a hapless vassal bound,
Pining in darkness, famish'd, and benumb'd
By damps, clanking my slavish chains, and counting
Many a weary hour of my dull life
Away, thinking that if I could but rend
The links that gall'd my heart, I'd quickly fly
To the dear pledge whom to my first-born hopes
Was known—one whose face I found in pride of
Beauty fair, and in whose lustrous blue eye
Her gentle spirit shone. O that Daisy
Now were nigh to hear my voice, I'd—"

Daisy felt

Like being lifted to the clouds, and fixed
Her eyes full on the stranger. "I see, I see!"
She cried, "thou art none else but Athol!
This yeoman's guise is all delusion!"
With one accordant pause an attitude
They struck; and mute awhile they stood in all
The silent eloquence of love; then rush'd
Into each others' arms.

Heart to heart they press'd—

Burning kisses seal'd their lips. Raptures raised
Their two embodied souls to heaven, for
They knew not where they stood. Creation, too,
Her grateful voice uplifted; as the sky,
Just then, with joyous light an unclouded
Aspect wore. Gaily the birds, in pairs,
On lithe wings flutter'd about them. Their jocund songs
Attuned made the welkin ring with mirth.

SHE GAVE A SHRIEK AND CRIED ALOUD

Soon from the wretched Daisy Athol's presence
Banish'd care; her falling tears dried, and caus'd
Life's mantling current high to mount her face.
Her humorous heart then dimpled her cheek with
Smiles. The lucid gladness over all
Her features spread. Sonorous and clear she vented
Forth a joyous laugh at seeing Athol
In disguise. He, too, in sweet astonishment
Smiled and said: " 'Tis done to cheat the rebel's sight;
For, the human mind, you know, is well versed
In deceit: The sire of falsehood practiced
It; the rebels follow him; we copy
Them—perhaps with more consummate art."

'Twas
Thus that their strange meeting on each other
Much unsullied pleasure did bestow. Then
Daisy mildly said: "Come, Athol, let us
Hasten from this place: It is the shrine of
Rebels, and the air around is tainted
With their breaths. Come, let us go ere the brood of
Vile cut-throats bar our paths."

"No, Daisy, no,"
Cried Athol, "Fame, honor, truth, forbid it.
The dastard sycophant who mock'd at me
Scarce heal'd of my wounds, and you an orphan
Made, to suffer from hunger and p'rhaps die,
Unpitied, among my friends a speedy fate
Must find: as justice for the wrongs the brute
Has done, the crimes which he's exulted o'er
Demand his doom. Yet, being a scout, it would
Be prudent, now to leave ere danger may
In direst form arise and disconcert
My well laid plans to capture the guerrillas [*sic*],
For our corps is now encamp'd upon the edge
Of this small stream just where it runs through yonder cedar grove."

Then they clasped their hands and sighed the vow that
They would, when the battle ceased and he had
Swept with giant strength the proud survivor
Of their wrongs from earth, be wed. So, Daisy,

Hailed the dawn of that bright day, thinking much
Of the sweet promise and of many years
Of bliss in store, and said whatever might
Betide, she'd share his fate on future fields
Of proud renown or fall with him in victory.
So, trusting in Heaven for strength and quick
With nimble feet she with him flew, to dare
The paths which Athol oft had dared before.

Then ere the redd'ning sun that day had set,
Sounds of drums and war's alarms were heard upon
The wind. Hosts of men with hollow eyes,
Haggard cheeks, and with their bright arms gleaming
In the sun, cross'd Potomac's flood to wage
Impious war upon Antietam's plain.
There McClellan brave, his country's pride, but
Short-lived faction's hate, unfurled his banner
To the vent'rous foe, and led in proud array
His daring thousands forth, who far and wide
Dispersed Lee's plund'ring hosts.

In Daisy's eyes
It was an awful sight to see, face to face,
Christian freemen stand in line of battle dread
Hurling ruin, waste, and death around her:
Terrible the vengeful shouts and horrid yells
Which rose amid the thundering cannon's peal:
Heart-rending cries of mortal agony,
And shrieks of death from mangled corse ascending.

And when the discordant din of strife had
Died upon the evening breeze, she bounded
'Midst the heroic slain, and called, with cries
Of sadness, the name of him who promised
Her, ere long, the nuptial ring. So, onward,
Wild in aspect, across the bloody plain
She flew, searching, with tearful eyes along,
With brothers o'er brothers bending, fathers
O'er slaughter'd sons, and friends loudly mingling
Their lamentations with the wounded's groans,
Her Athol's bleeding form; when soon, among

SHE GAVE A SHRIEK AND CRIED ALOUD

The ghastly slain, she spied, prostrate upon
The ensanguined ground, the guerilla chief,
Athol's mortal foe, 'gainst whom he strove in
Rage of battle hot, and triumph'd o'er at last:
For, a deadly minie ball from Athol's
Well-aimed carbine had gone whizzing where
The chieftain stood, urging on his men, and sank
Him 'mid the rebel dead.

Seeing his fate,
She raised her hands on high, and utter'd "God
Be praised, thy retribution's just:" then hurried
On in grief, low bending, scrutinizing,
In the moon's pale beam, ev'ry pallid face
That lay cold in death, to find her love.

Soon from the blood-stained grass a muttered prayer
With mournful groans upon her ears sounded.
Quickly whence the moans arose she hastened;
And there, alas! quite faint, expiring, saw
Her lover writhing in his wounds, bleeding
Fast, all welt'ring in his life blood, gasping
Hard for breath; his dark hair drenched with gore; his
Musket by his side, its handle firmly grasped.

Franticly [*sic*], she called him by his name; stooped
And fondly clasped her Athol to her heart,
Brushed the matted locks back from his brow and
Gazing on his dying eyes, she bade him speak
One dear fond word to her, his Daisy fair.
He muttered "Oh! is that you, love, my bride?"
Then gave a gurgling sound and lay a breathless corpse.

Swift frenzy lit her eyes. A mortal pang
Her heart struck. She gave a shriek and cried aloud,
"Oh! God, thy will be done," then fell upon
Her lover's clay-cold corse, kissed his bloodless lips
And on his mangled bosom died.

FINIS.

II. THEIR EARTHLY PATHS NO MORE SHALL SEVER

Apart from obvious divergence over the slavery issue, Northern and Southern war verse exhibits few differences. Far more poems than not bear no internal evidence, aside from obvious geographical allusions, to indicate whether their authors bore allegiance to the stars and stripes or to the stars and bars. This similarity can be seen by comparing Dagnall's *Daisy Swain* (see page 178) and a Southern verse narrative which appeared a year later, Mary Hunt McCaleb Odom's *Lenare: a Story of the Southern Revolution.* Mrs. Odom is no plagiarist, turning Dagnall's Northern dross into Southern gold, as a juxtaposition of the two poems might suggest. Rather, both Dagnall and Mrs. Odom are conforming to well-established formulae in the construction of their narratives.

Aside from the obvious similarities in plot, *Daisy Swain* and *Lenare* invite comparison through the heavy reliance both poets place on stereotyped phrases, often identical ones. Mid-nineteenth century poets felt that every noun needed its accompanying adjective. The more stereotyped the resulting combination, the more "poetic" the description. That Dagnall and Mrs. Odom plundered a common stockpile for some of their poetic diction is evident. Both Daisy and Lenare possess, at various times, "heaving bosoms," "beating hearts," "drooping heads," "tearful eyes." Both are thrown into "deep despair," which leads to "fervent prayer." Other characters share identical labels. The fathers of both heroines are "aged." Both heroes possess "fond hearts." Such conventional phraseology permeates both narratives. A survey limited solely to the descriptions of the heroines indicates that the duties of the mid-nineteenth century writer of verse narratives did not include searching his lexicon for unusual modes of expression.

An anatomizing of Daisy Swain shows her to have possessed, at one time or another, "fevered temples"; a "brow serene"; an "aspect mild"; a mien which ranges all the way from "languishing" to "mournful" and back; versatile eyes which can be "radiant," "weeping," "anxious," "glistening," "gleaming," and "languid"; cheeks "bloodless," "livid," "dimpling," "roseate"; "pale hands"; a bosom "chaste" but "gladsome." These parts, put together, result in a "gentle maid" of "graceful form" whose "fair face" reflects a "smile serene" and whose "budding charms" house a "pure heart." In times of duress, Daisy emits "tender sighs," "broken sighs," and "stifled moans."

A difficult standard, surely. But Mrs. Odom's Lenare is capable of matching Daisy's "roseate cheeks" with "crimson cheeks" of her own, Daisy's "languishing mien" with a "melting glance." And so on down the anatomy. Lenare comes equipped with a "forehead fair"; a brow which is variously "mournful," "marble," "sunny," "throbbing," "uplifted." From her "dark," "dauntless," "eager," "flashing," "gentle," "kindling," and "streaming" eyes come "eager gazes," "melting glances," "pensive looks." "Vivid blushes" make "crimson" a cheek which frequently is "marble" and "pale." Her heart is always "gentle," "loving"; frequently "bleeding"; occasionally "wildly beating." In her ability to emote conventionally, Lenare perhaps outdistances Daisy, although the race is close. Daisy, under stress, emits "broken sighs" and "stifled moans," while, variously throughout the course of her story, Lenare possesses a "trembling lip," a "trembling grasp," and erupts with "bitter tears," "fluttering sighs," and "wildest grief" on top of "wild despair."

Similar examples of the conventional expression which permeates both poems may be culled from any passage in either work. Clearly, neither *Daisy Swain* nor *Lenare* is a "language experiment," as Whitman once denominated *Leaves of Grass.* Most readers of poetry one hundred years ago, believing as they did that poetry should inculcate morals and advance the cause of Truth, would have been disturbed by a poetry which dislocated, or even jarred, language.

Mrs. Odom's poem is from *Lenare: a Story of the Southern Revolution; and other Poems* (New Orleans, 1866).

from LENARE: A STORY OF THE SOUTHERN REVOLUTION

I

THE MAGIC GLASS

[Lenare, as the heroine, has of course grown up amid sylvan surroundings. Her appearance, as described in this chapter and elsewhere, corresponds closely to what any fictional or poetic heroine of the time looked like.]

'Twas fair and bright the first of May,
God never formed a lovelier day;
The birds, the joyous morn to greet,
Sent forth a chorus, wild and sweet.
The zephyrs played with leaf and blade,
The sparkling dew begemmed the glade;

E'en Nature's self looked on the scene,
With smiling lip, and brow serene.
Deep in this lovely, magic dell,
'Tis whispered gentle fairies dwell.
Hard by a fountain, clear and sweet,
Is said to be their Queen's retreat,
Where love-lorn lads and lassies go,
To read their future weal or woe.
'Tis but to hold a mirror bright,
So it reflects the beaming light
That falls upon the waters clear,
That flow in gentle murmurs near,
The future will before thee pass,
Reflected clearly in the glass.
This bright and smiling morn in May,
A maiden takes her lonely way,
To read, in fairy's magic glade,
The future's dark, uncertain shade.
Her form was graceful as gazelle,
Her hair in jetty ringlets fell;
Her eye, large, dark, and full of fire,
Could melt in love, or flash with ire;
Both changing cheek and kindling eye
Betrayed her birth 'neath Southern sky.
'Twas in the time when Northmen came
To subjugate, degrade, and shame
The land of freedom and of right,
And make them bow to wrong and might.
The maiden's heart swelled proud and free
Beneath the skies of Liberty.
The blood that bounded in each vein
Flowed free from every Northern stain,
And backward, for a century,
She counted Southern ancestry.
The magic glass she raises now—
Tosses the bright curls from her brow,
Then turns, with eager gaze, to look
Into the future's mystic book.
Ha! maiden, what is written there
To blanch a brow already fair?
Why glares thine eye upon the sight?

Why turns thy crimson cheek to white?
Ah! seest thou not a lover brave,
As ever heart to maiden gave?
Then why this start of wild surprise?
Why flashes fire from thine eyes?
Ah! look within the glass so fair,
And view the picture mirrored there.
There mounted on a noble steed,
That well might serve his master's need,
A soldier, young in looks and years,
Within the fairy glass appears.
His forehead was both high and fair,
And curling flaxen was his hair;
His eye, a deep and restless blue,
Told of a spirit brave and true.
But ah! that spirit, bold and free,
Now wears a tyrant's livery.
His garb is not of greyish hue,
He wears the hated Northern blue.
Ah! maiden, dash beneath thy feet
The glass that marred thy visions sweet,
Then wring thy hands in wild despair,
And breathe to heaven a fervent prayer;
Of small avail 'twill be to thee,
When fate shall weave thy destiny.

II

THE PICKET

[Mrs. Odom joins a sizeable group of her literary brother- and sisterhood, both South and North, in suggesting that the Rebellion is the villain responsible for the separation of hero and heroine.]

'Twas night; on old Potomac's shore,
The stars ne'er shone so bright before—
The soldier slept upon the ground—
His single blanket wrapped him round;
The steady watchfires ruddy glow
Threw lurid light upon the snow,

And save the picket's measured tread,
The camp was silent as the dead.
As slowly o'er the frozen ground
He walks his weary midnight round,
His thoughts to by-gone pleasures roam—
His lone heart wanders back to home.
The father, on whose noble brow
The snows of age are sprinkled now,
Who breathed a prayer that he might be
True to the cause of liberty;
The mother, who, in infancy,
Had nursed him all so tenderly;
Ah! well her boy remembers now
Each furrow on her aged brow,
While o'er him steals, with thrilling power,
The memory of that parting hour;
The moment of her last good-bye,
When, with a sadly filling eye,
She bade farewell to him and joy,
And said, "God bless my soldier boy!"
Then o'er his heart a softness steals,
That every gallant soldier feels,—
A feeling manhood cannot smother,
When thinking of his absent mother.
Another form, to memory dear,
Drew from his eye the rising tear;
A face to his fond heart more fair
Than tenants of the upper air.
With sigh suppressed he fondly drew
From near his heart, so warm and true,
Where, e'en in battle it was laid,
The image of a lovely maid.
He stooped beside the vivid blaze,
That he might for a moment gaze,
With love, with adoration, on
The eye that beamed for him alone.
That girlish face was passing fair,
And beautiful that curl of hair;
Dearer than aught this side of heaven,
Save her by whom they both were given.
Long gazed he on that senseless thing,

The imaged maiden of the Spring,
That rises in the lonely dell,
Where fairies future visions tell.
Then with a quick, convulsive start,
He pressed it to his lips and heart.
"Oh, happy home! beloved Lenare!
When will thy Walter meet thee there?
When shall around his heart entwine
The echoes of that voice divine,
Where every well-remembered tone
Around this dreary hour has thrown,
A spell of quiet, pure delight,
To cheer his lonely heart to-night?"
Once more he gazed upon her face,
And then resumed his weary pace.

III

THE BATTLE

The cannon's roar booms on the air,
It tells that strife and blood are there;
Where foemen meet and deeply feel
The deadly thrust of foemen's steel.
There brothers meet in mortal strife,
And loundly [*sic*] cry, "no, life for life!"
Now clears away the battle smoke,
It shows the Northern columns broke,
While Southern valor dashes on
To make secure the vantage won.
The Northmen rally, charge again,
Again they are by thousands slain.
'Tis vain to cast more life away,
The Southern arms have won the day,
Defeated, foiled, compelled to yield,
The Northmen leave the gory field.
The Burg of Frederick long shall be
Bloodstained in Northern memory.
Night closed upon the gory scene,

And quiet all, where late had been
Such deadly and such murderous fray,
That fiends were glad to turn away.
Extended far o'er hill and plain,
Lay thousands of the ghastly slain,
Their rigid forms now cold in death,
Their hearts' blood crimsoning the heath.
What sight for human eyes to view!
Great heaven! can such tales be true?
Can brothers meet as mortal foes,
And strike such sure and deadly blows?
See! weltering lies, bathed in his blood,
The young, the gifted and the good;
A widowed mother's darling son
Lies cold in death—her only one—
The life tide ebbing from his side,
Alone upon the field he died.
A youthful Northman, too, is there,
Deep dyed with blood his flaxen hair;
The hissing lead had pierced his brain,
He ne'er will meet the foe again;
The silver cord of life is riven,
He stands before the courts of Heaven.
Hark! what low sound falls on the ear?
Is it a dying groan we hear?
Some wounded soldier's feeble moan,
Who scarce has strength enough to groan?
There, where most deadly was the fray,
Upon the ground poor Walter lay;
A bleeding wound upon his brow,
As pale as marble was it now
Save where the blood oozed from the wound,
And dripping, clotted on the ground.
"Oh, give me water!" is his cry,
"One cooling draught, or else I die!"
Stealing along, with coward tread,
A Northman, who, in strife, had fled,
Came creeping to that gory field,
To find the booty dead men yield,
This wretch, who feared the light of day,
Now neared the spot where Walter lay;

His feeble moan fell on his ear,
He started back, and then drew near;
Stooped o'er the young and fallen brave,
To steal some trinket from the grave.
There shone upon the nerveless hand,
A gift of love—a golden band
Of little worth, save as a token
Of vows pledged never to be broken.
With beating heart, and trembling grasp,
He siezed [*sic*] the circlet in his clasp,
Then turned to go—but paused again—
What might that other hand contain?
'Twas gathered closely to his breast,
Within its palid [*sic*] fingers pressed,
Something the darkness had concealed,
But which a rough grasp now revealed.
Oh, Walter! rouse thy swooning sense,
And spurn that thieving minion hence!
Reclaim that face, so passing fair,
The worshipped image of Lenare!
That nerveless hand and swooning brow
Can offer no resistance now.
Hark! who comes there, with heavy tread,
At this lone hour to seek the dead?
Some friend, perchance, to seek again
A comrade 'mong the gory slain.
The Northman trembled now with dread,
He grasped his sinful gain and fled.
He who would rob the dead by night,
Must hide the guilty deed by flight,
Nor stay to face an honest foe,
But deeper still in darkness go.

IV

THE BESIEGED CITY

[In Chapter IV, here omitted, the author describes how the Northerners subdued the Southern city in which Lenare lives. In the course of the bombardment, Walter's parents, along with Lenare's mother, are slain, and Lenare's father imprisoned. The death of Lenare's mother, and the imprisonment of her father, form conventional parts of the price which the heroine has to pay in order to qualify as a heroine. This chapter also paves the way for Lenare's eventually becoming an orphan.]

V

THE RECOGNITION—THE APPEAL

[Since a Southerner wrote the poem, the villain, who now makes his appearance, wears the hated Federal blue. Victor's hardness of heart, emphasized throughout the narrative, constitutes one of the distinguishing trademarks of the villain. Victor also acts in a prescribed manner in proposing marriage to Lenare as the price for granting some boon the heroine desperately desires.]

Whiling the summer hours away,
The Northern chief luxurious lay;
His vassals lingering at his side,
He care and trouble both defied.
One of his braves, his favorite knight,
With forehead high, and eye of light,
Thus to the Northern chieftain spoke:
"Say, Victor, wilt thou tell me now
About the maid with sunny brow,
Whose image is so fondly pressed
In slumber to thy doting breast?
Why still, with jealous care, conceal
A tale thou'st promised to reveal?
Lift now the veil from mystery—
Who can this hidden beauty be?"
"Thou't scarce believe me when I vow,
I just as little know as thou;
It is a trophy from a field,
Where Northern valor had to yield.
A paltry coward robbed the dead
Of this one priceless gem, and fled.
'Twas chance and gold that to me gave
The treasure of the fallen brave.
But since I gazed upon its face,
Where lingers beauty's softest trace,

My heart throbs with a passion true,
That other men ne'er felt or knew.
I tell thee, Gordon, I would sell
My soul to deepest, blackest hell,
If by the traffic I could buy
One tender beam from her dark eye."
"Why, Victor! by the gods, I vow,
I never knew thee weak till now,
To worship at a phantom's shrine,
When nations lowly bow at thine!"
Ere he could add a sentence more,
A menial stood within the door.
"What is it, Michael?" Victor said,
"What new plea is before me laid?"
"A lady, sir, with mournful brow,
Would beg to see thy lordship now."
"A lady! is she old or young?
Speak, sirrah! what hath bound thy tongue?"
"The lady, sir, is young, I'd swear,
By every lock of jetty hair;
I saw her face beneath her veil,
'Twas beautiful, but very pale."
"Then let her come, and nothing fear,
Go, tell her I await her here."
A moment passed, and, pale and fair,
Before him stood the young Lenare.
He raised his careless eye to seek
The beauty of her marble cheek,
Then flushed his brow with crimson dye,
As full he met her soft dark eye;
And her pale cheek grew paler still,
While both hearts felt a sudden thrill.
She saw, in his deep, restless eye,
His sunny locks of flaxen dye,
The Northman she had seen to pass
Across the future-telling glass;
While he beheld, with sudden start,
The image pressed against his heart—
A living, breathing maiden fair,
With flashing eye, and midnight hair.
"What wouldst thou, lady?" Victor said,

And lowly bowed his lordly head.
"What would I? oh! the boon I claim,
I scarce can find the words to name."
She clasped her hands in deep despair,
And urged her wild, heart-rending prayer.
"Victorious foe! behold me here,
In agonizing hope and fear;
'Tis for a father that I pray,
A father old, and weak, and gray;
In yonder cell he lies in chains,
Have pity for an old man's pains;
Or, if thy heart shouldst callous be,
Show mercy then to wretched me.
Of freedom, mother, all bereft,
Take not the only blessing left!
Oh, heed my heart's despairing cry,
If here thou wouldst not see me die!"
She sank imploring at his feet,
And raised her streaming eyes to meet
The glance of his, that she might read
Soft pity for her wretched need.
Young Victor's color went and came—
"Fair maiden, what thy father's name?"
"They call him Hargrave," low she said,
And bowed again her fair young head.
"Arise, and I will tell thee here,
All that thy father has to fear;
The power is thine alone to save
His grey head from the yawning grave.
Go, twine thine arms about him now;
Kiss each dark furrow on his brow;
Tell him thy young heart bleeds to see
Thy father in captivity.
Conjure him, with thy honeyed breath,
To leave the road that leads to death;
His *loyal oath* will set him free,
Fair maid, his fate depends on thee."
The maiden knelt no longer now,
But stood erect, with scornful brow.
"What! urge my father to forswear
His honor, country, all that's dear!

No, chieftain, I can see him *die*,
But can not hear him *swear a lie*."
She turned, with queenly step and mien,
To seek her wretched home again.
"Stay, maiden, stay!" the chieftain cried,
And hastened quickly to her side;
"Long have I worn thine image pressed,
With fond affection, to my breast.
It matters not from whence it came,
My love and purpose are the same;
Give but one glance of love to me,
And thou wilt set thy father free."
"In mercy, chieftain, tell me where
Was found the image of Lenare?
Oh, gracious heaven! can it be,
That Walter, too, is lost to me!
Oh, spare that crushing weight of woe—
In pity tell me 'tis not so!
By every blessing to thee given—
By all thy dearest hopes of heaven,
Do not confirm the pang I dread,
But tell me Walter is not dead!"
She stood, with wildly beating heart,
With eager eye, and lips apart,
Awaiting now, with doubt and fear,
The words she scarcely dared to hear.
Her melting, upward, beaming glance,
Seemed Victor's bosom to entrance;
Her wild, dark eye, veiled by a tear,
Her pale cheek, paler still with fear—
As like the bending lily flower,
That droops beneath the summer shower,
She bowed, in wretchedness and woe,
Before the deadly falling blow.
"Fair maiden, 'gainst my heart is pressed
An image from a soldier's breast;
Though not my hand that robbed the dead—
That crime rests on another's head.
"I—," "Give me proof!" the maiden cried,
"I'll bless thee still, if thou hast lied!"
The chieftain's brow grew dark with fire,

And paled his cheek with rising ire.
"Hold, maiden! thou art now the first
Of man, or womankind, who durst
Look Victor in his honest eye,
And dare to think that he could lie;
Still less to whisper, without fear,
That dark deceit could linger *here*."
Fiercely he smote his heaving chest,
And proudly raised his haughty crest.
"Chieftain, I have not known thee long,
Thy pardon if I do thee wrong;
But still the truth I'll dare to tell,
I think I know thee passing well.
When kneeling at thy feet, I plead
Thy pity on a father's head;
With tears, besought thy power to save
My last of kindred from the grave,
What came in answer to my prayer?
What mercy to my wild despair?
That freedom should be his again,
If he his spotless soul would stain,
Would wear upon his brow the brand
Of treason to his native land!
I tell thee, chieftain of the North,
The soul that gave that answer forth,
Would scarce perceive the *lesser* dye
That lingers in an *added* lie!
Aye, grasp thy sword with passion's hand,
And bid thy minions round thee stand;
I tell thee, chieftain, I would dare
To beard the lion in his lair!
I much have borne, and murmured not,
At what would seem a bitter lot
To one less gently reared than I—
For pleasures past I heave no sigh—
I've seen my country bathed in blood,
While foemen tread the reeking sod;
I've seen the crimson life-tide start,
Warm from my mother's gentle heart;
Received her last expiring sigh,
And closed myself her glazing eye,

As with a mortal wound she fell,
Slain by a hissing Northern shell.
It, too, is my unhappy fate,
To see my home made desolate;
To see my father, old and worn,
A prisoner from his portal borne,
While I must hush my bitter moan,
And bear my many griefs alone.
But now, I tell thee, chieftain, here,
By all that once to me was dear;
By every drop of Southern blood
That now bedews a Southern sod;
By every soldier's dying sigh,
By every orphan's tearful eye,
And by an all avenging God,
I pass to thee my solemn word,
My father's child shall never see
His honor sold for liberty;
But rather let him die in chains,
And let his conscience soothe his pains,
While I can stand, too, proudly by,
And see him for his honor die!"
Her hands were clasped tight o'er her heart,
While from her dark eye seemed to start
Her soul, with fiercely beaming ray,
As though it scorned its robe of clay.
The chieftain now all vainly strove
To curb his fast increasing love;
The more her Southern blood was fired,
The more her beauty he admired.
"Maid of the South, thou here hast dared
To do what all mankind have feared;
My power thou hast now defied,
Yea, thou hast told me that I lied;
A *man* could not speak thus and live,
A *woman* Victor can forgive.
I told thee once that naught could win
Thy father to his home again—
That thou wouldst never see him free,
Save through his oath of loyalty.
I told thee, too, that I possessed,

And to my throbbing bosom pressed,
An image that is wonderous [*sic*] fair,
And much resembles thee, Lenare.
Thine answer—well, it boots not now
For Victor to repeat thy vow,
Still less should Victor deign to prove
His honest word—his spoken love—
But here I hold," the chieftain cried,
"Strong proof, Lenare, I have not lied."
Young Victor from his bosom drew
A tiny case of magic blue,
Clasped by a simple golden band,
And placed it in the maiden's hand.
Lenare's brave heart seemed now to fail,
Her lip, and cheek, and brow grew pale,
As with a nervous, trembling grasp,
She soon undid the fatal clasp.
Ere Victor could her name repeat,
The maid lay senseless at his feet.
Oh! how can heaven look on and see
Such heartless inhumanity!
The ways of God are strange indeed,
But strength is given as we need.

VI

THE WOUNDED SOLDIER

[In Chapter VI, here omitted, Walter is shown convalescing in a convent which has been turned into a temporary hospital.]

VII

THE PRISONER

[In Chapter VII, here omitted, Hargrave is shown languishing in prison, where he prays to God for deliverance, putting himself in the care of the Almighty. Hargrave's trust in God warrants some notice, trust in the

Almighty being one of the chief means of differentiating the characters for whom readers are supposed to feel sympathy from those for whom readers are supposed to feel revulsion. That all manner of misfortune befalls those who repeatedly pray to God for help and deliverance seems not to have appeared paradoxical to poets or, for that matter, to the pious characters themselves.]

VIII

THE LOVER'S VOW

[In Chapter VIII, here omitted, Walter recovers fully from his wounds, and leaves the convent where he has been nursed back to health, vowing that he will yet win Lenare's freedom.]

IX

THE WARNING

[Chapter IX, here omitted, shows Victor struggling with his conscience, in the form of a vision, concerning his inhuman treatment of Lenare and her father. Since he is the villain, his conscience is not strong enough to overcome his depravity.

Throughout the chapter Victor is portrayed imbibing heavily. The chapter thus affords an example of the way in which the temperance movement, during the war period, was obliged to act in an auxiliary capacity. Moralistic poets, with notably few exceptions, were indisposed to waste their heavy artillery against demon rum when the nation at large was caught up in the whirlwind of war. Still, it was possible to use temperance—by which the era meant total abstinence—in convenient if subordinate ways. A relatively effortless way to earmark a villain was to let him be seen drinking.]

X

THE NORTHERN CHIEF AND REBEL MAID

[Mrs. Odom's Southern sympathies here first show themselves in an historical way. The detailed description of old Fleta's loyalty to her masters is too prolonged to be justified on artistic grounds. But Mrs. Odom is not concerned with artistic considerations; she is concerned with informing readers that slavery is not the ogre Northern radicals for several decades have been making it out to be.]

Cold winter laid him down to rest,
And gentle spring, with flowery crest,
With verdure crowned each hill and vale,—
Embalmed with fragrance every gale.
The heart of mother earth beat gay
Beneath the emerald foot of May.
Lenare's pale cheek still paler grew,—
Had lost the bright carnation hue
That bathed it in such kindling glow,
The same bright month one year ago.
In vain she prayed her Northern foe
To lift the burden of her woe;
When last she sought the haughty chief,
And at his feet implored relief,
A tear within his eye had stood—
He seemed to lose his fiercer mood.
Sweet thoughts of mercy seemed to roll
An instant o'er his heaving soul.
"Oh, maiden! in thy gentle breast,
Can Victor's image never rest!
And must I always feel the dart
Of disappointment in my heart?
Oh, God! 'tis worse than death!" he cried,
"Far better had I bravely died—
Had found, among the countless dead,
Sweet resting in a dreamless bed,
Than won the boasted laurel wreath,
To feel the piercing thorns beneath."
The chieftain paused before Lenare,
While, in his turn, he breathed a prayer.
"Lenare, within this heaving breast,
Thine image must forever rest!
I need not tell thee, maiden fair,
How fiercely I have held it there;
I could not, words would fail to prove
The boundless measure of my love.

Thou deemst him cruel, heartless, cold,
Who can thy father captive hold;
Whom all thy pleadings fail to move,
Yet still pursues thee with his love.
When thou hast sought me here before,
Thy father's pardon to implore,
One single answer did I give—
His oath—thy hand—and he shall live.
This hour, some softer feelings move
The heart that thrills for thee in love;
Before that soul-entrancing thrill,
I bend the fabric of my will—
Nay, speak not yet, till thou dost know
How much of mercy I shall show.
If I, Lenare, for love of thee,
Should set thy noble father free;
Recall my vow he should forswear
The sunny land to him so dear;
Couldst thou, to gain thy father's life,
Become a Northern chieftain's wife?"
"Oh, Victor, why with mercy seem
To mingle passion's darker stream?
Too well thou knowest my life would be
No sacrifice too great for me,
All youthful as I am, to give,
To bid my aged father live.
But long before mine eye met thine,
My love burned on another shrine;
I would not from my vows depart,
Or give my hand without my heart.
No, no! while Walter lives for me,
Still faithful I to him will be.
Though thou dost deem his spirit fled—
His heart now silent with the dead—
Kind heaven to my soul still gives
The darling hope that Walter lives.
Oh, chieftain! act the nobler part,
And seek no maid's unwilling heart;
But yield to mercy and to me,
And set my captive father free.
The God, to whom we bow in fear,

Blends mercy with his justice here.
We pray, as others we forgive,
That we may in that mercy live;
Then ask me not to be thy wife,—
I've sworn to bless another life."
"Lenare," the Northern chief replied,
"Think not to be a rebel's bride.
Thy lover coldly sleeps in death,—
He lies beneath the distant heath.
But still, if thou canst prove to me,
That Walter lives for love and thee;
If thou his life and truth canst prove,
Then Victor yields thee to his love.
But if I prove his certain death,—
The final yielding of his breath—
Then maiden, by the powers above,
I'll claim the right to win thy love."
Young Victor paused, with flashing eye,
To hear the Southern maid's reply.
A moment moved her lips in prayer
To heaven, in this her dark despair.
The maid then raised her dauntless eye,
And firmly gave him her reply:
"A something, I cannot define,
Within this beating heart of mine,
Breathes that I'll soon unbar to thee,
The golden gates of destiny.
Full soon my fate and thine thou'lt know,
The angels whisper it is so.
But still around my throbbing brow,
I'll bind no rash, or hasty vow.
For guidance, I will humbly bend
Before my God, my surest friend;
When thrice the dew has gemmed the lea,
I will return and answer thee."
"Fair maid, till then I must await
From thy fair hand, my coming fate."
Lenare passed slowly from the room,
Then swiftly sped toward her home.
Its portal gained, she sought a friend—
One true and faithful to the end—

Amid misfortune's wintry chill,
Her nurse was fond and constant still;
Still, to Lenare, she fondly gave
The love of a devoted slave.
In infancy, she lulled to rest
Her little nursling on her breast;
Then when the tiny feet could walk,
Had taught her baby lips to talk.
When childhood passed, she saw her flower
Bloom sweetly in her girlish bower;
And now, 'mid sorrows, dark and wild,
Lenare was still her "mammy's" child.
When first old Fleta met the foe,
They bade her from her shackles go.
They told her, *they* her freedom gave,
And bade her be no more a slave.
The old nurse answered, firm, but mild,
"I ne'er will leave Miss Ellen's child;
I'd not desert, my life to save,
The charge my dying mistress gave.
When thy accursed, unerring dart,
Transfixed her mother's gentle heart,
She turned on me her eye so mild,
And bade me guard her orphan child.
My hand upon her pallid brow,
I breathed to God a solemn vow,
That naught on earth should tempt my heart,
From those I love so well, to part.
Then go—I ask no better fate—
Go, if thou wouldst not win my hate."
Lenare now sought this friend, to share
Her slender hope—her great despair.
She soothed her darling's wretched fears,
Dried, for a time, her bitter tears;
Then bade the trembling, nervous maid,
To tell her all the chieftain said.
" 'Tis then to save her father's life,
My child would be a Yankee's wife?
No, no! heart-broken little pet,
If Walter lives, I'll save thee yet.

In three days thou again wilt go
To seek the presence of the foe;
With policy upon thy shield,
Appear, at least, to him, to yield;
Then when thy words his heart shall move,
Ask some brief time to learn to love.
Around this fort, I know, full well,
Each secret path, through wood and dell.
With whisky fully drugged, I'll start,
And play, for once, the tempter's part.
A colored guard the picket keeps,
I'll pass the postern while he sleeps;
The foe I soon will leave behind—
Thy lover I will surely find—
And ere two moons shall wax and wane,
Thou'lt rest upon his heart again."
Lenare drew closer to her side,
"A thousand thanks, good nurse," she cried;
"Though when to Walter thou hast gone,
I'll be, alas! left all alone;
Alone, with no one, save the foe,
I still can calmly bid thee go.
A something whispers in my heart,
'Tis better thou shouldst soon depart;
The darkness now will aid thy flight,
I'll even say farewell to-night."

XI

THE COLORED GUARD

[In Chapter XI, here omitted, old Fleta, on her mission to Walter, successfully gets by the colored guard, who tells her that he has not seen any freedom yet in his new role as a soldier in the Union army.]

XII

THE PLEDGE

[In Chapter XII, here omitted, Lenare tells Victor that, in return for her father's freedom, she will consent to become his wife if she fails within two months to prove that Walter is alive and loves her.]

XIII

THE RELEASE

[In Chapter XIII, here omitted, Hargrave is released, although Mrs. Odom is careful to point out to her readers that Hargrave will never recover from the deprivation he has undergone at the hands of the villainous Victor.]

XIV

OLD FLETA'S MISSION

[In Chapter XIV, here omitted, old Fleta arrives at Walter's camp, and lays the entire story of Lenare's perils before him. Walter, momentarily maddened with anger and grief, regains control of himself and hastens to the office of his commanding general.]

XV

THE RESOLVE

[In Chapter XV, here omitted, Walter's commanding general gives Walter permission to leave for home in order to free Lenare.]

XVI

THE MAIDEN'S PRAYER

It was a beauteous, heavenly night,
The sleeping earth, baptized in light,
Lay dreaming, like a happy child,
On whom its doating mother smiled.
Oh, words are cold and vain to tell,
The waves of thought, that rise and swell
In restless joy—in wordless bliss—
On such a matchless night as this.
Would to my soul the power were given,
To breathe its burning thoughts to heaven.
Oh, poesy! around thy shrine,
Bright garlands I would daily twine;
Would breathe, in soul-inspiring prayer,
The spirit-longings gathered there.
But, like sweet pearls in ocean's breast,
Those wordless visions still must rest;
Unspoken in my heart must lie,
In all their unseen purity.
Bathed in the moonlight's silent glow,
That softly kissed her brow of snow,
A maiden knelt in fervent prayer,
While sister spirits hovered there.
Alone she knelt, at midnight's hour,
No light within her sylvan bower,
Save here and there the fitful ray
Of moonbeams that around her play.
Pale, beautiful, alone, Lenare,
In anguish breathed her nightly prayer.
Her orisons of grief and love
Found echo in the courts above.
She knelt, in floods of liquid light,
A white-robed seraph of the night;
Prayed, that to her, would still be given
The guiding strength that comes from heaven.

The flowers of feeling sweetly wove
In garlands for the shrines above.
First, filial love stirred in her breast,
The thrilling chords that dare not rest;
The surging waves of anxious thought,
With pain and anguish ever frought [*sic*],
Now waft their incense up to heaven,
That Hargrave back to health be given.
Then o'er her gentle spirit stole
A tender thought, beyond control;
And melting words of pleading came,
For blessings on another name—
For him whose lightest tone would fill
Her bosom with a nameless thrill.
Then wildly rose a plea to heaven,
For freedom gained—for fetters riven—
That God would grant her power to prove
Her Walter's life—his constant love—
Would speed him swiftly to her side,
Ere Victor claimed her for his bride.
Then from her guileless heart arose,
A sweet petition for her foes.
A low, heart-felt, forgiving prayer,
And Victor's name was murmured there.
She rose, gazed on the star-gemmed sky,
Drew one long, quivering, bird-like sigh,
Then laid her down to guileless sleep,
While angel forms their vigils keep.
Ah! little thought the young Lenare,
That Victor heard her thrilling prayer;
That there, beneath the casement, stood,
Within the shadow of the wood,
Just shaded from the midnight's glow
The haughty chief—her Northern foe.
The vision vanished from his sight,
He saw no other lesser light;
The moon and stars grew pale and dim,
The world was rayless night to him.
"Oh, God!" he cried, "why dost thou fill
My soul with every maddening thrill?
Why agonize it thus with pain?

Why rend this aching heart in twain?
This worthless bauble would I give,
To prove that Walter does not live."
He tore the laurel from his head,
And buried it beneath his tread.
As deep in earth its leaves he pressed,
A "small voice" echoed in his breast.
To Victor's soul the voice thus spoke—
"The mighty God, thou dost invoke,
Heeds not—thy breath is vainly spent,—
Guilt brings its own just punishment.
Hadst thou not sought this Southern land,
With kindred blood to stain thy hand;
Not sold thy soul for sordid gain,
Or sought to bind the galling chain
Around this free and glorious land,
Thou hadst not felt the avenging hand."
Thus came, unbidden to his mind,
Thoughts of a now unwelcome kind;
He half resolved to yield the prize,
For which his soul now madly sighs;
Then rudely dashed aside the thought,
That heaven within his bosom wrought.
"No, no! by all the powers divine,
I'd forfeit heaven to make her mine!
Could I but meet her chieftain lover,
His dream of bliss would soon be over.
To win and wear this rebel maid,
His blood should stain my trusty blade.
If but this chief and I could stand
With sword to sword, and hand to hand,
Full soon, Lenare, to thee I'd prove
The death of him thy heart doth love."
Ah! Victor, thou wilt sooner meet
The form thy spirit longs to greet,
Than thou shalt wish—beware! beware!
When Walter draws to win Lenare.

XVII

THE RESCUE

[Mrs. Odom hastens to complete the orphaning of her heroine. The eternal warfare between the forces of Righteousness and the forces of Evil is enacted on the stage of mid-nineteenth century America as Walter and Victor clash. Justice and Mercy mutually triumph in the disarming of Victor and in his reprieve by Lenare. And the nineteenth century morality play draws near its close.]

At midnight's holy hour—a time
That lifts each soul in thought sublime—
When, bowed before its Maker's will,
The earth lay calmly, darkly still,—
Lenare gazed on her father's face,
Where death his signet soon would place.
The morning sunlight, warm and clear,
Perchance would fall upon his bier.
The prison drear, the heavy chain,
Young Victor had not used in vain.
Sweet freedom had, at last, been given,
When life's bright chain was almost riven.
The anxious heart—the loving care—
Could not its broken links repair;
It lay a shining, shattered band,
Beneath oppression's heavy hand.
Lenare, with low-bowed, anguished head,
Stood by her father's dying bed.
Her heart grew still with throbbing pain,
The blood congealed in every vein;
She read, in his fast glazing eye,
The bitter truth that he must die.
For long, long days, with hopeless care,
Alone had watched the young Lenare.—
No friend, upon whose loving breast,
Her heart could lean for needed rest;
Not one to soothe with tender love,
Save Him who rules the realms above.
She knelt within the chamber there,

And breathed a deep, heart-thrilling prayer,
To pitying heaven that it would send
To her, in this dark hour, a friend.
"Oh, God!" she cried, with bitter moan,
"Leave not thy helpless child alone!
My father, I must yield to thee,
Then give, oh, give a friend to me!"
A movement of the sick man's head—
A low, faint murmur from the bed—
And Hargrave softly called her name,
As quickly to his side she came.
She clasped his hand in both her own,
Suppressed the rising, bitter groan,
That almost rent her soul in twain,
With bursting throbs of hidden pain.
She felt the damps of death cling cold
About the fingers in her hold;
Watched anxiously each fleeting breath,
From lips that bore the hue of death;
And felt that ere the dawn of day,
His spirit would have left the clay,
To bind, in glory worlds above,
The broken ties of early love;
While she would linger here below,
A friendless orphan with the foe.
Nay, more; a sadder draught remained,
In hopeless sorrow to be drained;
Yea, hopeless, helpless, chilling sorrow,
Awaited her upon the morrow.
Her two months grace would then be over,
And still no tidings from her lover.
Her heart grew heavy with its sighs—
Hope folds its snowy wings, and dies.
Love's flowers, blighted in their bloom,
Lie mouldering upon its tomb.
To-morrow she must yield to fate—
Must wed the man her soul will hate.
Her father's moving fingers broke
Her mournful reverie—he woke—
His hueless lips moved once in prayer,
Then lowly breathed her name—"Lenare!"

"Dear father, I am here," she said,
And smoothed the pillow for his head.
"My child, my hour, at last has come,
The dews of death my senses numb;
I feel his chilling fingers now,
Like icicles upon my brow.
Ere morning gilds the mountain's crest,
Thou'lt be alone, and I at rest.
To dying eyes, I feel is given,
The quivering, dreamy lights of heaven;
The shades of earth before them flee,
Like morning mists from out the sea.
I feel a something, vague and wild,
Within me, that I'll see my child,
Ere I shall seek my final rest,
Clasped warmly to her lover's breast."
He paused—his fading eye he raised,
Full on her marble brow he gazed;
He saw her bosom heave and swell,
Watched the bright tear-drops as they fell
Upon the hand that clasped his own,
Like crystals on a lily thrown;
Then in the stilly midnight air,
A low voice breathes her name—"Lenare!"
A form upon the casement sprung—
Upon the floor a footstep rung—
Lenare sprang wildly to her feet,
Her lover's clasping arms to meet;
Her clinging form he madly pressed—
She fainted on her Walter's breast.
But soon his heart, so strong and warm,
Thrilled life into her senseless form.
She shivered—breathed a fluttering sigh,
And woke to meet her lover's eye
Fixed full on hers, in tender love,
Like rays of glory from above;
A beacon-light by angels given,
To lift her drooping soul to heaven.
Then memory dimmed her gentle eye,—
Her father yet was sure to die—

No mortal care, or love, could save
Him from the cold and narrow grave.
The dying parent faintly smiled,
And beckoned to his weeping child:
"Come hither, sweet dream of my heart,
Ere I from thee, forever part.
Come, kneel, Lenare, that I may give
My blessing while my senses live;
And Walter, too, my noble boy,
For thee I'd breathe a note of joy.
Oh, God hath answered well my prayer,
To raise thee up a friend, Lenare."
They knelt beside that dying bed,
A hand in blessing on each head.
In broken words he murmured there,
For each, a solemn, touching prayer;
Besought the God of heavenly light
To lead them in the path of right.
His accents, faint and fainter came,
Then ceased at last,—life's wasting flame
Flashed up, and sank to rise no more—
Hargrave had reached the shadowy shore.
Lenare but raised her drooping head,
To gaze upon her honored dead;
To feel within her bleeding heart,
Another rankling, reeking dart;
Then bursting sobs of wildest grief
Came to her wretched heart's relief.
Young Walter soothed, with gentle care,
The stormy sorrow of Lenare;
Though bitter tears his own eyes dim,
He prays her still to live for him.
To seek the night's reviving breath,
He bore her from the couch of death.
Ah! little recks he, in that grove,
Where he so oft hath told his love,
Another waits, in mad despair,
To see, unseen, the young Lenare.
Yes, Victor stands within the grove,
Where Walter bears his stricken love.
He hears the maiden's trembling moan—

He hears young Walter's loving tone—
He fiercely marks each fond caress—
The fervent kiss he dares to press
Upon the pure uplifted brow,
And thinks upon his plighted vow,
If young Lenare could fully prove
Her lover's living claim to love—
That vow sealed on his shining blade—
To yield the lovely Southern maid.
His heart rebels against the fate,
That on the morrow seems to wait.
He drove his hand against his breast,
His heart he madly, fiercely pressed,
As though a giant's mighty will
Could bid the tempest there be still;
Strode forward, with a haughty pace,
And met the lovers face to face.
" 'Tis Victor!" cried the frightened maid.
And gazed upon his glittering blade.
"Yes, Victor, who will firmly stand,
And with his sword shall win thy hand,
Or bravely yield his worthless breath
Upon the crimson shrine of death.
Draw, chieftain!" he to Walter said,
"Or be thy doom upon thy head."
Young Walter drew his trusty steel,
Which soon the Northern chief would feel;
But ere he raised it for a blow,
He thus addressed his hated foe:
"Since first my home came in thy power,
My soul has thirsted for this hour;
To meet thee thus, my mortal foe,
And thus to pay the debt I owe;
My honor to this blade be given—
My trust is in the God of heaven."
Kneeling beneath the shadows there,
In anguish bowed the young Lenare;
Her heart with hope and fear imbued,
To watch the struggle that ensued.
Ere Walter spoke the last low word,
Each foeman raised his gleaming sword;

Gazed each on each with stubborn glare,
Then plied their blades to win Lenare.
In deadly silence raged the strife,
On which depended more than life.
Naught save the clashing of their steel,
The midnight combatants reveal.
Lenare knelt in the dewy glade,
To wreathe in prayer her Walter's blade;
To heaven arose her tearful plea,
To bless his arm with victory.
Young Victor fiercely aimed each blow
Full at the brave heart of his foe;
While Walter, with unerring skill,
Delayed the final issue still.
But fierce and fiercer grew the fray—
More madly did their weapons play—
Once Victor's steel touched Walter's side,
And Walter's sword with blood was dyed;
While in its silent, crimson flow,
Each felt in each a worthy foe;
While victory alternate played
Around each crimson-tinted blade.
First, Victor's forehead lightly pressed,
Then laid her hand on Walter's crest;
But angels viewed the contest wild,
And on the Southern chieftain smiled.
That smile his trusty weapon charméd—
His struggling foeman falls, disarmed.
His knee upon that fallen breast,
He laid his hand on Victor's crest;
The laurel leaflets clinging there
He scattered on the midnight air;
Then, ere his foe could frame a word,
He plunged in earth the Northman's sword;
Its metal shivered in the clay,
Then tossed the bloodless hilt away.
"Now, Victor," [*sic*] now," the chieftain cried,
"Is my victorious hour of pride—
The boon for which I wearied heaven
To my proud soul at last is given.
Upon thy vanquished neck I stand;

Thy life lies quivering in my hand—
Yes, lies in my victorious clasp,
When I can crush it with a grasp."
His eye gleamed with triumphant fire—
It darkly flashed with inward ire,
While fallen Victor seemed to wait,
With sullen bravery, his fate.
Though fortune bowed his haughty head
Beneath the hated foeman's tread;
Though fairly vanquished in the strife,
He seemed to urge no plea for life;
But calmly gazed on coming death
As though he wooed its icy breath.
Lenare gazed, through the shades of night,
In terror on that sanguine fight.
She saw the Northman's broken sword;
She heard each proud, exultant word
That Walter uttered to the chief.
One moment—but an instant brief—
Ere Walter drew again his blade,
A trembling hand his passion stayed.
"Nay, dearest, bid the chieftain live,
Thy mother taught thee to forgive."
Like oil on troubled waters thrown,
Upon his heart her gentle tone
Fell, soothing with its breath of prayer,
The mighty tempest raging there.
One glance upon her angel form
Would quell in him the fiercest storm.
Now, gazing on that worshiped maid,
He slowly dropped his thirsty blade,
And, 'neath the spell of her dark eyes,
He bade the fallen chieftain rise.
Young Victor raised his crownless crest,
Obedient to his foe's behest;
But not on Walter fell his eye—
No, not for him that long-drawn sigh—
He felt, with silent, mad despair,
He had forever lost Lenare.
With flushing cheek, and throbbing brow,
The maiden turned her to him now:

"My chief, in heaven's holy name,
Thy plighted word I now may claim.
My lover lives—hath proved to thee,
His deep, undying love for me;
Then here, beneath the stars of heaven,
I claim thy knightly pledge thus given."
Young Victor stood, with folded arms,
And viewed Lenare in all her charms;
With anguish felt they soon must part—
But buried deep within his heart,
The keen, half-maddening, bitter thrill
That lashed his soul and senses still.
His pride forbade his cheek to show
His crushing sorrow to his foe.
He stood before the Southern maid—
"To thee, I'll keep my word," he said.
"This signet ring thou wilt display
To each guard in thy outward way;
Full well they know the gilded sign,—
Thy safety will around it twine;
Thou, and thy chief, can pass out free,
Protected by this pledge from me.
Now, maiden, I have kept my word,
Pledged on my then unbroken sword.
For me, thy young heart may not swell—
Take, take the ring—and now—farewell!"
He placed within her trembling hand,
The heavy, golden, magic band;
A moment bent before the maid,
Then plunged into the forest's shade;
Nor word, nor look, did he bestow
Upon his haughty Southern foe,
Who watched him vanish from his sight,
Through rising mists of morning light.
The shades of night had passed away,—
Had paled beneath the smile of day—
The rosy wings of morning hover
Above the maiden and her lover.
So passed their night of grief and care,
Its morning rose serene and fair;

Round their united hearts shall twine
The light of love and hope divine.
But one sad thought the future gave,
That lingered round an open grave;
With tearful eye, and bended head,
They thought on their unburied dead.

XVIII

THE NUPTIALS

[Mrs. Odom arbitrarily chooses to give her readers a "happy" ending, unlike John M. Dagnall, who, in *Daisy Swain,* chose with equal arbitrariness to afford his readers a good cry instead.]

Twelve hours passed—the grave had closed,
Where Hargrave's stiffened limbs reposed;
Lenare had dropped her farewell tear
Upon her martyred father's bier;
Had left her childhood's fallen home,
With him she loved so well, to roam.
With signet ring, the guard they passed,—
The captive maid was free at last;
Free in her own dear "Dixie" land,
Where waited Walter's gallant band.
With tears of pleasure, glad and wild,
Old faithful Fleta met her child;
The one lone idol whom she prest
In worship to her sable breast.
The stars shone clearly bright in heaven,
Their beams of silver light were given
To gild the bonds of wedded love,
With radiant glory from above.
They knelt in holy rapture there,
The chieftain brave—the maiden fair—
The knightly legion gathered round
In silence. No discordant sound
Awoke the echoes of the wood,

Where all the brave twelve hundred stood.
The man of God, a solemn prayer
Breathed over Walter and Lenare—
The spoken vow—the golden band—
The clinging pressure of the hand—
Two loving hearts are bound for life—
The maid is now the chieftain's wife.
Their earthly paths no more shall sever,
But wind as one through time forever.

Bibliography

Abbey, Henry L. *May Dreams.* New York, 1862.

———. *Ralph, and Other Poems.* Roundout, [N.Y.], 1866.

[Adams, Ann Olivia]. *Poems. By Astarte.* New York, 1865.

Aldrich, Thomas Bailey. *Poems.* Boston, 1865.

Allen, William. *Poems of Nazareth and the Cross.* Northampton, 1866.

Ambler, A. I. *Jessie Reed, and Other Poems.* Philadelphia, 1867.

Anderson, Joseph. *Two Victories; a New England Idyl.* New York, 1867.

[Augustin, John Alcee]. *War Flowers, Reminiscences of Four Years' Campaigning.* 1865.

Avery, David. *A Poem on the Origin and Suppression of the Late Rebellion.* Willimantic, 1865.

Ayres, D. *The Warning; or, the Birth, Youth, Manhood, and Danger of the Nation, a Poem.* Rochester, N.Y., 1868.

Baker, George M[elville]. *An Old Man's Prayer.* Boston, 1868.

Baker, John R. *Gettysburg.* Philadelphia, 1866.

Ball, C[aroline] A[ugusta]. *The Jacket of Grey, and Other Fugitive Poems.* Charleston, 1866.

Barnes, G. H. *Poem, Read at the Soldiers' Welcome, Franklin, Delaware Co., N. Y., August 5th, 1865.* Binghamton, N. Y., [1865].

Benton, W. C. *The Past—the Present—the Future.* Hudson, 1865.

Birdseye, George W. *Woman and the War.* New York, 1865.

Bishop, Putnam P. *Liberty's Ordeal.* New York, 1864.

Bissell, Champion. *A Poem Pronounced before the Phi Beta Kappa Society of Yale College.* New Haven, 1861.

Blackwell, Robert. *Original Acrostics; on Some of the Southern States, and Most Eminent Men of the Southern Confederacy; and on Various Other Subjects, Political and Personal.* 1863.

———. *Original Acrostics on Some of the Southern States, Confederate Generals, and Various Other Persons and Things.* St. Louis, 1869.

Boker, George H[enry]. *Poems of the War.* Boston, 1864.

———. *The Second Louisiana.* Philadelphia, [1863].

———. *Tardy George.* New York, 1865.

Bolton, Sarah T[ittle Barrett]. *Poems.* New York, 1865; 1867.

Ye Book of Copperheads. Philadelphia, 1863.

Booth, Mary H. C. *Wayside Blossoms.* Philadelphia, 1865.

[Bourne, William Oland]. *The House That Jeff Built.* New York, 1868.

———. *Poems of the Republic.* New York, 1864.

Bradford, J. Stricker. *Autumn Winds, and Other Poems.* New York, 1869.

Bristol, Augusta Cooper. *Poems.* Boston, 1868.

A Broadside for the Times; by E. Pluribus Unum. New York, 1861.

Brooks, Sarah Warner. *Even-Songs and Other Poems.* Boston, 1868.

[Brown, John Sullivan]. *This War, a Satire for the Times.* New York, 1863.

Brown University. Class of '66. The Oration and Poem Delivered in Manning Hall, on Class Day, June 15, 1865. Providence, 1865.

Brownell, Henry Howard. *Lyrics of a Day: or Newspaper-Poetry.* 2d ed. New York, 1864.

———. *War-Lyrics and Other Poems.* Boston, 1866.

Buell, P. L. *The Poet Soldier. A Memoir of the Worth, Talent and Patriotism of Joseph Kent Gibbons, Who Fell in the Service of His Country during the Great Rebellion.* New York, 1868.

[Burke, John]. *The Burden of the South, in Verse, or, Poems on Slavery, Grave, Humorous, Didactic, and Satirical.* New York, 1864.

———. *Chivalry, Slavery, and Young America.* New York, 1866.

———. *Stanzas to Queen Victoria, and Other Poems.* New York, 1866.

Butts, B. J. *The Angel and the 'Slaver; a Radical Poem.* Hopedale, Mass., 1860.

C., M. T. *Flowers from the Battle-Field, and other Poems.* Philadelphia, 1864.

[Caldcleugh, William George]. *The Branch: a Sacred Poem, and Other Poems.* Philadelphia, 1862.

[Cameron, Hugh]. *The Troublesome Trio.* Washington, 1867.

Campbell, Gabriel. *War Pictures: a Poem.* Ann Arbor, 1865.

Carmichael, Sarah E. *Poems.* 2d ed. San Francisco, 1866.

Carr, George P. *The Contest: a Poem.* Chicago, 1866.

Celebration at Tammany Hall, of the Ninetieth Anniversary of the Declaration of American Independence by the Tammany Society, or Columbian Order, Wednesday, July 4th, 1866. New York, 1866.

Celebration of the Eighty-Sixth Anniversary of the Independence of the United States, in Chicago, July 4th, 1862. Chicago, 1862.

Ceremonies at the Dedication of the Soldiers' Monument, in Newton, Mass. Boston, 1864.

Chester, A. T., and Long, J. C. *The Lessons of the War. An Oration and Poem.* Westfield, N.Y., [1865].

[Clarke, Mrs. S. M.] *Our Country.* San Francisco, 1864.

Clarke, Thomas. *Sir Copp. A Poem for the Times.* Chicago, 1865; 1866; 1867.

Coloney, Myron. *Manomin: a Rhythmical Romance of Minnesota, the Great Rebellion and the Minnesota Massacres.* St. Louis, 1866.

Congdon, Charles T. *The Warning of War: a Poem Delivered before the United Societies of Dartmouth College, Hanover, N. H. at the Annual Commencement, July 30, 1862.* New York, 1862.

Cook, William. [*Poems*]. Salem, 1852-70.

Cooke, Samuel Walden. *Cobwebs: a Poem.* New York, 1865.

Cox, Sanford C. *The Evangelist, and Other Poems.* Cincinnati, 1867.

[Cromwell, Ruth N.] *Nancy Blake Letters to a Western Cousin.* New York, 1864.

Cutler, Elbridge Jefferson. *Liberty and Law. A Poem for the Hour.* Boston, 1861.

———. *Stella.* Boston, 1868.

———. *War Poems.* Boston, 1867.

Dagnall, John M. *Daisy Swain, the Flower of Shenandoah. A Tale of the Rebellion.* Brooklyn, 1865.

Daniel, Charles T. *William and Annie: or, A Tale of Love and War and Other Poems.* Guelph, 1864.

[Dannelly, Elizabeth Otis Marshall]. *Destruction of the City of Columbia, South Carolina. A Poem by a Lady of Georgia.* Charleston, 1866.

[David, Mrs. Mary Evelyn]. *Minding the Gap and Other Poems.* Houston, 1867.

The Days of Sixty-Three. Philadelphia, 1864.

Dedication of the Memorial Hall, in Dedham, September 29, 1868. Dedham, Mass., 1869.

Dedication of the Soldiers' Monument at Dorchester, September 17, 1867. Boston, 1868.

Denison, F[rederic]. *Army Hymns; Written for the Third Regiment R.I. Heavy Artillery.* Providence, 1863.

The Devil in America: a Dramatic Satire. Spirit-Rapping—Mormonism; Woman's Rights Conventions and Speeches; Abolitionism; Harper's Ferry Raid and Black Republicanism; Defeat of Satan, and Final Triumph of the Gospel. By Lacon. Mobile, 1867.

Devon, W. A. *War Lyrics.* New York, 1864.

De Warrdenau, D. *The Gift,* [1866].

Doty, G. Dexter. *Corn-Husks: a Poem for the Times.* New York, 1863; 1864.

Duganne, A. J. H. *Utterances.* New York, 1865.

Earle, Pliny. *Poem Delivered before the Alumni Association of the New England Yearly Meeting School, at Their Third Annual Meeting, at Newport, 1861.* Providence, 1861.

[Eastman, Mrs. Mary Henderson]. *Jenny Wade of Gettysburg.* Philadelphia, 1864.

Ely, A. B. *"Pro Patria Mortui Sunt." Oration Pronounced before Post 62, Grand Army of the Republic, Newton, Massachusetts, in Memoriam, May 29th, A.D. 1869.* Boston, 1869.

Everett, William. *Hesions: or Europe Unchained. A Poem Delivered before the Φ.B.K. Fraternity of Harvard College, July 16, 1868.* Boston, 1868.

Everhart, James B. *Poems.* Philadelphia, 1868.

Ewing, E. E. *The Story of the Ninety-First. Read at a Re-union of the Ninety-First Regiment Ohio Volunteer Infantry, Held at Portsmouth, Ohio, April 8, 1868, in Response to the Toast, "Our Bond of Union."* Portsmouth, O., 1868.

[Fields, Annie A.] *Ode.* [Boston], [1863].

[Ford, Mary A. McMullen]. *Poems: by Una.* Cincinnati, 1863.

Francis, Valentine Mott. *The Fight for the Union.* New York, 1863.

Ganyard, A. O. *The Talisman of Battle and Other Poems.* Rochester, N.Y., 1864.

Gardette, Charles D. *The Fire-Fiend, and Other Poems.* New York, 1866.

Gazelle, A True Tale of the Great Rebellion; and Other Poems. Boston, 1866.

Gray, Amy. *The Lily of the Valley; or, Margie and I: and Other Poems.* Baltimore, 1868.

The Great Organ in the Boston Music Hall. Being a Brief History of the Enterprise from Its Commencement, with a Description of the Instrument; Together with the Inaugural Ode, and Some Account of the Opening Ceremonies on the Evening of November 2, 1863; to Which Is Appended a Short Account of the Principal Organs in England and on the Continent of Europe. Boston, 1865.

[Greene, Richard Henry]. *Cannon-Flashes and Pen-Dashes.* New York, 1866.

Grenell, Z. *Democracy! in Five Parts.* New York, 1867.

Gunnison, E. Norman. *Our Stars.* Philadelphia, 1863.

Guthrie, W. E. *The Betrothed. A Nation's Vow.* Philadelphia, 1867.

[Harlan, Caleb]. *Ida Randolph, of Virginia. A Poem in Three Cantos.* Philadelphia, 1869.

Hewes, George Whitfield. *Ballads of the War.* New York, 1862.

[Hickox, Volney]. *Palmetto Pictures.* New York, 1863.

Holmes, Oliver Wendell. *Poems.* Boston, 1869.

Holmes, S. N. *Holmes' Patriotic Songs, for Coming Campaigns.* Syracuse, N.Y., 1867.

[Homes, Mary Sophie Shaw]. *Progression; or, the South Defended. By Millie Mayfield, of New Orleans.* Cincinnati, 1860.

Hoskin, A. A. *Flowers and Leaves.* Chicago, 1867.

How McClellan Took Manassas. New York, 1864.

Howe, Julia Ward. *Later Lyrics.* Boston, 1866.

[Howison, George Holmes]. *Abraham Lincoln. A Threnody.* St. Louis, 1866.

Hunt, C. M. *Greenbacks and Tin. A Poem Delivered at Emory Hospital, Washington, D.C., July 4, 1864.* Washington, D.C., 1864.

Janvier, Francis De Haes. *Patriotic Poems.* Philadelphia, 1866.

Jones, Amanda T. *Poems.* New York, 1867.

Jordan, Cornelia J. M. *Corinth and Other Poems of the War.* Lynchburg, 1865.

———. *Richmond: Her Glory and Her Graves.* Richmond, 1866.

A Journal of Incidents Connected with the Travels of the Twenty-Second Regiment Conn. Volunteers, for Nine Months. In Verse. By an Orderly Sergeant. Hartford, 1863.

Keefer, Justus. *Slavery: Its Sin, Moral Effects, and Certain Death.* Baltimore, 1864.

Kennedy, Evender C. *Osseo, the Spectre Chieftain.* Leavenworth, 1867.

King, Henry F. *The Rebellion; an Historical Poem.* Portland, 1865.

Latimer, E. *"The Unknown."* 2d ed. Philadelphia, 1867.

Letters from a Maryland Mail Bag. [1863].

Longfellow, Henry Wadsworth. *Poetical Works.* Complete ed. Boston, 1868.

Loring, Geo. B. *An Oration, Delivered at Bolton, Mass., December 20, 1866, at the Dedication of the Tablets, Erected in the Town Hall, to Commemorate the Deceased Volunteers of the Town in the War of the Great Rebellion.* Clinton, 1867.

Lowe, Martha Perry. *Love in Spain, and Other Poems.* Boston, 1867.
[Lowell, James Russell]. *The Biglow Papers.* 2d series. Boston, 1867.
———. *Poems.* 2 vols. 8th ed. Boston, 1866.
[Lowell, Robert Traill Spence]. *Fresh Hearts That Failed Three Thousand Years Ago; with Other Things.* Boston, 1860.
———. *Poems.* New ed. Boston, 1864.
Lownsbury, C. W. *Gloria: and Other Poems.* Ypsilanti, 1864.
———. *Leoline, and Other Poems.* Detroit, 1866.
[McAfee, Nelly Nichol Marshall]. *Gleanings from Fireside Fancies by "Sans Souce."* Chicago, 1866.
McDougal, Fanny Green. *The Genius of American Liberty. A Patriotic Poem.* San Francisco, 1867.
[McLaughlin, J. Fairfax]. *The American Cyclops, the Hero of New Orleans, and Spoiler of Silver Spoons. Dubbed LL.D. By Pasquino.* Baltimore, 1868.
McNair, John. *Eighty Original Poems; Secular and Sacred, and Chiefly Adapted to the Times.* Lancaster, Pa., 1865.
Mangum, Adolphus W. *Myrtle Leaves; or Tokens at the Tomb. A Book Peculiarly Adapted to the Times.* 2d ed. Raleigh, 1864.
Markham, M. Roland. *The Parlor Book of Poetry.* New York, 1869.
Marshall, J. U. *The Times, or Chaos Has Come Again.* Charleston, 1868.
Melville, Herman. *Battle-Pieces and Aspects of the War.* New York, 1866.
Memorial Ceremonies at the National Cemetery, Arlington, Virginia. Under the Auspices of the Grand Army of the Republic. May 30, 1868. Washington, D.C., 1868.
A Memorial of Brevet Brigadier General Lewis Benedict, Colonel of 162d Regiment N.Y.V.I., Who Fell in Battle at Pleasant Hill, La., April 9, 1864. Albany, 1866.
A Memorial of Major Edward Granville Park, of the 35th Massachusetts Volunteers. Boston, 1865.
A Message from the Army. [1864].
Mitchell, Walter. *Poem Delivered at the Flag-Raising, Stamford, July 4th, 1861.* Stamford, 1861.
The Modern Gilpin. A Ballad of Bull Run. New York, 1866.
The Mongrelites: or, the Radicals—So-called. A Satiric Poem. New York, [1866].
Moore, James. *The Kimeliad. A Poem in Three Cantos.* Philadelphia, 1867.
[Morris, T. H.] *A.D. 1862, or How They Act in Baltimore, by a Volunteer Zouave.* Baltimore, [1862].
Morse, D. S. *Brazen Age.* [Manchester, N.H.], [1862-63].
Moschzisker, Clara H. von. *Poems.* Philadelphia, 1868.
Neal Neff's New National Poems, Composed by a Captain of the Line, Belonging to the 54th O.V.V.I., of the 2d Division, 15th Army Corps, of Gen. Sherman's Army, Who, While at the Front, in Moments of Idleness, Wrote for His Own Amusement. Cincinnati, 1866.
[Nelson, T. A. R.] *Secession or Prose in Rhyme and East Tennessee; a Poem by an East Tennesseean.* Philadelphia, 1864.
The New Pantheon or the Age of Black. Rollo, N.Y., 1860.
[Newell, Robert Henry]. *The Martyr President.* New York, 1865.

Nichols, G. W. *Reconstruction: a Poem.* Beloit, [Wis.], 1868.

North and South, or, What Is Slavery? By Jehu Geeup, of Jackass Alley, 1861.

Nowell, Edward P. *The Ballad of Jefferson D.* Portsmouth, 1865.

Nunes, Joseph A. *Day Dreams.* Philadelphia, 1863.

[Odom, Mary Hunt McCaleb]. *Lenare: a Story of the Southern Revolution, and Other Poems.* New Orleans, 1866.

O'Donnel, Kane. *The Song of Iron and the Song of Slaves: with Other Poems.* Philadelphia, 1863.

Oration and Poem. Alumni Association. Tufts College, July 12, 1865. Boston, [1865].

Original Poem, Written and Dedicated to Post 15, Grand Army of the Republic, by High Private. Boston, 1868.

Owen, Moses. *Fragments.* New York, 1868.

[Parks, Martha A.] *Echoes,* [1865].

Parmly, Eleazar. *Thoughts in Rhyme.* New York, 1867.

Peckham, Robert. *Historical Poem, to be Read at the Dedication of the Soldiers' Monument, in Westminster, Mass., July 4th, 1868.* Fitchburg, 1868.

Peffer, W. A. *Myriorama: a View of Our People and Their History, Together with the Principles Underlying, and the Circumstances Attending the Rise and Progress of the American Union.* Clarksville, Tenn., 1869.

Phelps, S. Dryden. *The Poet's Song for the Heart and the Home.* New York, 1867.

Piatt, John James. *Western Windows and Other Poems.* New York, 1869.

Plumb, David. *The Slaveholders' Rebellion.* [New York], [1865].

Poyas, Catharine Gendron. *Year of Grief, and Other Poems.* Charleston, 1869.

Preston, Margaret J. *Beechenbrook; a Rhyme of the War.* Richmond, 1865.

Proctor, Edna Dean. *Poems.* New York, 1866; 1867.

[Putnam, Mary Lowell]. *Tragedy of Errors.* Boston, 1862.

———. *Tragedy of Success.* Boston, 1862.

[R., E. B.] *Comprising a Few Thoughts Suggested by the Assault on Our Glorious Flag in 1860-'61.* New York, 1861.

Randolph, P. J. *The Slave-Mongers' Convention: a Satire on American Despotism, and Men-Stealing Religion.* Sauk Co., Wis., 1861.

Read, Thomas Buchanan. *A Summer Story, Sheridan's Ride and Other Poems.* Philadelphia, 1865.

Redden, Laura C. *Idyls of Battle and Poems of the Rebellion.* New York, 1864.

Reed, George E. *Campaign of the Sixth Army Corps Summer of 1863.* Philadelphia, 1864.

Rhymed Tactics, by "Gov." New York, 1862.

Ripley, Mary A. *Poems.* Rochester, N.Y., 1867.

Rogers, J. Henry. *The California Hundred.* [California], 1865.

[Rutherford, George S.] *The Poetic History of the Seventh Iowa Regiment, Containing All Its Principal Marches, and All the Battles They*

Have Been Engaged in, from the Day of Their Entering Service to the Present Time. Composed and Written by One of Their Number Who Has Passed through, or Borne His Part in, Nearly All the Scenes He Has Described. Muscatine, Ia., 1863.

Sanford, W. S. *"Soldiers' Welcome." A Poem Delivered in North Haven, July 19th, 1865, on the Reception of the Returned Soldiers of That Town. Respectfully Dedicated to the Members of the 15th Regt. C.V.* New Haven, 1865.

[Sargent, Lucius Manlius]. *The Ballad of the Abolition Blunder-Buss.* Boston, 1861.

Savage, John. *Faith and Fancy.* New York, 1864.

Sayles, F. O. *Follies of the Day, a Satire.* Author's ed. Springfield, Mass., 1867.

[Sealey, Celia]. *Echoes from the Garret.* Buffalo, 1861.

Searle, E. *Agatha; and Other Poems.* Morrison, Ill., 1867.

Silsbee, S. *D. D. D. or, Death, the Devil and the Doctor, on the War. Read, for the Benefit of the St. John's Hospital, at the Union Hall of the Catholic Institute.* Cincinnati, 1862.

Smith, Dexter. *Poems.* Boston, 1868.

Smith, E. Delafield. *Brief Appeals for the Loyal Cause.* New York, 1863.

Souder, Mrs. Edmund A. *Leaves from the Battle-Field of Gettysburg. A Series of Letters from a Field Hospital. And National Poems.* Philadelphia, 1864.

Southern Chivalry. The Adventures of G. Whillikens, C. S. A. Knight of the Golden Circle; and of Guinea Pete, His Negro Squire. An Epic-Doggerel, in Six Books. By a Citizen of the Cotton Country. Philadelphia, 1861.

Southern Odes, by the Outcast, a Gentleman of South Carolina. Published for the Benefit of the Ladies Fuel Society. Charleston, 1861.

Spaulding, Anna Marie. *Poems.* New York, 1866.

Sperry, H. T. *Country Love vs. City Flirtation; or, Ten Chapters from the Story of a Life. Reduced to Rhyme for Convenience Sake.* New York, 1865.

Sprague, A[chsa] W. *I Still Live. A Poem for the Times.* Oswego, 1862.

Stedman, Edmund C[larence]. *Alice of Monmouth. An Idyl of the Great War, with Other Poems.* New York, 1864.

Stockwell, William W. *New Songs and Poems for the Camp and Fireside.* Cleveland, 1864.

Stoddard, Charles Warren. *Abraham Lincoln. An Horatian Ode.* New York, 1865.

Sumner, Samuel B. *A Poem Delivered at the Reunion of the Forty-Ninth Regiment Massachusetts Volunteers, at Pittsfield, Mass., May 21, 1867.* Springfield, 1867.

———. *A Poem, Delivered July 4th, 1865, at Great Barrington, Mass., and Repeated the Same Day at Pittsfield, Mass.* Springfield, 1865.

S[wain], M. P. *Mara: or, a Romance of the War.* Selma, Ala., 1864.

Telfer, William Dugg. *A Reminiscence of the First Battle of Manassas: A Camp-Fire Story of the Seventy-First Regiment, N.G.S.N.Y.* Brooklyn, 1864.

Thayer, Christopher T., and Buswell, H. F. *Address and Ode Delivered at the Dedication of Memorial Hall, Lancaster, June 17, 1868*. Boston, 1868.

Torrey, H. D. *America; or, Visions of the Rebellion; a Poem in Four Cantos*. Reading, Pa., 1862.

[Torrey, Mary Cutler]. *America: a Dramatic Poem*. New York, 1863.

[Tremain, Lyman]. *Memorial of Frederick Lyman Tremain, Late Lieut. Col. of the 10th N.Y. Cavalry. Who Was Mortally Wounded at the Battle of Hatcher's Run, Va., February 6th, and Died at City Point Hospital, February 8th, 1865*. Albany, 1865.

Trumbull, Truman. *The New Yankee Doodle: Being an Account of the Little Difficulty in the Family of Uncle Sam*. New York, 1868.

Underwood, T. H. *Our Flag. A Poem in Four Cantos*. New York, 1862.

Vandenhoff, Geo. *Life: or Men, Manners, Modes and Measures, a Poem for Union*. New York, 1861.

Vinton, Francis, and Curtis, George William. *An Oration on the Annals of Rhode Island and Providence Plantations, and a Rhyme of Rhode Island and the Times, Delivered before the Sons of Rhode Island in New York, May 29, 1863*. New York, 1863.

Vosburg, John Henry. *Virginia, and Other Poems*. New York, 1865.

Ward, Thomas. *A Lyrical Poem, Delivered at the Commemoration of the Two Hundredth Anniversary of the Settlement of Newark, before the New Jersey Historical Society*. Newark, 1866.

———. *War Lyrics*. New York, [1865].

Watkins, Frances Ellen. *Poems on Miscellaneous Subjects*. 14th thousand. Philadelphia, 1864.

Weeks, Della Jerman. *Legends of the War*. Boston, 1863.

Westlake, J. Willis. *Success: a Poem*. Philadelphia, 1866.

Whitehead, L. *The New House That Jack Built. An Original American Version*. New York, 1865.

Whiteside, Mrs. L. T. *Freedom's Banner*. Long Bottom, O., 1867.

Whitman, Walt. *Drum-Taps*. New York, 1865.

Whittier, John Greenleaf. *Poetical Works*. Complete ed. Boston, 1869.

Woodward, B. W. *Our Country. A Poem, Read before the Students of Hobart College and the Citizens of Geneva, on Washington's Birth-Day, Feb. 22, 1862*. Geneva, N.Y., 1862.